DISCARDED

DISCARDED

*Foreign Travelers in America
1810–1935*

*Foreign Travelers in America
1810–1935*

Advisory Editors:

Arthur M. Schlesinger, Jr.
Eugene P. Moehring

OBSERVATIONS

ON

PROFESSIONS, LITERATURE, MANNERS.

AND

EMIGRATION,

IN THE

UNITED STATES AND CANADA,

MADE DURING A RESIDENCE THERE IN

1832

REV. ISAAC FIDLER

ARNO PRESS
A New York Times Company
New York—1974

Reprint Edition 1974 by Arno Press Inc.

Reprinted from a copy in
 The University of Illinois Library

FOREIGN TRAVELERS IN AMERICA, 1810-1935
ISBN for complete set: 0-405-05440-8
See last pages of this volume for titles.

Manufactured in the United States of America

Library of Congress Cataloging in Publication Data

Fidler, Isaac.
  Observations on professions, literature, manners, and emigration in the United and Canada, made during a residence there in 1832.

  (Foreign travelers in America, 1810-1935)
  Reprint of the 1833 ed. published by Whitaker, Treacher, London.
  1. United States--Social life and customs--1783-1865. 2. United States--Emigration and immigration. 3. Canada--Social life and customs. 4. Canada--Emigration and immigration. I. Title. II. Series.
E165.F45 1974   917.3'03'56   73-13129
ISBN 0-405-05452-1

OBSERVATIONS

ON

PROFESSIONS, LITERATURE, MANNERS.

AND

EMIGRATION,

IN THE

UNITED STATES AND CANADA,

MADE DURING A RESIDENCE THERE IN

1832.

BY THE REV. ISAAC FIDLER,

FOR A SHORT TIME MISSIONARY OF THORNHILL ON YONGE STREET,
NEAR YORK, UPPER CANADA.

LONDON:
PUBLISHED BY WHITTAKER, TREACHER, AND CO.,
AVE-MARIA LANE.

1833.

BAYLIS AND LEIGHTON,
JOHNSON'S COURT, FLEET STREET

CONTENTS.

BOOK I.
UNITED STATES.

	Page
PREFACE	iii

CHAPTER I.
Reasons for Emigrating—The Voyage, and First View of New York—Impressions on Landing, and High Price of Lodgings and Fuel—Miscellaneous Particulars, upon Delivery of Letters of Introduction—Remarks on the Episcopal Church and Clergy in the United States—American Marriage............................ 1

CHAPTER II.
Sanscrit Printing—Poverty of Clergy—Influence of Clergy—Changes in Professions—Emoluments of Clergy—State of Learning—Prospects of English Clergymen in the States—Character of American Clergy—Methodist Bigotry 25

CHAPTER III.
Reasons for Abandoning the Idea of Teaching the Eastern Languages in the United States—Day Schools—Insubordination of Pupils—Anecdote of the Blind Teacher—Of an Irish Classical Teacher—Sad Tale of a Village Schoolmaster—American Insensibility—Farther Opinions concerning American Schools.................. 46

CHAPTER IV.
Story of a Stranger and his Travels—Of his Book, and his Teaching Experience—Case of a Young Schoolmaster from England—His Sanguine Hopes, and his Disappointments—The New York Proprietory School—Low State of Greek Teaching in New York—Distaste for

iv   CONTENTS.

Page

Improvements in the United States, that do not Promise Immediate Return in Money—Determination to Proceed to Boston.................................... 64

CHAPTER V.

Journey to Boston—Conversation with a Man of Letters there—Visit to the State House—To the University of Cambridge—The Dock-yard—Specimens of American Learning—Boston Evening Party—Prejudices in America against the English Aristocracy, and General Unfairness of Opinion there concerning England......... 88

CHAPTER VI.

Return to New York—Resolution to Proceed to Canada—Retrospective Incidents—Story of an American Merchant—Professions in the States, as described by an Englishman—American Superiority—Our Removal to Canada Predicted—Custom-House Dues—Effect of Captain Hall's Travels—Visiting on New Years' Day—Washington's Birthday—Miscellaneous Observations 111

CHAPTER VII.

Visit to the Passaic Falls—Conversations on English Reform—On the Condition and Disappointments of English Emigrants in the United States—Description of the Falls—The Proprietor—American and English Decorum—An English Clergyman—Miscellaneous Remarks... 148

CHAPTER VIII.

Democracy—Brutal Conduct of Americans towards such as Speak Lightly of their Government—May-Day in New York—Silence and Haste at Meals—Vanity and Illiberality—Americans Fear the Reproach of being Descendants of Felons—Change of Surnames—Frequent Fires—Value of Ground Lots—American Fruits—Servitude—Complaints of Emigrants—American Dispatch—Juvenile Delinquents—Work-House—Outraged Indians—Boundary Line between the United States and Canada.................................. 170

CONTENTS. v

Page

CHAPTER IX.

Journey to Niagara—Accident in a Steam-Boat—Albany —American Travelling—Mode of Location—Inns— Beautiful Scenery—Roads—Two Female Passengers— Methodist Preachers—Ancient Banks of Lake Ontario —Niagara Falls—An Eccentric English Gentleman precipitated down the Cataract—a Solitary Female.... 196

BOOK II.

CANADA.

CHAPTER I.

Arrival in Canada—Irish Deserter from the American Fort—Reception in Canada—Called on the Governor of York—On the Archdeacon—Journey to Newmarket —Want of Clergy—An Officer—A Deputation—Insurrection—Mode of Judging among Uninformed Men— Demagogues and Republicans—Journey to Montreal and Quebec—Return to New York.................. 205

CHAPTER II.

Second Journey to Canada—Salt Works at Syracuse— Voyage over Lake Ontario—A brow-beaten Irishman— Fare on the Lake—Arrival in York—Lodgings—Fellow Lodgers—New Church—Market-house—Parliament Houses—Kindness of the Archdeacon—Our Parsonage —Kindness of Parishioners—Mode of Living—Landlady—Yankee Impostures 250

CHAPTER III.

Cholera—Our Preservation—Its Prevalence in the States —In Canada—Canadian Philanthropy—Preventives of Cholera—Effect of Forest Rambles—Remedies for Cholera—Its Infectious Nature—Cases of Cholera— Death of a Medical Gentleman—Of a Young Lady.... 274

CONTENTS.

CHAPTER IV.

Desire for Ministers—Canadians fitted for Clerical Orders—College and University—Bishop of Quebec—Clergy and Congregations—Funeral—Prospects of Clergy—Methodists—A Reformed Presbyterian—Roman Catholics — Presbyterians — Shaking Quakers — Medical Profession—Education—Definition of Comfort 307

CHAPTER V.

Emigration—Farming—Forest Trees—Fertility of Canada—Its Inducement for American Democrats—Liberality of Government—Canada better for Englishmen than the United States—Distress of Emigrants—Advantages of Emigration—Who ought not to go—Price of Labour—Emigrant's Fondness for Canada......... 343

CHAPTER VI.

Farming—Gardens and Orchards—Cheap Government—Badness of Roads—Price of Various Articles—Fuel—Negroes—American Improvement—A Machine—Canadian Improvement—Thunder-Storm—Temperance Societies—Character of Canadians—Canadian Houses—Canada Company—Emigration ought to be Encouraged... 368

CHAPTER VII.

Clerical Emigrants—A German Missionary—Removal to the Falls—A projected City—Law-suit—Republican Revenge—The Indians—Spread of Christianity—Character of the English Emigrants—Custom-house Officers American Integrity—A Michigan Lady—Buffalo—American Judgment of Mrs. Trollope—Episcopal Synod of America—Political Absorption..Church of England and America—Return to England 401

PREFACE.

The Author of this volume had prepared materials for a much larger work than he here ventures to offer to the public.

While in Canada, and after most of his observations had been written, the Author read Mrs. Trollope's well known publication, and found it necessary, in consequence, either to abridge his plan, or to repeat what that lady had already said in a very popular and attractive style. On his return to England, Mr. Stuart's book next appeared: this also he perused, with a view that nothing contained in it might by him be needlessly repeated. He flatters himself, therefore, that what he has retained and given in the following pages, belongs pretty exclusively to his own opportunities and his subjects, and that those who have read the above works may yet peruse his with some advantage.

Sensible, however, that the period which he spent in the United States and Canada was too short to allow of such maturity to his observations, as might make them of value in the eyes of the judicious, the Author has preferred giving what he has collected in the form of conversations on the several points of his inquiries, with known or named individuals, whose nativity to the Transatlantic soil, or long residence in the country, may entitle their statements and opinions to respect. His great aim has been authenticity, as well as that degree of novelty in respect to subject, which may be included in the nature of his professional inquiries.

The following observations, and much more, were originally conveyed in a series of letters to a friend, who deemed them of sufficient importance for publication, but with whose name the Author is not at liberty to grace his pages.

Clapham, May 1st, 1833.

BOOK I.

UNITED STATES.

CHAPTER I.

REASONS FOR EMIGRATING—THE VOYAGE, AND FIRST VIEW OF NEW YORK—IMPRESSIONS ON LANDING, AND HIGH PRICE OF LODGINGS AND FUEL—SICKNESS—MISCELLANEOUS PARTICULARS, UPON DELIVERY OF LETTERS OF INTRODUCTION—REMARKS ON THE EPISCOPAL CHURCH AND CLERGY IN THE UNITED STATES—AMERICAN MARRIAGE.

At the latter end of 1831, I left England for America, with a view to adopting the United States as my future country. My reasons for taking this step were similar to those of most emigrants. Dissatisfaction with the government and the state of things in my own country, by which I had, as I concluded, been hitherto kept back in my fortune, and disappointed in my aims, together with a high admiration of the American Republic, formed the foundation of my reasons for emigrating.

This admiration had been conveyed to me, in some measure, as an hereditary opinion, and was made almost sacred by parental authority. For many years before his death, my father had cherished the intention of becoming himself an American. Whenever, therefore, any real or fancied evil oppressed me, my imagination and my hopes took refuge among the free wilds and rising communities of the great republic.

Educated for the church, but destitute of interest or patronage, I remained a mere teacher at home, with little to encourage my ambition even in that laborious profession; although, in addition to competent classical acquirements, I had made myself master of several of the languages of the East, which are but seldom studied in England. In the United States, these advantages would, I anticipated, either be the means of introducing me into the Episcopal church, or would at least enable me to live there, in a degree of respectability which I could scarcely hope for in England. With these views I emigrated; and my observations will, therefore, be more full in reference to my own particular pursuits, than those of most travellers who have written upon the prospects of English settlers in the United States or in Canada. Circumstances, however, ultimately induced me to return and fix myself again in my native land; and I now offer to my countrymen, with all candour, and in some detail, the result of my inquiries, and the nature of my disappointments.

On the 28th of October 1831, our ship sailed from London for Portsmouth, at which we arrived in three days, and in this latter place we were detained four days more. Setting sail again, we soon found ourselves in the wide ocean, and made the usual observations which landsmen are accustomed to make during the tedium of a voyage across the Atlantic. Many plans I had formed for industry on the passage, but I found Bishop Heber's observation correct, that a man can seldom study to much purpose at sea. Sickness first, and lassitude after, the uncongeniality and discomfort of a sea life;—the weariness of its sameness, and the consequent eagerness for amusement to excite or divert the mind; together with eating, which in these circumstances is a real pleasure, and sleeping, which is a grateful oblivion—leave little time or inclination for steady application of mind. Then we had the usual variety of weather, foul and fair; a competent share of storms and perils; and felt the customary anxiety for the termination of our voyage. My fellow-passengers were also of the mixed sort common on such occasions, some of them being English and some Americans; and their long conversations, and many arguments upon the comparative advantages of the old and new countries, served to enlighten me considerably as to what I had to expect in the trans-atlantic country. Of these conversations I took careful notes, and their substance I may have occasion to allude to in the sequel, as corroborative of my own observations.

At length, after a voyage of seven weeks, American land was discovered from the mast-head, and we soon after found ourselves approaching the protruding wharfs of New York. It was now about the middle of December, and the severity of the American climate began to be sensibly felt by most of us.

The first glimpse we had of trans-atlantic land was reflected from snow-clad hills. A biting frosty wind also, blowing from the coast, conveyed anticipations of what we might experience on shore. During all the voyage, till three days before our arrival, there had been no fire in the cabin; but the intensity of cold was at last so great, that fire could no longer be dispensed with. When the vessel had approached near enough for a signal to be made, a gun was fired for a steam-boat to tow us to the wharf. After one had arrived, we ascended rapidly and smoothly that delightful harbour. Several picturesque islands, crowned with batteries, appeared in different directions; but as a deep covering of snow overspread the landscape, the natural beauties of the harbour were indistinctly visible. The vessel was soon at the landing-place. Most of the passengers, among whom was myself, quitted the place of our long incarceration, and by one leap found ourselves at large in the land of freedom, independence, and equality. These mystic and magic words are there on every one's tongue. I shall hereafter give my opinion of how they apply to this favoured land— a land after which my soul had panted many years; and the government of which my imagination had painted as perfection itself.

The first business we had to attend to on landing, was seeking lodgings. For two rooms, badly furnished, three meals a day, and water to drink, I paid twenty-one dollars a week. Myself, my wife, and two children, with a servant, constituted the members of my family. Fire and candles cost us four dollars a week; and would have cost double that sum had we continued longer at the same house. Our landlady informed us that, from the price of fuel, she could not supply us with fire for less than one dollar a day. We had but one fire-place, which, had we submitted to such exaction, would have cost, in four months, nearly £25 sterling.

We afterwards rented unfurnished apartments, which allowed us to be more private than any boarding-house in New York admits of. It was our intention at first to take an entire house; but on finding that one of any respectability, would cost from one to two hundred pounds a year, we contented ourselves with lodgings. For unfurnished lodgings, in most parts of the city, more is demanded than for *furnished* lodgings in many parts of London. It required some time to arrange things necessary for our convenience, which imposed more exertion and less comfort than we had been accustomed to. Our servant in the mean time left us. She had been ascertaining the value of a dollar, and how many made a pound; and most probably conceived, that she could obtain more elsewhere. On making inquiries at the house where we had previously boarded, we found that the mistress of it had seduced her from us. This is so universally the practice as to be no matter of surprise. But as the former, with three of her family and domestics, died of cholera, and our servant returned to England six months before ourselves, I shall make no further animadversions. The servant appeared to be dissatisfied with America and its people.

The person, at whose house we had taken lodgings, was an Englishman, a painter, who informed me that he had lived some years in

Liverpool; but that from the heavy weight of rates, tithes, and taxes, he had not been able to gain a living. He still had a shop there, and intended to return if the Reform Bill should pass. He so often spoke with contempt and bitterness of kings, nobility, priests, and taxes, that it was evident at once under what denomination he might be classed. He was a radical, a gambler, a frequenter of Tammany Hall,* and of the lowest society. I blushed to think that such a person and myself should have entertained similar sentiments on such a subject. He had gone to America to improve his condition, but had not found that improvement realized. He hated, and cordially railed at, the American people, their manners, and the prejudices they entertained against the English. His wife, a most worthy and industrious woman, told us, that had her husband been industrious and careful, they might have saved money, and been independent, but that they could, with the same means, have been much more comfortable in Liverpool.

---

* A place where the lower and more restless orders meet to discuss political and religious questions, and not a few of whose frequenters, as I was informed are professed Atheists.

After we were somewhat settled, I found time to look around me, and consider what was passing. It seemed to me probable, that there was as much distress in New York, in proportion to the population, as in London. We saw and relieved several beggars in the streets of that city. The number, also, of paupers who were relieved by charity, was very great. I think the excessive charges for house-rent and fuel must be severely felt by persons of slender means. There must be a great want of capital among coal and wood-merchants, or a total absence of proper regulations. Sufficient fuel had not been provided to supply the regular consumption of the city; and its value became so enhanced in consequence, as to be almost out of the reach of the poor. The coals we consumed were double the price of what coals had cost in the summer. The coal-merchants had promised, before the winter commenced, that they would supply the people at summer prices. But promises are slight obligations, when put into competition with interest. We paid for coal at the rate of seventeen dollars a ton. While in England, we thought forty shillings a chaldron a high price; but in New York they were twice that sum.

As my object in going to the States was to be professionally employed, my proper interest required that I should lose no time in gaining every necessary information. For the sake of all inquirers on the same subject, I will, at some length, explain the prospects, which English clergymen in general will have before them in these States. Some of the gentlemen with whom my letters of introduction brought me into contact, possess considerable distinction. I was introduced to the Catholic and Episcopal Bishops, to Dr. Milnor, Dr. Wainright, Dr. Hossack, some of the professors of Columbia College, and several other gentlemen of all professions.

The intercourse I had with Americans was often confined to short calls and occasional confabulations. This, perhaps, arose from the circumstance, that I had illness in my family almost all winter; and also from the clergy, with whom I associated more than with any other class, being much engaged in sacred ministrations among the sick, the dying, and the dead. There were, according to the statements of some clergymen, more sickness and mortality in New York, and more calls on their time for private visitation and prayers, than they had ever known in any preceding winter. There was a great mortality among all ranks, and much sickness prevailed. I myself had an attack of quinsy. Having known previously its troublesome and dangerous nature, I took every means for my recovery, and suffered the less in consequence. This whole winter we suffered much illness and hardship.

I think the prevalence of sickness and death in New York, arising probably from severity of climate and extreme changeableness of weather, might be greatly counteracted, could skilful physicians be induced to settle there. But the depressed state of professions is striking to an Englishman, accustomed to see them in their high state in his own country. This arises from a want of classification in society, a want of aristocracy, independent of sordid interest, and consequently a want of due encouragement of literature and science. In that vast assemblage of people, there is no person able to promote the object of a stranger, nor to take him by the hand. High recommendations from England are a man's greatest detriment. The Americans, confident that no respectable professional man will leave England for their shores, unless engaged beforehand, look upon such recommendations as English lies, intended to impose a worthless wretch on their notice. This was hinted to me by several; and, among others, by the rector of one of the principal churches in the city. " Many," said he, " come to our country with flaming pretensions; but Americans are not too easy to be caught by such artifices." Englishmen will, hereafter, know better than to enter America in pursuit of respectable employment. If they will stoop to menial offices, these they may obtain.

I made several inquiries respecting professorships in colleges throughout the United States, and was candidly informed by many persons capable of giving correct information, that no man, whatever be his worth or acquirements, has much chance of obtaining either collegiate or clerical promotion there, unless he have personal influence with a majority of the electors. A stranger is entirely excluded by such a system. The only thing open to an English clergyman, in a regular way, is the employment of a common schoolmaster ; or a situation far back in the country, where an educated American will not go. An English clergyman of great oratorical powers may receive a call from some congregation to be their pastor ; but this is mere chance, and depends much upon the degree of his servility. He must entirely abandon every thing like English refinement, and submit to things never heard of in his native country.

I had no letters from England to any of the episcopal clergy in New York, or indeed in the States. A gentleman, to whom the king's physician in London gave me a letter of introduction, took me, on the morning I delivered it, to Dr. Milnor, an episcopal minister of great celebrity. He inquired if I had any papers with me by which he might be satisfied of my being a clergyman. These I had left at my lodgings ; but I shewed him letters to persons of distinction, in New York, Boston, Philadelphia, and Washington. After some conversation on various subjects, he desired me to call again with my clerical papers ; promising that he would, on the following day, introduce me to their bishop, should my papers be satisfactory. Before we parted, he had recollected that none of the letters I had shewn him were addressed to clergymen, and inquired if I had brought any such. My answer was in the negative; but that the letters I had produced before him must be as respectable as if from clergymen. He replied, the clergy of America will think differently. I then told him, that among those clergymen in England with whom I was more intimately acquainted, there was no one personally known to any of our profession in the States, nor indeed to any respectable person settled there. He remarked, such testimony will here be considered as indispensable. I must mention, in justice to myself, that I had with me a testimonial, regularly drawn out, and signed by three beneficed clergymen, countersigned by the Bishop of London, in which diocese I had resided for the ten preceding years.

I waited on Dr. Milnor the day following; who, after having examined my letters of orders, and my other papers, expressed himself satisfied that they were correct. " Your letters of orders are on parchment," he said; " but one person from

England presented to the clergy of this place similar documents on plain paper, and written instead of being printed. Of course he was an impostor. He exhibited letters of correspondence between himself and the Bishop of Chester, written in terms of gross familiarity, and not signed Chester, but the sirname of the person who then filled that see. These excited the suspicions of the clergy of New York, who demanded a sight of his letters of orders. He exhibited them written on plain paper. In addition to this, they were not canonically correct; and he was desired to call again with them on the morrow for further examination. He did so; but his papers had, in the meantime, been re-written more canonically, in another hand, and on English paper : they were before on American paper. He was now fully detected, and obliged to withdraw from this city." Dr. Milnor described him as of gentlemanly deportment; and was, upon inquiry being made in England respecting him, found to have been a teacher near Knutsford. " But," continued the Doctor, " this is not the only clerical imposture practised upon us. Another instance was by a person from England of a low grade, who, having by some means gained possession of the papers and other documents belonging to some episcopal English clergyman, was admitted through them, under an assumed name, to ecclesiastical employment in America. He was detected in a way natural enough, but not very flattering to the judgment of his auditory. He had collected around him a large congregation. One Sunday, a person of mean condition from England entered his church, and was surprised on finding one of his fellow-workmen in the pulpit. He mentioned the circumstance to those around him. This announcement, like all bad news, soon spread far and wide, and found its way to the preacher himself, who instantly disappeared, and was never seen again in his former place. Hence it has arisen, that we pay no attention to letters of orders, or testimonials of character, be they ever so flattering, unless they come authenticated by clergymen in England of well-known respectability. Any person may produce high testimonials, forged, or from persons of no standing; but America will not be imposed on in any such way."

"Impositions like the above," continued he, "occasioned a regulation to be introduced into the episcopal church of America, to prevent any clergyman from England being admitted to a benefice, until he should have resided twelve months in the country." I acknowledged that this is a very judicious and necessary regulation; but I also observed, that it seems hard that such as arrive with every requisite testimonial, should be debarred from the advantages of their profession, because others have acted improperly. "We think otherwise," replied he: "a three years' testimonial is required from an English clergyman in England itself, previous to his induction to a living, yet we admit him, upon proper testimony, after one. Should we suppose emigration reversed, and an American clergyman to flee to England, he is debarred altogether, whatever may be his character, from officiating in an English church." "You have placed the subject," said I, "in a striking point of view, and such as does credit to the liberality of America. I could not desire it otherwise with respect to myself."

It is a curious circumstance, that an American

clergyman, or one ordained by an American bishop, cannot hold any preferment in England, nor a mission in Canada ; whilst an English clergyman, whether from this country or from Canada, can hold one in the States after twelve month's residence. This arises from a deep laid policy in the American government, which has the peopling of their country for its object. Yet I much doubt if any clergyman from England finds himself in a better condition from such regulations in his favour.

Dr. Milnor, after this, accompanied me to the house of Dr. Onderdonc, Bishop of New York. On our way thither, he informed me that there are in America, as in England, two church parties, the high and the low. The late Bishop Hobert was of the former, and rather violent in his proceedings; or, to use a more lenient and modified phrase, very firm in his conduct and principles, and determined in his opposition to such as differed from him. The present bishop, although of the high church number, has in a great measure disarmed party-spirit of its rancour, by being exceedingly moderate. Dr. Wainright is the leading minister, in New York, of the former, and Dr. Milnor of the latter party. Both of these gentlemen are excellent and amiable, and stand deservedly high in the estimation of their flocks, and of the public in general. This proves that no party possesses exclusively, or is debarred from possessing, those characteristic features of true Christianity which consist not in particular views of non-essentials, but in a cordial belief and sincere practice of the doctrines and precepts of the gospel. But it also shews, that no form of church Government which human reason can devise, can so unite its members and blend them together, as to render them perfectly harmonious and unanimous.

The Bishop examined my papers, and expressed himself pleased with them; but on learning that I had no letters from or to clergymen, he observed, that it would be desirable I should write to my clerical friends and obtain some, which might testify that I had not quitted my country for any impropriety, nor been on unhandsome terms with the dignitaries of our church, and that I was a decidedly religious character. This observation I immediately complied with, and received several letters from England in the course of a few months. But in the States I did not profit by them; not because they were inadequate to establish my character, but because I had, previous to their arrival, relinquished the design of remaining there. They had, however, sufficient weight with the Bishop of Quebec, when I shewed them to his lordship, to procure me a mission in Canada.

The Bishops of America enjoy no title as in England, nor any civil distinction. Their church, not being a national church, is not represented directly or indirectly in their houses of legislation. In other respects it much resembles the established church of England, if we except the manner in which ministers are paid, and the power of the American church to reform or regulate its own concerns. The liturgy is, as far as a difference of government will allow, nearly the same in both countries. The clergy of New York, and of them only can I form an idea, having heard none elsewhere, are very efficient, and very pious. All the churches I entered are well attended, and the clergy of all of them devout and earnest. I do not wonder that those who have visited America, and have compared the clergy of one country with those of the other, should imagine some change necessary in the established church of England. Yet there is a dignity of manner in the English clergy which those of America have not, and also a much greater extent of sound learning, which I should be extremely sorry to see lost or discontinued. These remarks I have made from no interested views, never having held, nor likely to hold, any church preferment.

The clergy of America are prohibited, by an act of the legislature, from sitting in the chamber of representatives. This was not always the case, but was brought about after the following manner. One of the members of Congress, a clergyman, was very desirous that some permanent provision should be made for the episcopal church, and was urgent with a friend of his, a member also, to use his endeavours to accomplish it. This friend, probably annoyed by frequent solicitations, and being, as Americans in general are represented, a summer's-day friend, promised his word of honour, that he would do something for the church. Accordingly, he mentioned this circumstance in Congress on the first opportunity, and, relating his promise, moved that no clergyman should thenceforth sit in that house. The motion was carried by a vast majority, and clergymen, with their golden anticipations, vanished from it for ever. This was told me by a divine of eminence.

From an introductory letter from Lady Wellesley, I was privileged to call on the Catholic Bishop of New York. He is a pleasant and intelligent man, and has a cast of countenance very similar to what we often find in pictures of Cardinals and Popes. With this gentleman I had a long conversation, during which he flattered me, by saying, that I should obtain much encouragement in America. He informed me that there are upwards of thirty thousand Roman Catholics in and about New York. A large flock, he observed, and many of them very ignorant; but I find a great deal of good feeling among them, and a tractableness which is very gratifying. A few months after this, when dining at the table of his Excellency the Governor of Upper Canada, his Excellency mentioned that he had learned from the British Consul at New York, that there are forty thousand Irish people in that city and its neighbourhood. It consequently contains between five and ten thousand Irish Protestants.

The Catholic Bishop made a somewhat curious remark, which I did not soon forget: that the Protestants and Roman Catholics are approximating rapidly towards each other, and that we shall all be Catholics in the end. I replied, " a moderation and liberality of feeling is springing up, and rapidly diffusing itself throughout the world; and it is therefore probable that the difference between Catholics and Protestants may gradually disappear." Before I withdrew, he gave me an introductory note to Dr. Wainright, saying, " that he had great respect for the episcopal clergy," and then dismissed me, with a warm invitation to repeat my call, whenever I could find an hour of leisure. I related the remark he had made respecting the converging of Protestants and Catholics to a common creed, to Dr. Milnor; who smiled, and said, " I hope all members of the Christian family may become true members of the Catholic faith, but not of the Roman Catholic."

With the above introduction I waited on Dr. Wainright, who invited me to take tea. We had some conversation together on various subjects, particularly Eastern literature, and the progress it has made and is making in Europe. During our conversation, a marriage party was announced, and I rose up to depart. " If," said he, " you have any curiosity to see the ceremony performed, you can stay." The party was immediately introduced, and the ceremony took place, without any hesitation, in his study. It was much like our own, only curtailed. The parties were not of full age, but this is almost universally the case of young people in the States at the time of marriage. A relation of the bride, a mere boy, attended to affirm that the parents knew of the match, and that there was no impediment. After the retiring of the party, I inquired, with some surprise, if it were frequent for parties to be married in the clergyman's house, and at night too ? " Yes," replied he, " and in their own houses also, or in any other place, by day or by night, whenever they desire it. Any industrious man can support a family, and that is as much as most people here expect. There is also plenty of room to spread in, without any danger of over-population. If a family is in difficulty at one time, it can generally make up the deficiency at another."

CHAPTER II.

SANSCRIT PRINTING—POVERTY OF CLERGY—INFLUENCE OF CLERGY—CHANGES IN PROFESSIONS—EMOLUMENTS OF CLERGY—STATE OF LEARNING—PROSPECTS OF ENGLISH CLERGYMEN IN THE STATES—CHARACTER OF AMERICAN CLERGY—METHODIST BIGOTRY.

Soon after my arrival, I called on an American bookseller, to whom I had a letter of introduction, and requested he would inform me if I might be able to get something in Sanscrit printed. He answered, that even Greek printing, much more Sanscrit, of which he had never before heard mention, could with difficulty be executed; and that, if I would even pay him for importing Sanscrit types into the States, and pay also for warehouse room, he would not take them in. Both they, and books in that language, would be worse than useless lumber. I had similar conversations with other persons, confirming the above statement; and was informed, that if I commenced any such work in the States, from any apparent encouragement, or from subscriptions of professional men, I might depend upon ruining myself. Many, I was told, are ready to subscribe to, or encourage literature, but hang back at the time of payment. I was also assured by some, from their personal knowledge, that subscriptions for any work, from which no profit could be gained, unless advanced before hand, would never be paid. The only method of preventing disappointment in collecting subscription-money, is the getting it in advance. "The clergy and literary men of this country," said they, "are notoriously poor, and the worst payers in the world. You will find them ready in promises and encouragements, but backward in discharging them. Their salaries and incomes are often so small, as not to enable them to pay their bills, and many of them are frequently years in arrears." This statement was confirmed by the testimony of so many, that no doubt remains in my mind of its truth. A minister in

INFLUENCE OF CLERGY. 27

New York had raised, a short time before our arrival, a large collection among his hearers, to defray the accounts of his tradesmen, which had been accumulating for years.

Every person in business, with whom I conversed, described the little influence possessed by professional men, and by the clergy in particular. Yet, I could never perceive any reality in this representation; nor do the clergy themselves perceive it. They imagine themselves to be, what I believe they really are, among the best informed and most consequential in the commonwealth. They uniformly stated, that they possess as much influence among the people, as is necessary to ensure the respectability of their order.

A person in New York, living in a most respectable house of his own, and conducting a flourishing business, advised me to change my profession. The reason he urged was, that the clergy are without wealth, or influence or respect. He told me that, if I would transfer my capital and talents to some other pursuit than my profession, I should find that I had acted for my best interests. He also gave me an anecdote, respecting the clergy there, which, he thought, demonstrated their want of influence in society. The condition of the negro slaves in the southern States has often been a subject of deep consideration, with the religious portion of the community; and their instruction, through means of missionaries, has been attempted. But the missionaries are, in some of the States, prohibited by law from imparting information of any kind to these degraded people; and some were arrested for violating that law. A meeting was convened in New York by desire of the clergy, at which an immense multitude of persons of different classes were assembled. The clergy attended in their canonicals, and were seated on the elevated front of the Town Hall. The arrangement respecting proper speakers had not, among the friends of negro instruction, been properly preconcerted; and none were prepared to explain the object of the meeting. An officer of the army, adverse to the purposes of the clergy, rose up, and in a short and expressive speech, addressed the surrounding multitude. He informed them, that since those who had intermeddled in matters not concerning them, had nothing to offer, he would move a resolution that the meeting should instantly dissolve, and that every man should return to his home. This speech was cheered enthusiastically by the assembled multitude, which immediately dispersed amidst ribaldry, and laughter.

This anecdote, whatever might be its truth, was told me, as I perceived, to induce me to change my profession. But it had the contrary effect. I had known, by frequent intercourse, the estimable character of several clergymen of New York; their desire of discharging their sacred duties conscientiously; and the salutary influence which their labours have over a great portion of the people. A statement like the above, kindled only feelings of sympathy; and I asserted immediately, that my attachment to the sacred duties of the church was stronger than ever.

The same advice having been given me from other quarters, I thought proper to make some inquiries respecting it. In the course of these I was told, that it is no unusual thing for a person to have been schoolmaster, doctor, lawyer, clergyman, and to have been engaged also in other professions; and in the business classes of society, to have followed almost all the circle of trades. This is becoming less frequent than formerly. Yet I was most credibly assured by some workmen, that an American will frequently undertake numbers of jobs in various trades, none of which he has ever learned himself, and then advertise for workmen to complete the jobs. The Americans are skilful calculators; and can generally find out, what are the probable expenses in any undertaking. The workmen they employ are, for the most part, poor Irish or English emigrants, whom they can hire at low wages, which must be taken out in shop goods. The contractor, without having had the labour of learning these trades, thus contrives to reap a double advantage from them. He secures both the profits which accrue from the jobs, and likewise a per centage from the goods, in which the wages are paid.

The salaries of ministers in the States, depending generally on pew rents or on contributions, cannot be stated as permanent. Yet there are churches in New York, which are liberally endowed. Ministers in large towns, are said to receive from two to six hundred pounds sterling a year; yet I have heard this amount contradicted, by persons, who asserted, that there are episcopal ministers in New York who do not receive two hundred, and none receive six hundred pounds. The salary of the bishop is stated to be about seven hundred pounds. The salaries of country clergy vary from thirty to one hundred and fifty pounds. If a country minister's income be small, his parishioners in some cases allow him to keep a school in his neighbourhood. But their consent is necessary, since they, and not he, regulate this. He is entirely at the mercy, and under the control of his flock. He is, in fact, their creature, however desirous he may be of concealing it from himself. But still, while he conducts himself to their satisfaction, and is able to perform his clerical duties, he is in no danger of want. I have heard of some pastors, who have been able to save as much out of their salaries and schools, and the earnings of their wives and children by knitting, sewing, spinning, &c. as enabled them to buy an estate, and build themselves a comfortable house. When a minister has not been able to anticipate the approach of sickness or age by savings from his income, it must find him wretched; for there is no permanent fund from which relief can be obtained, and the motto of his country is, " No work no pay." The annals of pauperism scarcely contain more distressing cases, than those which poor superannuated American ministers sometimes exhibit, if I have been veraciously informed. I hope, however, such instances are rare. Yet no American clergyman can look forward to support in old age, independent of what he may have laid up in the season of activity. Parishioners in general, are either unable or unwilling to bear any burden. He must prepare in youth and manhood for old age, or else, suffer the consequences of his own improvidence, with none to give him sympathy.

I was informed that in large towns, a clergyman was seldom suffered to divide his time between clerical and scholastic duties. The people also, who are jealous of professional and priestly wealth, and who imagine that the clerical character should be that of poverty, abstinence, and self-denial, do not wish that even the talents of a minister should obtain other pecuniary recompense, than what arises from his preaching, A clergyman of acknowledged abilities would, in England, add lustre to his character, by sending shining scholars to our universities or public schools. Americans view things in a different light. Shining scholars, with them, are neither known nor wanted. And every one there is fully persuaded, that dollars shine brightest in his own purse.

From the manner in which ministers are rewarded, it is clear to me, that America can never, under her present form of government, possess a body of divines so learned and respectable as those in England. Science and sound learning require more fostering aid than they yet receive in that country. Americans possess, in an eminent degree, talent and energy; but these are exerted, almost exclusively, in other than sedentary studies. Few in that part of the world are born to wealth. The great majority are compelled to fight their way in the best manner they are able, and professional men among others. As the clergy depend almost entirely, except in a few instances, on pew rents, voluntary contributions and donations, it is evident that no minister can confidently look forward to any permanent provision. And since the remuneration of even the more respectable congregations to their pastors is barely adequate to maintain respectability, none of them will be eager to increase his qualifications beyond the point at which they can be estimated and rewarded. The demand for eminence in learning must exist, before that eminence will be generally sought. Literary distinction is not attainable, otherwise than by great sacrifices of time, labour, and expense. These, American clergymen have not to bestow. Admitted at the age of twenty-one to clerical orders; removed from connexion with seats of learning, before the maturity of studies or of judgment have been reached; frequently placed in extensive parishes, with numerous important duties to discharge; and living among people, who are incompetent to estimate mental attainments, or to reward them if they were; it is not in their power, perhaps not in their aspirations, to reach proficiency in the higher walks of literature.

There is a clerical college established in New York, for the reception of divinity-students in-

STATE OF LEARNING. 35

tended for episcopal ordination. After having passed through the university, they there prepare themselves peculiarly for sacred functions. This appears a proper and judicious plan. It will generally impart a serious tone to the candidates for orders, and enable them to accommodate their energies to their future destinations. This college may bear some features of resemblance to the clerical institution at St. Bees. Yet it cannot stand so high in point of learning; nor its students so matured in point of experience. In England, literature is incalculably higher than in the States. And at St. Bees, the divinity students are generally twenty-three years of age; whereas, in America, candidates are admitted to clerical offices, at the age of twenty-one.

One day, when in conversation with Dr. Milnor, he alluded to an address, published in England by Dr. Chase, late Bishop of Ohio, encouraging English clergymen of the Established Church, to emigrate to the United States, and promising them a hearty welcome and a liberal support. "The promise and encouragement," said he, "was contrary to my advice; for I knew that it could not be fulfilled, and might occasion much distress and disappointment. The bishops of this country," he added, " have no power whatever to appoint a minister over any congregation. The only thing they can do for a clergyman is to recommend him. His nomination rests with the people who support him." On explaining to him the nature of my own views, as to teaching, and the reasons for my abandoning a country, where patronage and aristocratic interest were every thing, and where heavy exactions eat up the earnings of industry; he smiling replied, " In our country, every man can repose under his own fig-tree and his c n vine, and can eat without molestation the fruit of *his own labours.* But it is not *every* person, who visits this country, that finds his expections realised in it. Instances are neither rare nor solitary, of persons coming hot from Europe, and returning soberer than they came."

A clergyman from Ireland, with whom I had a short conversation soon after my arrival, on being told my object, and learning that I was not immediately pressed to seek employment, said, " It is well for you that you are not so. Look around deliberately, before you enter on any thing; and if afterwards you decide upon a permanent residence, you must adopt this proverb in its literal sense. ' When at Rome, act as do the Romans.'"

I was repeatedly asked, if I would accept a situation in Ohio, and as repeatedly declined such a place of exile. My habits had fitted me for other scenes, and required more domestic comforts than a wilderness can furnish. Besides, I was early made acquainted with the sort of people I was likely to find for associates in places remote from the frontier. As I perceived that persons of the same standing, even in New York, are not the most amiable or liberal, I feared their manners would not be improved, by contiguity to forests, bears, and Indians.

During the year preceding our emigration, the pastor of St. Thomas' in New York, was obliged to resign, and retired with his family into the Ohio territory. His great crime was, his being an Englishman. He had, moreover, not been so submissive to the free-born Americans as to endure passively, various things in their conduct, which to him appeared unpleasant. As the purse-strings of the clergy are generally in the hands of their flock, they can always clothe and feed them and their families as they please. For although, by a canon of the Episcopal church, no minister of that denomination is liable to be expelled by his hearers, yet, presents and subscriptions can be withdrawn when they please. The minister of St. Thomas' had given some offence to a few individuals, native Americans. The thing was canvassed among their countrymen, and the result was, that the greater part of his congregation withdrew their subscriptions and attendance. The minister, finding himself forsaken, and without resources, was obliged to relinquish the place of his sojourn, and to bury his griefs and necessities in the solitudes of Ohio.

Such was the statement of an English lady in New York. Similar statements have been made to me by various persons, whose narrations I could not disbelieve, respecting several different English clergymen, who, after years of laborious duties, have been turned adrift by those who had been benefiting from their instructions. My fair informant expressed a wish that I might be so fortunate as to obtain that church. " But," added she, " if you have still a friend in England, return again. America is a place of refuge, but to such only as are of doubtful character, or completely distressed. You will always be considered as having fled your country on account of something which had blasted your comfort at home ; and any success or respect, however small, will be considered greater than your merits and character deserve, or than you could have obtained in England. I myself came thence several years ago, allured by the flattering promises of Americans, whom I then considered as friends, but whom I have since found to be heartless beyond description. There is no dependence to be placed upon the promises or friendship of any person in this country. There is not, indeed, sir," she added, " therefore return to England, if you have *one* friend there, and do not suffer any thing they may tell you to induce you to accept a situation here, if you can live elsewhere. But you know best your own circumstances. I would have returned to England had I not lost every thing, and my sons not being apprenticed, or placed in business."

Such were the sentiments of one who could not possibly have a motive to mislead me; and they are worthy the attention of clergymen, who are friends to democracy.

During my sojourn in New York, Dr. Milnor once granted me the use of his pulpit, and I enjoyed the pleasure of delivering a discourse to his highly respectable flock — the only sermon I preached in the States. The Dr. praised my discourse, but stated that my plain manner of delivery would not suit Americans, from their fondness of high declamation, action, and attitude, so different from the chaste style of the English preaching. Effect is more aimed at in American, than in English churches; and is, I believe, more necessary in the dawn than in an advanced state of society. But perhaps other causes are in operation, to require rhetorical action there more than with us. The people are remarkably active and restless; and a dependent minister must use every exertion to adapt his mode of delivery to the taste and temperament of his hearers. Yet, I must say I have seen it carried too far.

It is impossible for me to quit the subject,

without giving almost unqualified praise to the worthy and estimable character of the episcopal clergy of New York generally. Their church discipline and government is admirable; and is making rapid advances, not only in that State, but throughout all America. The episcopal church is gaining strength there, fully equal to the spread of knowledge, and the increase of population ; and will ultimately be matured, in my opinion, into a national church. Its members are adopting every available means for rendering the ministers of their order as competent as possible to sustain the sacred character with becoming dignity ; and to merit, and consequently secure, the respect and support of every well informed and rationally pious christian. If they have not yet attained to that elevation of character, that dignity, and learning, enjoyed by ministers of the established church of England, we must remember, that they have neither the means nor the incentives to attain it ; that they have not British audiences to preach to ; that their church, and the society around them, are in a state of infancy ; and that their means of instruction, and the manner of imparting it, correspond with their institutions, and the habits of the people. The episcopal clergy are greatly in advance of those of all other denominations, and march in the van of learning, improvement, and public virtue.

One Sunday morning I entered a methodist chapel, without being previously aware that it was one. What a difference in the language and manner of the preacher, from what I had heard and seen elsewhere! It reminded me forcibly of an observation made by the Catholic bishop when I called on him. " Although," said he, " all sects and denominations are said to be placed on an equal footing here, yet I respect the episcopal church more than any other. Its ministers are men of greater learning than the rest, and the most respectable citizens are included within its pale." The same thing occurred to my recollection, when returning through the States from Canada. A methodist printer, who had struck off some hundred copies of a portion of Watts' hymns, and who was wandering up and down to vend them; on learning that he was in company with an episcopal minister, coarsely asserted that our church was the devil's house, and that the wise and prudent, the mighty, the learned, and the wealthy, everywhere belong to it. " How surprising," continued he, " it is, to find that the best informed and the wealthiest are the devil's own children, and belong to his house!" Ignorance and illiberality are generally found to go hand in hand.

The congregations of ministers are generally the best criterion of their pastor's worth. All the churches I had an opportunity of entering, while in New York, and they were not few, were numerously and respectably attended. The devout behaviour of episcopal congregations could not be exceeded by that of any congregation of any church in London. If I were asked whether, in the churches I attended, a greater number of males or females were present, I should feel great hesitation in deciding.

Those only who have travelled to a distance, can conceive how gratifying it is to an English clergyman, properly imbued with the spirit of his calling, to find, in places so far from his former home, and even in another hemisphere, not only the same language spoken, but the very customs of his native country imitated and adopted, as far as a change of circumstances and a diversity of governments will allow. Here he finds the same prayers, the same ceremonies, the same version of psalms and tunes in psalmody, the same decent solemnities of worship, the same sort of discourses, as in our churches, with but a slight and immaterial alteration, and that alteration generally for the better. Our Saviour's words force themselves strongly on our recollection, on going into an American church, after arrival from England: " Other sheep I have which are not of this fold. Them also I must bring, and they will hear my voice; and there shall be one fold, and one shepherd."

Having found that I could not be the appointed minister of any episcopal church in America, before the expiration of twelve months, I deemed it most adviseable to make inquiries respecting the other branch of my professional life—school-teaching. I had long been engaged laboriously in education; and from protracted and arduous pursuits of learning, had believed myself well qualified for a teacher My introductions also, several of which were to professors of colleges, would confirm the respectability of my character. The result of my inquiries in this particular I shall now proceed to detail.

CHAPTER III.

REASONS FOR ABANDONING THE IDEA OF TEACHING THE EASTERN LANGUAGES IN THE UNITED STATES—DAY-SCHOOLS—INSUBORDINATION OF PUPILS—ANECDOTE OF THE BLIND TEACHER—OF AN IRISH CLASSICAL TEACHER—SAD TALE OF A VILLAGE SCHOOLMASTER—AMERICAN INSENSIBILITY—FARTHER OPINIONS CONCERNING AMERICAN SCHOOLS.

When I had held two or three conversations with a gentleman, to whom I had a letter of introduction from London, with reference to my plan of teaching, particularly the languages of the East; he told me that, in his opinion, my best measure would be to go back to England. " The Americans do not yet want any thing with the East Indies. They are not colonizing other countries, but peopling their own; and have more need of being taught how to handle the axe or the spade, than how to read Hindoostanee. Had you been a strong active hardy ploughman, you might have been worth encouragement, but as it is, I can give you none." What this gentleman and his family told me, I found to be perfectly correct. The attempt would be useless and absurd to persuade a people, in love with money, and with themselves; doating upon their own perfections, and their superiority over all the nations of the earth in learning, arts, and arms; and despising, or pretending to despise, the English most heartily, that an individual from Great Britain had arrived in their country to teach them languages they do not know. It would be equally useless, to attempt inducing them to pay for information, which they could not at once convert to purposes of gain. A little further inquiry among those, with whom my letters and introductions brought me in contact, soon induced me to abandon the intention of opening a school for instruction in Eastern languages. Dr. Milnor himself thought the attempt could be only futile and followed by disappointment. He imagined, however, that another kind of school might be opened, which would be more likely to succeed. A day-school, with liberal terms, he said, *might* answer my expectations.

As the same thing had been suggested by other gentlemen of some consideration, it became worthy the attention of one, circumstanced like myself, to investigate more closely the character of day-schools in general, and the mode of conducting them. I soon found, that a common schoolmaster, in that country, is not regarded with much respect; and that education, in such schools, is on a contracted scale. It is true, that high claims to skill are advanced by teachers, and parents are flattered with reports that their sons are in such and such classes, and have studied such and such books.

The hours of attendance in day-schools are about five and a half each day, for four days, and four for the remaining two days of the week. In some seminaries, there are sixty or eighty pupils taught by one, or at the most, by two masters. Such schools, generally close at three in the afternoon.

SCHOOL INSUBORDINATION. 49

Here insubordination prevails to a degree subversive of all improvement. The pupils are entirely independent of their teacher. No correction, no coercion, no manner of restraint is permitted to be used. It must be seen, from this picture, that general education is at a low ebb, even in New York. Indeed, all who know any thing of teaching, will see at once the impossibility of conveying extensive knowledge, in so few hours per day, and upon such a system. Parents also have as little control over their offspring at home, as the master has at school; and the leisure hours of idle boys are, in all countries perhaps, alike unproductive of improvement.

Two or three anecdotes were related, to convey to me an idea of American schools. The best teacher whom the United States could ever boast of was a blind athletic old man, who was so well acquainted with the books he taught, as to detect immediately the slightest incorrectness of his scholars. He was also a great disciplinarian; and, though blind, could, from constant practice, inflict the most painful and effective chastisements. From the energetic mental and bodily powers of this teacher, his pupils became distinguished in the colleges and universities of America. They were generally, at their admission into public seminaries, so far in advance of other students, that, from the absence of inducements to steady application, they there, for the first time, contracted habits of idleness. They also became less obedient and subordinate to collegiate regulations than the other scholars, when the hand of correction, of which they formerly had tasted, was no longer extended over them. Thus, a two-fold evil was produced by the discipline and skill of this blind teacher. Since that time, corporal punishment has almost disappeared from American dayschools; and a teacher, who should now have recourse to such means of enforcing instruction, would meet with reprehension from the parents, and perhaps retaliation from his scholars.

My inquiries, when this statement was made to me, were naturally directed to the real means of which a teacher might be allowed to avail himself, in order to inculcate his instructions on the more inattentive of his pupils.

" He must," replied a gentleman, " put up

SCHOOL INSUBORDINATION.

with their behaviour, but by no means punish them; and should his patience be exhausted, he must then acquaint the parents with their conduct. Allow me," continued he, " to mention to you a circumstance which occurred under my immediate observation:—A school-master was appointed to a parish or district school, over which I had some influence. A rumour was circulated that he made use of chastisement, and an investigation took place. The report was confirmed by a public examination; and a notice was, in consequence, conveyed to him, that he must relinquish either his rod or his school. His answer imported that the latter, if either, would be abandoned. I entered one day whilst he was employed in attending to some lessons with which his scholars were engaged. He was, himself, rather an odd-looking person, and his visage frequently assumed involuntary contortions and grimaces, when his mind was ruffled or agitated. I observed a little boy, who was very deaf, amusing himself with laughing at the grotesque figure and odd contortions of his master. The teacher observed this act of impropriety, and after reprimanding the little fellow for neglect of his books, threatened to punish him in case of repetition of the offence. The master, on observing that what he had said produced no effect, forgetting the deafness of his pupil, inflicted on him immediate punishment. I felt indignant at this conduct, and, after sharply rebuking him before his boys, convened a meeting of the trustees, of whom I was one, and had him summarily dismissed."

I inquired what course a schoolmaster must pursue if any of his scholars should turn out obstinate and refractory, or if he have one more intractable than the rest. Is the master still obliged to tolerate patiently the most insubordinate conduct?

" He should expel the offender," was the reply. " In a college of ours, there was a student notoriously offensive and ungovernable. On one occasion, his instructor having observed something improper in his conduct, deemed him worthy of reprehension, and summoned him to his desk. The young man, suddenly extending his hand to the watch-chain of his teacher, jerked his gold time-piece out of the pocket, and dashed it instantly on the desk. A meeting of the trustees and members was convened, and the young man was *dismissed.*"

In a country like America, where there is nothing in the patronage of colleges, and where expulsion from a public institution entails no disgrace, nor disqualifies for any kind of business or pursuit, it appeared to me improbable that much attention to instruction could be secured. I therefore asked if such a system of education could lead to eminent acquirements?

" In our country," he replied, " education is generally completed at the age of sixteen or seventeen, even in colleges and universities. Young men enter at that age and sometimes earlier, into business or professions. The clerical profession must be excepted. Learning, to a great extent, is not required for store-keepers and merchants' clerks. Yet the students in our colleges are generally acquainted with the rudiments of Greek and Latin; also with common arithmetic, and the usual course of mathematics. This is sufficient to enable them to comprehend any allusions which occur in reading or conversation. And a foundation being once laid, it is in their power, if choice induce, or opportunity allow them, to prosecute any branch as far as they please."

"But yet," said I, resuming the subject of common schools, " if schoolmasters are allowed no coercive influence over their scholars, is it not a difficult matter to meet with respectable persons willing and able to undertake a task so laborious and ungrateful ?"

" There are always found," he replied, " some respectable young men, who, intended for other professions, are willing to devote two or three years to a parish or district school, in order to improve themselves, and save a little money to help them forward. And even others, on leaving the university, frequently begin their career by conducting an inferior school. These, becoming noted, by degrees, for their good conduct and steady application, rise from one station to another, till at last they fill a professor's chair in some college or university."

" It appears then," said I, " that common schools in the States are regarded as very subordinate situations; and are not of sufficient importance, to secure the continued residence of a really respectable person. There must either be teachers of doubtful character and qualifications, or a continual fluctuation, in your district schools."

He assented to the correctness of these remarks; and then proceeded in the following narration:—
" There are always found persons both qualified and willing to conduct such schools, notwithstanding their subordinate situation, and also the smallness of salaries annexed to them. The following anecdote will convince you," he continued, " that we are at no loss for teachers. Sometime ago, a gentleman came over from Ireland, with high and satisfactory testimonials, desirous of obtaining a professorship in some of our schools or colleges. He applied to several gentlemen in the States; and to me, among others. I was very desirous of promoting his object, and recommended him to the trustees of several colleges and schools, one after another, yet he could never succeed. His failure did not arise, in the least degree, from deficiency of talents or of character; but merely because he was a stranger, and was opposed by many candidates, who had greater personal in-

terest than himself. Disheartened, at last, by frequent disappointments, and reduced in his circumstances, he supplicated me to use my utmost exertions in his behalf. There happened soon after to be a school on Long Island vacant, and I had sufficient influence with the electors to procure his nomination. The stipend, indeed, was rather small, but was enough to furnish a subsistence. This Irish gentleman, after filling the situation for some time, fell sick, and grew desirous of returning to his native country, and to his relatives, from whom, during his American sojourn, he had heard no account. He had been unable to save any thing, or, to speak more correctly, was in debt. How to return, he did not know; and in this forlorn condition, he again applied to my benevolence. I made his condition known to some friends of mine, who subscribed a few dollars, and procured him a passage to Ireland. He promised to write to me, on reaching his native country; but his gratitude evaporated, and I heard of him no more."

The foregoing anecdote was related to me by a person of conspicuous standing in New York, and the truth of it is unquestionable. A story, in some respects similar, but with a tragical and melancholy ending, was told, to dissuade me from emigrating far back, or accepting any office in America out of the Atlantic States. The person who related it, was possessed of elegant manners, and from England.

A person from England. with every characteristic of a gentleman, who had moved in better circles, solicited the place of school-master in a country village, and was successful. The emoluments arising from his teaching were barely adequate to the supply of indispensable necessaries, and left him without any of those little comforts which sweeten civilized life. The boors and storekeepers of the village, unaccustomed to such a schoolmaster, observed, indeed, the propriety of his conduct, and his sad and silent mien; but took no interest in him, beyond the education of their children, and the exercise of a prying curiosity, which he was unwilling, and all others were unable to gratify, by any information or disclosure. He entered into none of their parties, partook of nothing cheerful, nor joined in any pastimes. He found, in the contracted souls around him, no kindred spirit with his own; none, with whom to interchange ideas, or communicate his griefs. His mind had, consequently, no intervals of social relaxation; and his bodily wants were but scantily supplied. His nights were spent in a wretched apartment, and on a bed of straw; and his days, in educating those, who were strangers to the feelings of civilized life, and whose earthly existence would be bounded by rustic toils, or sordid calculations. This situation he filled for some time, with increasing sadness, but without a murmur or complaint. At last, his strength became completely exhausted; and, unable longer to attend his school, he was confined to a solitary room. Too poor to hire attendance, he prepared his own food, and lived by himself. Some of the neighbours, not having seen or heard of him for a longer time than usual, entered his lonely abode, and found his lifeless body stretched upon the straw, where, bereft of every earthly comfort, he had sickened, without a hand to aid him, and died in absolute solitude. His pockets and apartments were ransacked, to discover his real name, and the place of his nativity; but every inquiry was useless. An impenetrable secrecy rested upon his birth and misfortunes; and his remains were deposited by strangers in unconsecrated ground, without a sigh of sympathy, or even common Christian burial.

"The Americans," continued my informant, "are, in general, strangers to the finer feelings; and take pleasure in humbling those whose manners differ from their own. If you retire back from the larger cities, which have received a tincture from European residents, you will have ample opportunities of realising this tale, in almost every particular. Your family, indeed, will keep you from utter solitude; but if your children mix at all with those around them, their conduct towards yourself will be so contaminated with republican principles, as will become a source of hourly vexation. Such places are fitted only for the rudest people, and offer no correspondence with minds in the least refined by good society, or humanized by literature."

In conversation with an American clergyman, I once expressed myself thus:—" It appears strange to me, that so many should be found willing to engage in school-teaching, which, even here, must require expensive qualifications, and which, notwithstanding, is so little respected, and so badly paid." "The expensive preparation, of which you speak," he replied, "is generally defrayed by the public; and the respect is perhaps greater than you have been led to imagine, although not equal to what a clergyman or a lawyer receives. A schoolmaster's character is less obtrusive or conspicuous, than that of other professions : but he is not, on that account, less respected. His standing in society is equal to respectable traders, and persons in the minor professions. But perhaps it may afford you some insight into this subject, when I tell you, that in the New England States alone, there are between one and two millions of dollars, of public funds, annually expended, in affording education to the children of those, who could not otherwise obtain it. The sons of these people, after having obtained a grammatical, and, in many instances, a collegiate education, go abroad into the world without a dollar, to fight their way. No school or college affords an opening, which cannot instantly be supplied. And a small salary is perhaps as much as they could obtain by labour, or in business. Besides, in point of respectability, a school possesses some advantages ; and may lead to higher degrees of advancement, if filled by merit." To this I merely observed, " that I never before felt so strongly the force of Alexander's reply, when asked if he could contend at the Olympic games." " I could readily contend," he answered, " if kings were my competitors." " If clergymen of eminence in learning were frequently so engaged, I could open a day-school in your country. But at present, I will content myself with pushing my inquiries," " You had better," said he, " consult other teachers."

In one of my interviews with Dr. Wainright, he advised me to open a school in New York, and to charge the following terms; ten dollars per quarter for boys under ten years, fifteen for those above that age, and twenty for such as might read the higher classics. These, although not the highest terms, are considered respectable. He supposed I might soon have a school of fifty or sixty scholars. The terms above mentioned are two, three, and four pounds sterling, per quarter, respectively. It would be difficult to raise a day-school in England with higher terms and greater numbers; especially when we take this into consideration, that the higher classics in America would be lower classics in this country. Perhaps a person would imagine that a considerable saving might be made from such a school. Yet I believe most people, engaged in schools, in New York, relate a different tale. They deduct house rent, which is nearly double of what it is with us; and clothes, which are fifty per cent. higher; and fuel, which is also higher. They then remember, that sickness is more prevalent, and that medicines are more expensive. After years of experience, they learn the fact, that a few hundred dollars go but a little way in housekeeping.

When I delivered an introductory letter to Dr. Moore, of Columbia College, he recommended me to take a house immediately, and receive pupils; for, by expressly preparing them for the college, or for professions, I might have a large and respectable school. We had once thought of taking an entire house; but when we made inquiries, and found house-rents excessive, we contented ourselves with lodgings. We determined, ultimately, not to embarrass or distract ourselves with any engagements, till the arrival of Spring ; when, as we were universally informed, all houses are to let, and all people are migratory ; when the rivers and canals are open, and trade revives ; and when our own prospects, now overcast by contradictory statements, doubts, and indecision, might brighten up, and be relumed and renovated into vernal promise. I continued, therefore, to be arranging my Sanscrit work ; and to keep my ears and conviction open to every source of intelligence from every quarter

CHAPTER IV.

STORY OF A STRANGER AND HIS TRAVELS—OF HIS BOOK, AND HIS TEACHING EXPERIENCE—CASE OF A YOUNG SCHOOLMASTER FROM ENGLAND—HIS SANGUINE HOPES AND HIS DISAPPOINTMENTS—THE NEW YORK PROPRIETORY SCHOOL—LOW STATE OF GREEK TEACHING IN NEW YORK—DISTASTE FOR IMPROVEMENTS IN THE UNITED STATES, THAT DO NOT PROMISE IMMEDIATE RETURN IN MONEY—DETERMINATION TO PROCEED TO BOSTON.

ONE winter evening, when seated by the fire, a book from some stranger was brought up for our inspection, accompanied by a request from its owner, that we would allow him to be introduced. The request was complied with. He entered immediately, and soon found himself at home by our fire-side.

" The book which preceded me, said the stranger," was " written by my uncle, a person of some eminence as a literary man; and a physician. I myself received a commercial education, and was placed in a house of great note in London. When I became my own master, I possessed thirteen hundred pounds sterling; and having heard much in praise of America, I formed the design of adopting it for my home. I had no sooner landed in this country, than the report was circulated, that a wealthy Englishman had made his appearance; and I was not long unsought. Being young and inexperienced, I was easily prevailed on to enter into various schemes of business, which required, indeed ready money, but which promised abundant and speedy profits. I need not occupy much time in telling you, that no scheme succeeded with me. I was completely cheated and plundered; and in less than two years, was without a dollar in the world. In my reduced situation, I could not dig, and to beg I was ashamed. I therefore determined to retire from the scene of my disgrace and ruin, and to go up into Canada to try my fortune. That extensive region I travelled on foot, with the intention of choosing some favourable place, in which, to commence schoolmaster. After having rambled up and down in it from one end to the other, and having found no resting place, I relinquished the British territories once more, and turned my attention to the States. To return destitute to England, was a step, which my pride, still unhumbled and unsubdued, would not allow me to take. I had, whilst living among Americans, frequently remarked, how exceedingly defective their education is, when contrasted with that of Europeans; and was eager to convert this circumstance to an honourable source of profit. I therefore began to collect materials for a book, which I intended to publish as a school-book; but, from being destitute of the pecuniary means, I had no other alternative left than to publish by subscription. I therefore turned pedestrian once more; and travelled up and down over all the States, as I had before done over Canada. I canvassed every place, in which as many people could be collected as would form a school. I sought all possible publicity. Wherever I went, I made it my business to seek out the principal persons of the neighbourhood. I explained to them the imperfections of their own system of education, and the necessity incumbent upon them of procuring a better. I then recommended them to give impartial encouragement to one from England; and proposed my own. In every village I entered, I followed the same plan; and then solicited subscriptions to my book. The thing succeeeded beyond my utmost wishes, or most sanguine expectations. I told every person, whose subscription I requested, that my book should not be printed, until ten thousand copies were subscribed for, and I had security for the payment. Before the expiration of two years the greater part of which time had been spent in perambulating the States, I had obtained twenty-five thousand subscriptions; with security for the payment, as soon as the book should be delivered.

" You will very naturally wonder, how a poor man, without a single dollar, contrived to feed and clothe himself (and let me tell you I lived and dressed sumptuously) during almost two years, without expense to himself, or any inconvenience. Wherever I entered, I followed the Scripture precept, " Peace be to this house." I had become so completely divested, not only of English money, but of English feeling also, that I might be considered as Yankeefied altogether. I had discovered that a foreigner cannot affront an American more, than by telling any truth which offends his prejudices. I therefore talked as they talked. I ran down the English, I praised Americans to the skies; I assured them that nothing was wanting to render them the wisest and happiest upon earth, but a more perfect system of instruction; which I myself was qualified to impart. I thus enlisted their prejudices on my side; and that is every thing with Americans. They took me by the hand wherever I went. They invited me into their houses. They caressed and honoured me. When I was hungry they fed me; and when thirsty, they gave me drink. When I was naked, they clothed me; and sheltered me in their houses whenever I sought their hospitality. By these means, I contrived to pass almost two years; and with improved health, strength, and spirits; with a perfect knowledge of America and its people, their propensities, failings and prejudices, I returned to New York, and published my book. The profits of its sale realized for me six hundred pounds, and also gained me reputation. I might almost say, that this was diamond cut diamond. It brought back nearly half the money of which I had been previously deprived. Furthermore, it procured me a prosperous school, and an American lady for my wife. My scholars have been regularly increasing, since I first commenced, which is six years ago, and I have now seventy pupils.

" I suppose you save," said I, " several hundreds of pounds every year, by your profession."

" You must not suppose," he replied, " that it is all gold which glitters. I do not save one hundred yearly. Indeed, to speak the truth, this is the first year, in which my riches have increased by teaching. House rent is very high; and I am obliged to rent two rooms, one for boys, and another for girls."

"Have you a mixed school of boys and girls?" I inquired. "Yes," replied he; " and two rooms for them; or, more properly speaking, one large room, which I have made into two, by suspending a curtain across the middle of it. I have been at a great expense in fitting up my school with forms and tables, so that hitherto my savings have been trifling. I now have hopes, that the up-hill part of my life is already past; and look forward to the future with brightening expectations."

" But how is it," observed I, " that nothing is saved, from so large a school?"

"I have told you, he replied," that house-rent is excessive. My expenses, also, in fitting up, have been great. And besides all this, no person in America, in any kind of business, expects to obtain all his dues. Many parents never pay at all; and the bills of others I am often obliged to take out in shop goods, with perhaps some addition to ready money prices laid on them. In short, I get paid as I can. But I do not complain of this; for my success, in this respect, equals that of most people. But there is one very remarkable circumstance, which befalls all English people who settle here. I do not recollect a single instance, of any Englishman succeeding in the States, who had not first been freed from all his English money. There is a kind of pride about persons from " the old country," which prevents their stooping to the practices of this, till compelled to do so by absolute want. When they have found, that either compliance, or starvation, is the consequence, they prefer the less

of two evils, and turn Americans in self-defence
And indeed we often find them lending their endeavours, in their turn, to assist such as come with
money in their pockets, to become Americans as
soon as possible."

With this intelligent teacher I had a long conversation ; which ended in convincing me, that a
common school would never serve my purpose.
He confirmed every thing I had heard, respecting
the insubordination of children in America, and
the impossibility of instructing them in any thing,
to which their own inclinations were adverse. His
experience led him to believe, that every family is
a republic. The children are independent of parental control, and the *helps* are independent of
their employers. But yet he had become reconciled to American manners, and looked forward
to comfort in his family. To save much, he
believed, was impossible.

" Do you find the life of a school master very
laborious ?" I asked.

" A teacher," he replied, " is not, in America, so
great a slave as in England. We begin our labours at nine in the morning, and end them at

three in the afternoon ; after which hour, the business of the day is over. We have no trouble with the boys, out of school hours ; so that we are better paid, perhaps, for our time and exertions, than persons of the same profession in England."

"Do you find," said I, " that the boys make much progress, by having so much leisure time ?"

" It pleases the parents," he said, " and it pleases the scholars ; and you must know, that where this can be accomplished, the battle is won. Indeed, it is more to the interest of a master, to keep on good terms with the boys, than with their parents ; for, instances are not few, in which boys have left one master, and gone to another, without consulting their natural guardians. A boy, in this country, who has acted in this manner, when the thing comes to his parents ears, will generally carry his point, and compel them to sanction his choice. All children in New York are taught to read, and write, and keep accounts. This is all that is absolutely necessary. And even those who go to Columbia college, or who receive the best education, are not instructed like boys in England. But education is perceptibly improving.

" Will you do me the favour," said I, " to allow me the sight of your book?" for a strong desire had entered my mind, of inspecting that wonderful volume, which had performed the double purpose, of replenishing his coffers with money, and filling the minds of Americans with useful knowledge."

" I have not brought a copy with me," was the answer. " But I shall be very happy, if you will do me the pleasure of calling at my house. Here is the list of my terms, and of the classes of my school. It will also direct you to both my school and residence. When you call, I will present you with a copy of my book. It is a poor performance; but the sight of it may afford you some amusement." He then wished me a good night; and I never had an opportunity to call on him, or to speak with him again.

This little adventure was not without some useful effects. It afforded me an insight into American teaching, and the modes of being remunerated for the same. It also exemplified the necessity, under which every emigrant must find himself, of bending to the prejudices, and flattering the vanity, of the American public, if he have any well directed prospects of success. It moreover showed me, what I had antecedently learned from many other sources, that an honourable Englishman has no business in the States, except as an eye and ear-witness; and can only arrive at a knowledge of the real nature of things there, by mixing in some measure with all classes of society, and comparing their statements with each other. The school-master, of whom I have been speaking, possessed evidently considerable talent; and was, I am sure, a worthy and useful man. There was about him something so lively and interesting, that my feelings were entirely engrossed in his descriptions; and when, on departing, he called his book a poor performance, his modesty brought to my recollection an anecdote related to me by a gentleman who called on Mr. Abernethy to consult him.

" Mr. Abernethy," said he, addressing the eccentric philosopher " being from Scotland, and feeling honoured in so illustrious a countryman, I have paid myself the compliment of calling on you, to avail myself of your skill." " Sir," replied the surgeon, "some people are pleased to esteem me skilful; but yet I assure you, that I am no great proficient after all.' His prescription, however, proved invaluable; and this, contrasted with his modesty, forms the moral of the anecdote.

A young man, with whom I had been well acquainted in England, arrived in New York a few weeks after us. He had been employed in England as teacher, first in a highly respectable school belonging to another person, and afterwards in an establishment of his own. He accepted a similar situation in New York; and an adventure which befel him will illustrate my statements.

An elderly person in the city, who had long conducted a day school, had received intelligence of some property bequeathed to him in England; and became desirous, in consequence of this addition to his income, of meeting with some one, to whom he could,—for twelve months at least, and perhaps finally,—intrust his pupils. My friend received, through some channel, timely intimation of this matter, and lost no time in attending on the schoolmaster. He was approved of; and entered almost immediately on his duties. He called at our apartments the following day, and announced his good fortune." He had at last," he said, " been favoured with genial zephyrs and prosperous gales; and had reached the mooring ground, where he desired to anchor. He loved America. He loved its people. Their kindness to him was unbounded. He had never before witnessed so great civility, nor met with such encouragement." In short, he seemed to be transported from his wonted feelings, as far as he was from his native country, and to be in raptures with his prospects. How gay and charming, thought I, is the fickle goddess, when she displays before us her glittering pinions! I congratulated him sincerely on his flattering prospects, and expressed my wish, that his anticipations might be fully realized.

A few days after, he called again, with unabated expectations. He had obtained employment, which he conceived would yield him a handsome income; and he found his school was increasing. His predecessor still attended, for the purpose of establishing him in the good graces of his pupils; whom he found, indeed, very noisy; but this he conceived to arise from the circumstance of their seeing two masters instead of one, and that the noise would gradually subside "My predecessor," he observed, " has plainly told me, that his scholars are so tractable and well behaved, as to need no correction. And I certainly believe him; although I confess I have never before witnessed such procedings in a school. "However," continued he, " I am credibly informed, that Americans have a law, which forbids the correction of horses; and that the horses themselves are sensible of this; and evince their acknowledgments, by performing as much labour, and being as obedient, as any horses in any part of the world. And from what I see of the Americans, I believe them to be as sensible, and as well behaved, as their horses. I have no doubt, therefore, of finding scholars here do more *without*, than in other countries *with*, the chastisement of stripes." " You enter on the performance of your duties," said I, " with high opinions of your pupils. May your present sentiments be fully justified. Go on and prosper."

" I have not, yet," resumed he, " told you all my errand. There is a school vacant on Long Island; and also one in New York, the master of which is enfeebled by illness, and wishes to resign.

Either of these, it is my opinion, you might obtain on application."

" I shall take great interest," said I, " in watching the progress of your school, and the confirmation of your fortunes; and if these prove satisfactory, I may afterwards apply."

A few days after this, he paid us another visit; but with altered looks, and less of sprightliness than before. " How now?" said I, " what is the reason of this alteration in your conduct? What has befallen you?" " I regret," said he, " that I ever engaged in the school. I have been obliged to expel *eight* of my scholars. The noise and uproar of my school had been increasing every day, till at last it reached so high a pitch, that neither I nor my pupils could be distinctly heard. I reprimanded such as appeared most riotous, but some of them told me they would not be restrained by any English tyrant; so I visited one of them with a stroke. Hereupon, the whole school became a scene of anarchy. I was pelted on all sides, with books, and slates, and copies, and obliged to leave my seat. All the scholars pressed on, and endeavoured to strike or kick me. I was compelled to take refuge behind a pillar, against which I placed my back, and protected myself in front, by a chair. Such as approached near enough I knocked down, and kept the whole rabble of them at bay. At last, snatching a piece of wood out of the hands of the oldest, I put my pupils on the defensive ; and when I had completely subdued every appearance of resistance, I turned the ringleaders out of doors. Every symptom of insubordination has vanished ; but you cannot conceive how much mortification I have experienced." " I can conceive," I replied, " very well, the trouble you have undergone ; but I advise you to adopt no sudden or inconsiderate measure. It is scarcely three weeks since you were exceedingly elated by flattering prospects, and now you seem as greatly depressed by reverse and of fortune. Perhaps the storm will blow over."

My friend continued to conduct the school ; and as I was desirous of seeing it, he gave me an invitation. What was my surprise, to find no boy above the age of nine or ten years ! These, some of them not above six years old, had but a little time before threatened annihilation to his authority. What brave people these young Americans may become, it is difficult to predict; for they are certainly courageous. Their progress in studies would, I think, be accelerated by discipline; for they were under no proper restraint, and were playing on the tables.

I had now no further need of debating, in my own mind, the propriety of a day-school in America. If any English teacher doubts the literal correctness of my statements, or still imagines he would like the country, the field is open before him;—let him go and examine for himself.

Dr. Milnor once informed me that a proprietory school had been established in the city of New York, which, after a trial of two years, was abandoned. There was no unanimity among those concerned; and as it offered no advantages above what might be gained at Columbia College, nor any saving to parents, its utility was questioned. " But," continued he, " there is in contemplation the establishment of an university, in which the highest branches of education will be taught. It is possible that, if your powers of teaching be approved of, you may be elected to fill some situation in that establishment."

" Is there any degree of certainty?" inquired I, " that this would be the case, should my character and testimonials prove satisfactory?" " No promise could be given you," said he, " on which reliance should be placed. There is yet no certainty that an university will be built, although ground for it has been purchased. The projected institution has been agitated for two or three years, and a longer time may elapse before it be erected. The Americans are fonder of talking than of acting." " This," said I, " is at variance with the improvements effected, and effecting, in various parts of the country." " The improvements," he remarked, " are directly and visibly accompanied with pecuniary results, which an university does not promise. " There appears, then," I asked, " only a probability, but not a certainty, of such institution being founded?" " The case," he replied, " is just as I have stated, and I do not wish to encourage expectations which might end in disappointment."

The Greek language is yet but little known in

America. Few re-prints of Greek authors have appeared there; and of the few which have, some appeared quite improper for a country so young and so unlettered. Whilst engaged in examining school-books in an American bookseller's, I found a New York edition of Longinus, edited, I was told, by a professor of Columbia College, and from the antiquated text of Dr. Pearce. Columbia College is regarded, in the States, as nothing more than a public grammar-school. In a country, where literature in general is at an exceedingly low standard, and Greek literature in particular, a school-book like Longinus appears exceedingly unsuitable. His work is a critique upon the best authors, in a language which had, previous to his birth, declined from its purity; and his treatise itself is not only difficult, but also is not classed among those of the golden age. To read such a work as a school-book, whilst the authors which it criticises are but little understood, appears like beginning at the wrong end. If it has been selected with a view to instruct Americans in chasteness of style, or sublimity of ideas, the intention might be good; but the issue, I am sure, has not equalled the intention. There are some native Americans, whom all allow to be elegant authors; but we must always bear in mind, that their education is rather European than American. A great majority of transatlantic writers have no refinement of sentiment, nor elegance of diction; and their compositions exhibit a curious medley of prejudice, ignorance, and bombast.

The Greek plays are hardly read at all in America. Metres are little understood, and versification less. I speak confidently, when I say, that boys in good schools near London have, at the age of from twelve to fourteen, a more solid and thorough classical education, than the young men who have passed through Columbia College; and, I believe, than any persons educated altogether in America. Mathematical knowledge is much upon a par with classical. The professors of Columbia College made some attempts to raise the study of languages to a higher standard. Such elevation of studies would require additional exertion from pupils, and additional expenditure from parents, and has been vigorously opposed by both. Many, even of the supporters of that college, question the utility of high literary attainments. They cast their thoughts and glances upon such as have gained distinction in collegiate exercises, and find that, when contrasted with others, they are neither better clerks, better shopmen, nor more thriving traders. They then begin to ask the advocates of learning, what are the advantages it is expected to confer. Instead of rendering its votaries more attached to business, more eager for dollars acquired in any manner, more wedded to narrow and sordid gains, they perceive that it generates a taste for reading, a love of scientific and rational pleasures, and a freedom from the coarser manners which distinguished their forefathers. I have heard it gravely argued, that Columbia College has proved a source of bitterness to many in New York, by rendering their sons too much the gentleman, and disqualifying them for business.

I distrust, however, extremely, the correctness of this inference. It reminds me of a scene which took place in my presence, between the late Bishop of Chester, and a number of miners in the mountains of Yorkshire. His lordship suggested many little alterations and improvements in their chapel, which would render their place of worship much more convenient, with but little cost. All such improvements, they told him they would waive, on the score of economy. " There is one alteration, at least," resumed his lordship, " pointed out by your minister, which you cannot but admit the expediency of making. The small gallery is erected so near the roof, that no full-grown person can stand upright in it. A small expense would remedy the evil." Upon which they answered, " Our fore-fathers went to Heaven from this gallery, and why cannot we?" " My good people," said his lordship, " an incommodious temple is not essential to your going to Heaven. I came to recommend improvements, not for my own sake, but yours." And afterwards, addressing himself to one of his attendants, he said, " I perceive, that any thing which deprives them of money, is as keenly felt, as the drawing a drop of their heart's blood." " Our fore-fathers," say the older inhabitants of New York, " gained their independence, and we abundance of dollars, without extensive learning; and why, therefore, should our sons adopt refined innovations?"

Admission into colleges and churches in America being so uncertain to an Englishman, more especially to one whose principles of conduct are settled and inflexible, I now gave up my purpose of locating in the States, Whilst in a wavering and doubtful temper, I walked out one day and visited the consul. " Captain L., of the Royal Navy, and his sister," said the consul, " have arrived from Canada. I would recommend you to call at their lodgings, and that immediately. They are about to return to England, but an interview will afford pleasure to both, ince you are already acquainted."

The consul gave me the address of their lodgings, and I straightway called on them. After mutual inquiries respecting each others experiences in the New World, and reciprocated congratulations at having survived the hardships and rigours of the winter, I expressed the pleasure it would give me to have their company some evening at tea in our apartments. They readily acquiesced. The evening was appointed, and I returned to my family to relate the news.

We were overjoyed at having an opportunity

of hearing, from persons so well able to inform us, what is the state of the country through which they had passed; the accommodations on the road; and the advantages or disadvantages in the British provinces, to persons circumstanced like us. We soon found, from their descriptions, that their views of America coincided with ours; and that a journey through the States had produced no other result, than to bind them to their native land by stronger feelings of affection. They advised me, however, to visit Boston before my return to England; and promised to convey to some of our friends our intentions of returning, on their arrival in London.

I had, whilst in England, procured letters to two literary gentlemen of Boston; the one a professor in Cambridge University, the other an author, well known in that city. To these I trusted for further introductions, and admission to all places there, which are considered as worthy the attention of a stranger. A passage in a steam-boat to Providence was secured for me, which was the commencement of my travels in America.

CHAPTER V.

JOURNEY TO BOSTON—CONVERSATION WITH A MAN OF LETTERS THERE—VISIT TO THE STATE-HOUSE—TO THE UNIVERSITY OF CAMBRIDGE—TO THE DOCK YARD—SPECIMENS OF AMERICAN LEARNING—BOSTON EVENING PARTY—PREJUDICES IN AMERICA AGAINST THE ENGLISH ARISTOCRACY, AND GENERAL UNFAIRNESS OF OPINION THERE CONCERNING ENGLAND.

WE set out from New York at four in the afternoon of the last day of March, consequently night soon prevented our observation of the country through which we had to pass.

Travellers have generally stated, that the duration of twilight in America is much shorter than with us. That part of our trip, in which we were favoured with day-light, was pleasant. We had the city of New York, its steeples and its prisons, visible on one side, and the heights of Brooklyn studded with mansions, the navy and dock-yards, and a long extent of fine cleared farms, possessed for the most part by Dutchmen, on the other. The air was still too cold to be considered agreeable; and the season too early to present nature advantageously to our view.

That part of the landscape, however, which the following morning disclosed to us, was very beautiful. In one place the country seemed to ascend gradually from the margin of the water, by a gentle slope, till it attained a considerable elevation; and to mingle at last with the circumambient sky. In another place, the prospect was arrested by steep acclivities, covered on the sides and summits with trees of stinted growth. There were scattered up and down, in various places, and in a great variety of shapes, farm-houses, or diminutive villages, painted white. These are generally frame-houses, built of wood. We reached Providence, the place of debarcation, a little before nine in the morning; and travelled over land in coaches the remainder of our journey, about forty miles.

The face of the country between Providence

and Boston is rocky and broken; in some places undulating; but furnishes nothing in itself which can attract much attention, or on which the fancy can dwell with pleasure. I had been advised on my arrival at Boston to take up my residence at the Tremont House, an hotel which possesses as high a reputation as any in the States. As soon as I had arranged my matters there, I called upon one of the persons to whom I had letters from England. I found the gentleman, who was a *litteraire*, and an author well known in Boston—reading some work on Egyptian Hieroglyphics, of which he spoke favourably; but as this was a subject I had never studied, I could not enter into its merits. At last, after many desultory observations on numerous topics, as rapid and evanescent as mental and lingual volubility could render them, we alighted on a subject of mutual interest, frequently discussed by persons I met with at New York. I had always observed, that native Americans do not enter on such debates with half the warmth or bitterness, as European refugees. The Americans appear to employ dependant strangers on the outworks of their republic, to sound the political sentiments and principles of every approaching emigrant, and to convey to the democratic sensorium a timely and accurate impression, before they welcome him into the capital of their patronage and support.

"Captain Hall," said he "was the base tool of a flagitious and corrupted aristocracy, and was hired to come over to this country, and to insinuate himself into the houses of the people, for the purpose of spying out all their failings, and holding them up to ridicule." "If you think," answered I, "that he held up all their failings, or all their foibles, to public observation, you do not yet know the most obvious points in the American character. There are ample materials yet unnoticed, which future travellers will describe. As to his being sent over in the manner you imagine, no English gentleman would credit it."

"The English," resumed he, "are the rudest and most ungrateful people in the world. They are received with open arm by the Americans, and repay their kindness by detraction and insolence. I witnessed the great hospitality exercised towards Captain Hall in this city, and have seen in his book the manner in which he has returned it. Mrs. Hall treated several American ladies with extreme rudeness; and turned from them with contempt, even in the midst of their discourse. Of the manner in which Captain Hall and his lady behaved, while in this country, the English," answered I, "know nothing except what is conveyed through channels, polluted by illiberality, prejudice, and wounded sensibility. You must acknowledge, that their detractors have drawn the picture. But Captain Hall has, in his travels, transmitted his grateful remembrances, in characters sufficiently legible, and too plain to be mistaken."

"Captain Hall," he again observed, "has related many things entirely false. What could he know, respecting the laws and customs of a country, in which he made but a cursory sojourn, and through which he passed with too much rapidity to allow of his obtaining accurate information. His travels contain partial and incorrect and garbled descriptions, to vilify a nation which never injured him, and to mislead or prejudice his countrymen." To this I replied, "several Americans have admitted the correctness of that traveller's observations, and content themselves with attacking his ingratitude. Even those," I added, " who are the most inveterate against him, admit that his writings have done good in America. A native of this country, who appeared a person of considerable intelligence, compared Captain Hall's strictures on America, to those of Dr. Johnson on Scotland;—severe, yet salutary. A well-informed gentleman, from the highest circles of England, whose whole life has been little else than a succession of travels, is not in much danger of mistaking American manners and laws."

In the usual style of republicans, this gentleman hereupon quitted the censure of Captain Hall, in order to abuse the English nobility "All aristocracies," he exclaimed, " are hateful and oppressive; that of England is particularly so— they are rapacious and tyrannical. They devour all the good things of the nation. They neglect all learning, neither acquiring it themselves, nor rewarding it in others. They fill, both at home and abroad, every lucrative post in all civil and military employments, at the bar, and in the church. They usurp and trample on the rights and privileges of the inferior classes. They are intoxicated with haughtiness and pride!" He had passed, he said, some time in London, on his passage from Germany to America; for he was a German; and had witnessed the mal-admnistrations of the higher orders there, and the slavery and degradation of the lower. "The professions" he went on " are depressed for want of encouragement, and literature and science are humbled in the dust. In America, any native may become president; and multitudes might be mentioned, who have risen to be members of the national legislation, from the humblest parentage and birth. In England, it is impossible for talents to be rewarded, or to meet with encouragement."

" To all this," I replied, " that had I seen him on my first arrival in the States, I should have cordially agreed in his views and observations. I had harboured, whilst in England, bitter and aggravated sentiments against the aristocracy; and had believed, that the country would be better without that privileged body. This opinion I might always have indulged, had I always lived in England; but America is an infallible corrector of such erroneous judgment, in every man of intelligence and capable of observation. I have never met with any person from Great Britain, worthy to be called respectable, whose opinions, however a radical before, did not become completely altered. You cannot, when in England," I added, " have obtained satisfactory information on these points ; otherwise your, mind must be singularly formed A third rate talent in professions there, is certainly equal to the highest in the States. I am greatly mistaken, if any first rate professional man exists in all America. There are certainly men of eminence ; but they are eminent only among their own countrymen, and would not obtain a high rank in England. And although it is true, that many lucrative and important situations are held by noblemen, yet all such places are not exclusively so. England can enumerate more persons raised from a low to a high station, than any other country. In short, there is hardly any village in England, which does not possess residents of greater learning and professional talent, than is to be found in almost any large town in the United States. Besides, that which is a low reward for literature in England, is a high reward in America. No man there, who possesses more than ordinary learning, can remain long unnoticed. His reward often depends upon himself. The nobility are bountiful rewarders of merit, when it makes itself conspicuous."

I left this German author rather abruptly, some offence being apparent, from the difference of our views and the tendency of our arguments; and went to deliver another letter of introduction I had to one of the professors of Cambridge University. At his house I was introduced to Mr. Bowditch, professor, but not teacher of mathematics; the best mathematician in the States, and president of an insurance office, apparently between sixty and seventy years of age: this gentleman's look was venerable, and his countenance expressive and intelligent. At the professor's, I was introduced also to Mr. Pickering, a lawyer of great eminence in Boston. This party I found agreeable, and I was not again troubled with unseasonable remarks against existing aristocracies. Americans do not themselves revile kings and nobles, so much as foreigners do; but they listen to depreciating statements with visible pleasure.

Mr. Pickering accompanied me home, and invited me to call at his office the next morning early, when he or his son would accompany me to different places which he imagined I would choose to visit. Accordingly they conducted me to the State-house, Court-house, public reading-rooms, which form also a kind of museum, the dock-yard, market-house, university, &c.

On arriving at the State-house, I found it to be a noble building, and was particularly struck with its admirable situation. It stands on a lofty eminence, which commands a complete view of the town, and is ascended from the park side by a fine flight of steps I mounted to the cupola, which is almost as high from the water as the top of the Monument in London, and affords a prospect of vast extent on all sides. A great number of towns and villages were observable, scattered over the surrounding country; some of them at the distance of twelve or fourteen miles. The numerous bridges over the estuary appeared beautiful, and gave variety to the landscape.

The University is not within the city of Boston, but stands three or four miles without, and on the other side of the river. The buildings do not impress a stranger with ideas of magnificence. They are plain brick buildings, some of them very old, and destitute of ornamental architecture. We were so late in going that the students, generally mere boys, were coming out from evening prayers. The only thing which Mr. P's son deemed worthy of notice at Cambridge, as the university is called, was the library, which occupies two large rooms, and contains between thirty and forty thousand volumes. There are not many works in it, which can be regarded as valuable. Most of them have been purchased at second hand bookstalls in London. A small Greek M.S. was shewn to me, most exquisitely written; also a beautiful Persian M.S. These were both secured under two locks and keys, on account of their rarity. I had often seen splendid eastern M.S. on the shelves of London booksellers, without any such security; and could not help smiling at this characteristic protection.

The market-house is a long line of buildings of

hewn stone. There is a foot-path down the centre. On each side are stall for venders, and doors at convenient distances. It did not appear to me that there was any place set apart for butchers or fish stalls, &c., but that any person of any calling might pitch his stand where he pleased. The whole market was under cover, and had storerooms above.

My friend next accompanied me to the house of the Commodore, who, with great complaisance and condescension, carried us through the dock-yard, and showed us every thing it contained. The only object which filled me with admiration, was the dry dock just finished, into which no vessel had yet been admitted. This excavation, which the Commodore informed us was much longer and broader than any at Portsmouth, was lined with massive blocks of granite, larger than I had ever seen employed before in building. There is a steam-engine erected in the neighbourhood of the dock for pumping out the water, which, when completed, will possess sufficient power to empty it in a short time. Should greater celerity be wanted, the diameter of the well is sufficient to admit a greater number of pumps. There was nothing which the Commodore left unnoticed; and my obligation to him, and to various other gentlemen in America, require me to acknowledge that I believe there is no trouble they would think too great, in order to oblige and gratify a stranger.

In Boston, there is nothing to be seen very interesting to one who has lived in London. Their Libraries, Museum, Court-house, Town-hall, and other public buildings, present little worth noticing. There is some tradition respecting the Court-house, which may render it interesting. It was in front of that place, where the British forces were drawn up, during the time that riots existed in Boston, respecting the duties on tea. It was there that the soldiers were brutally insulted and stoned by the American rabble, previous to any bloodshed in revolutionary battles. It was there that the first shot was fired by the English, and the first American killed. The spot is still pointed out where the first man fell.

The gentleman before-named, whose kindness I thus experienced, expressed a wish to learn the Persian and Nagaree characters, and the euphonic changes of Sanscrit letters; and for this purpose, spent the greater part of two evenings at my lodgings. His ready acquisition of them was truly wonderful; and I had great pleasure in witnessing it. He also introduced me, with many commendations, to a congregational minister, Dr. J., whom he represented as the best orientalist in Boston. That gentleman, after expressing the satisfaction it afforded him to meet with a person, with whom he could converse on Oriental learning, withdrew into his study, and returned with an armful of Persian, Sanscrit, Arabic, and Hindoostanee books.

No sooner had I examined these works, than I began to think that I had already made a premature estimate of American literature, and that what I had frequently heard in New York must be true. When on my first arrival in the States, I mentioned to several scholars my surprise at the extremely low state of learning and the professions, I was always answered thus: "New York is not a literary, but a commercial city. If you are desirous of seeing the lions of American literature, go to Boston." As I had long been engaged in such studies, and had lately arrived from London, the hot-bed of languages, arts, and sciences, I thought I could have little to apprehend from any Orientalist in the United States: I therefore summoned up a fitting self confidence, expecting, with my new friend, a trial of skill. " Do you, Dr J., understand these authors?" I asked. " I have some knowledge of them," he replied, " but not very extensive." He then took a German selection of Sanscrit passages from various authors, the first of which was the opening passage of the Laws of Menu. This he requested me to read, which I did, and when I paused, and perceived that he made no inquiries, nor added any observations, I began to suspect that he did not understand the language. I therefore requested him to tell me, if he knew the letters. His answer amused me; I have written them over several times; but the truth is that they are so confoundedly difficult, that I could never remember them. I cannot therefore read any of the words, nor have I ever before heard them read; but have seen some accounts respecting the language, that it is a very engaging study."

To this latter statement I of course agreed;

adding, that the Sanscrit is certainly the most perfect and regular in its grammatical forms, of all languages with which I am acquainted; and its euphonic transformations the most accurately systematic. Moreover, it is now thought by the best judges to be the origin of the Greek language. Many roots, and prepositions, and the numbers and voices, are nearly the same in both. Also every euphonic change in Greek, and in every other language, can be referred to the principles of Sanscrit. After having held a short conservation with Dr. J., and discovered that his Oriental knowledge might be compressed into a nut-shell, he informed me, that some duties he had to perform required his absence, and requested I would call again on the following day. I promised to repeat my visit at the time he mentioned, and we took forthwith our departure.

As we were returning from this characteristic farce, Mr. P. informed me, that he had once resided in London, as secretary to the American Minister, and had seen the dignity and greatness which learning in England frequently obtains. " It is the prospect of rewards," added he, which stimulates and encourages. In America there is no inducement for enthusiastic perseverance in literature. Indeed we have no literature in this country." To this I could not help adding, "A well educated Englishman will always make the same discovery, after the residence of a day. It is impossible to be concealed or disguised."

On the day following, I paid a second visit to Dr. J., and read over to him some Persian and Hindoostanee. I then requested him to allow me the pleasure of hearing his pronunciation of some Persian sentences; but he begged I would dispense with his performance of it; and then added, "This is the second time in my life, in which I I have heard a Persian word pronounced. A young gentleman, who had been in India, once before indulged me in a similar manner with yourself; but it is several years ago, and I have no recollection of the sounds." The books he possessed must be considered as rarities in America, and as inexplicable puzzles even to himself. They must be, however, amusing companions to an American Orientalist. Had I not been well able to penetrate into the den of the Bostonian Lions, and to estimate its profundity and extent, I might have quitted that celebrated place, with the erroneous impression, that it contains at least one extraordinary linguist. But I must confess, that it appeared not a little amusing, that every thing of literature in the States, with which one grapples, dwindles into mere pretence, and vanishes in air. I observed, when in the Cambridge library, a copy of Dr. Wilkin's Sanscrit Grammar, and found its pages free from the finger marks of transatlantic students. May it long continue so, and be a true index of university intelligence, where it has been so carefully preserved. Whilst literary honours and emoluments are so sparingly dispensed, there is no fear of its derangement or disfigurement.

Mr. P. conducted me one evening to a party of gentlemen, assembled at the house of a physician, in honour of a distinguished lawyer, having been appointed a judge of the Supreme Court at Washington. The company was large and promiscuous. There were present, I was informed, lawyers, physicians, professors, merchants, mechanics, students, &c. &c. The rooms were crowded, but not uncomfortably so. Refreshments of various kinds were served round, among which were stewed oysters, of which I partook, in memory of a parting supper which I once ate in company with my much revered preceptor, the Rev. James Tate of Richmond; whose name I found to be held in great esteem among scholars in America.

On the evening previous to my leaving Boston, Mr. P. invited me to take tea at his house. There were four literary gentlemen invited to meet me, but they were not all present at tea. Some of them came later in the evening. Dr. J. and the German gentleman I have already mentioned were two; and besides these, a student, and a young gentleman who had spent some time in the Levant —a Mr. H. The student, a youth of sixteen, was introduced as a prodigy of learning, and an Arabic scholar. Mr. P's son had been employed two years in tuition, between his leaving the university, and engaging in the profession of the law. This youth had been his pupil, and was reported to be an extraordinary specimen of genius. Sir William Jones' Persian Grammar was produced, and I desired him to pronounce a few of the first words of the story of the Bulbul. He commenced spelling the first word, as a child does his a-b ab's. " Can you not read the words," inquired I, " without mentioning the letters." To which he answered, that he knew most of the letters, but could not pronounce the words. I inquired how long he had applied himself to Arabic, to which he answered, two years. I then explained to him the discipline of our schools in England, which is generally so strict as to preclude the possibility of a student's time being so long occupied, in acquiring the characters of a language. " You must many times," continued I, " have endured the infliction of chastisement, for such unprecedented neglect and idleness, had you been educated in England." I peceived that *discipline* and *chastisement* sounded harsh upon his ears, and he retired from the party at an early hour.

The German author, who had before vented his indignation against the aristocracy of England, now resumed the same subject; and repeated many accusations entirely unfounded, and which nothing but prejudice could dictate. This he did, to demonstrate his attachment to a republican form of government, and to expose my political views,

He dwelt particularly on the pride and immorality of our nobles. I ventured to dispute his statements and inferences, thus unnecessarily obtruded and reiterated; and witnessed also his hasty and untimely exit. As this second attack was unpardonable, being unprovoked, I afterwards addressed a note to Mr. P., in which were the following sentences: " Your friend, Dr. L. appears to have imbibed either in England or elsewhere, notions of our aristocracy, which do himself no credit, and them no harm. They are not likely to be injured by illiberal observations made in a sweeping manner against their order, by persons who could never have an opportunity of knowing their real character. As to their being the proudest aristocracy in Europe, it is true; and it is equally true that the very shop-keepers of respectability in London are, in talents, education, and wealth, higher, generally speaking, than the aristocracy of any other nation. England, as a nation, is among nations, what her aristocracy is, among the aristocracies of the earth; she stands supreme, and will do so for generations yet unborn, unless she persist in her present infatuation, forgetful of her high state, and of the Being who conferred it.

" I perceive, that a foreigner, to gain the favour of the American public, must vilify his own nation, and condemn all hereditary rule. The native Americans sit wrapped up in self-complacency, and inhale the grateful fragrance of slavish adulation. The swindler, the profligate, the idle, the disaffected,—they who have deprived others of their property, or who have squandered their own, find that the price of American patronage is cheaply paid : they flatter and falsify. A person of higher principles, who is able by his talents and industry to maintain himself in Europe, will never stoop to this sort of baseness."

Dr. Milnor, of New York, once informed me of the generous reception he had met with, while in England, from some of the nobility. He had been employed on matters connected with religious missionary societies. The object nearest to a good man's heart, is the accomplishment of his duty ; and this brought him into intimate communion with many of the aristocracy. He found there so much of sound and genuine piety, and of truly Christian feeling, that he had never seen religion in so beautiful a dress before, nor more pure and fervent. He did not say that every nobleman is such. Yet he did not, like most republicans, and illiberal and foolish Englishmen, condemn all aristocracies as proud, immoral, rapacious, and oppressive. He is a strong republican; yet this does not prevent him from observing, or from acknowledging, the existence of worth and virtue, and true religion, in persons of a higher station and a rival country. I introduce this, merely to prove, that a gentleman, of true magnanimity, will not stoop to make ungenerous statements against the members generally, of any existing order. I agree, therefore, in the judgment of Dr. Strachan, Archdeacon of York, Upper Canada, who had been introduced to this German author, and who described him to me as prejudiced and narrow-minded.

CHAPTER VI.

RETURN TO NEW YORK—RESOLUTION TO PROCEED TO CA-
NADA—RETROSPECTIVE INCIDENTS—STORY OF AN AME-
RICAN MERCHANT—PROFESSIONS IN THE STATES, AS
DESCRIBED BY AN ENGLISHMAN—AMERICAN SUPERIORITY
—OUR REMOVAL TO CANADA PREDICTED—CUSTOM-HOUSE
DUES—EFFECT OF CAPTAIN HALL'S TRAVELS—VISITING
ON NEW YEAR'S DAY—WASHINGTON'S BIRTH-DAY—MIS-
CELLANEOUS OBSERVATIONS.

DURING my journey from Boston back to New York, I had much conversation with a gentleman of Boston, a person of considerable wealth, the substance of which I thought worthy of noting.

On learning that I was an English clergyman, and that my object, in going to the States, was to settle, he expressed his opinion to be, that the clergy of America are better provided for than those of England generally. I reminded this gentleman of the small salaries which I had been informed the American ministers in country places usually obtain. He replied, that I was tolerably correct; but reminded me, on his part, that they frequently receive presents of various kinds, and that they are not required to keep up much external appearance; as also, that an American clergyman's wife, in country places, can frequently earn something by knitting and spinning. A careful clergyman, he said, may often save as much as will purchase a farm, and may become comparatively wealthy. Moreover, added he, our clergy are all their own masters, which is an advantage not enjoyed by a great majority of English ministers. " In short, I will venture to assure you," he continued, " that the clergy of this country are more independent and comfortable, and respected, than many ministers of the Established Church of Great Britain and Ireland. The higher clergy, and the professors of colleges, are of more consideration in England than here; but they do not constitute a majority."

I had heard something to this intent once before; and on expressing my surprise how a country minister could save any thing out of his income, I was told, that the salary and presents he received were all intended for his private use, and the use of his family. His taxes and rates were trifling, and he was seldom called upon for charity.

" The income of professors," I observed, " in Cambridge University, does not, I am informed, exceed upon on average, more than three hundred pounds a-year ; and not so much, if the professor does not reside within the walls. I imagine that a professor can hardly keep up his respectability with so scanty an allowance." " The professors of our colleges and universities," he replied, " are considered amongst the most respectable class. That salary is a great sum with us." I replied, that a common schoolmaster in England often gains a greater income, and probably greater respect. " I do not," said he, " agree with you. I have travelled through England and Ireland, and perceived that many of your country schoolmasters, as well as country clergymen, are worse circumstanced than ours. Near London it is different."

" The learned languages"—I went on, " are very superficially understood in the United States." To this he assented, and added : " the classics are too little read in America, and *too much* in England. Could a medium be adopted, and the Americans gain what the English would loose, it might be better for both nations." There are many Americans, thought I, who would rejoice to witness such a consummation.

This gentleman's acuteness and liberality of sentiment, on various other subjects, much pleased me. He had travelled over the continent of Europe, and was evidently acquainted with its passing events. The same I had observed in several I conversed with in New York and Boston. Although under a republican government, their more extended intelligence raised them above the narrow prejudices of their less informed countrymen; and justified the saying in common circulation, and which the Archdeacon of York, in Upper Canada, applied to the clergy and influential classes of America, " Gentlemen are the same all the world over."

On my return to New York, I went immediately to the Consul, and acquainted him with my purpose of returning to England, since I perceived that no sufficient opening presented itself to me in that country, and I felt no disposition to tarry longer. He replied, " You have committed a great error, in ever coming hither; but since you have come, do not be guilty of a greater, in immediately returning. Let me prevail with you to travel a little more in America, and to go into Upper Canada. I will give you a letter of introduction to my Lord Bishop of Quebec, a most estimable man, who is by this time in York, the capital of the Upper Province. I have no doubt of your meeting with something worthy of your acceptance. You will also find living there more reasonable than here." I complied with his advice, accepting the letter of introduction, and forthwith set about preparing to leave the States, not and journey at once towards Upper Canada.

Before entering upon the subject of my further travels, however, I think it right to return almost to the period of my first outset, to give sundry details on various points, with which my interim opportunities furnished me, but to which I have not hitherto alluded.

I have said, that during my passage from England, I obtained considerable enlightment upon various points, in the manners and opinions of the

Americans; particularly from one native of the Union, who happened to be passenger along with me. This person had been master of a small trading-vessel, which he had lost by shipwreck. The detail he gave us, one day, of the history of a friend, brought out various opinions and views, for which neither myself, nor the other English passengers, were prepared.

The person this American spoke of, he described as having embarked in business, without being possessed of a dollar; and as trading for a time, according to the custom of his country, upon speculation and credit. A series of bills, and promissory engagements, entered into with acquaintances similarly circumstanced, formed the chief means of these commercial speculations. When I expressed surprize at this sort of responsibility, and such a mode of conducting business, the American made answer, " Being in a profession, you are not yourself, Sir, much exposed to the difficulties of the world, and consequently do not know the contrivances which others feel it necessary to adopt. If any person in America should refuse to do a favour of this kind I speak of, for his friends, he would find similar accommodation withheld from himself. The friend of this gentleman was thus circumstanced, and soon failed, through the misfortune of another. During the period of his conducting business, however, he kept a carriage, and lived up to his imagined gains, without providing against the contingencies of an evil day. When all went wrong, his effects were disposed of for the benefit of his creditors; and he was obliged to exchange a comfortable for a wretched state. As he had married during his prosperity, and a family was the consequence, his greatest exertions were requisite to obtain even the necessaries of life. He was no longer regarded as belonging to the same class of society, but felt himself degraded, and was obliged to perform the most menial offices. While in this condition, his brother, more successful than himself, having made a fortune, died without issue, and bequeathed his property to a public seminary." The American, who told us the story, strongly condemned the conduct of the deceased brother of his friend, calling him an unnatural monster, for having violated, in his opinion, every principle of duty and justice. Hereupon, a discussion ensued, and it was debated with considerable warmth, whether one brother, in such circumstances, had any *natural* claim upon the other.

I made a remark, which kindled a burst of indignation. " In England," I observed, "a man unfortunate, from no cause of his own, does not forfeit his place in society. And I should imagine there was some cause for the desertion of your friend by his brother and acquaintances. But, even supposing him perfectly worthy of their continued approbation, he could not, according to Paley, have any natural claim on his brother; collateral branches of a family having no pecuniary claims from consanguinity. The only grounds for supposing, that one brother ought to render assistance to another, rests upon the probability, that if he does not, no other person will." The American, hereupon, lost all government of himself; and, brandishing his knife, for we were then at dinner, asserted that I had introduced this sentiment from motives of priestcraft; and that if neither pay for schoolmasters, nor loaves and fishes for priests, had been augmented by the bequest, I would have condemned it as well as himself.

I mentioned the above anecdote to some in New York; and received for answer, "That some time ago it was not uncommon to see persons, who had once lived in affluence, suddenly reduced by the circumstance above mentioned, and obliged to retail oysters, or do something equally mean to gain a livelihood. But, that now, such is the spirit of reformation and improvement, a *smart* man need not be reduced to any such extremity. He has only to close his store, or his business, with his pockets full of money, and take the benefit of the act; after which, he can, without loss of character, and with undiminished credit, if he has proved himself a *smart* man (by which is meant a keen insight into the highways and bye-ways of money-making), re-establish himself either in the same place, or in any other district of that extensive country." I heard of some men, who had called their creditors together several times, for the purpose of compounding with them; and who, immediately after each compounding with them, re-opened their business with renovated splendour, like a Phœnix from the ashes. This statement, however, it is but justice to mention, I had from Englishmen; some of whom had been disappointed, some cheated, and some returning to England, or removing to Canada. Yet, as it was a subject repeatedly introduced by English residents, it must have had some foundation.

Another cabin-passenger was a tallow-chandler, an Englishman by birth, who had been resident in the States fifteen years. He had a friend in England, a teacher by profession, who, from reading in various publications, unmeasured praises of America, had entertained the desire of emigrating, and of resuming his profession in that country. Before he adopted any decisive step, he applied to his friend, the tallow-chandler, for authentic information. " My answer," continued this person, " convinced my friend, who enjoys a comfortable home in England, that it is his interest to continue there ; and I may venture to predict your return, unless there are weightier reasons for your voyage than any you mention. You will not find the country what you deem it. The people there have so many opportunities of obtaining education for their children, free of cost, or nearly so, that tuition is very cheap, and schoolmasters a drug. A teacher in the States, also, will profess to teach more branches of education, than one English schoolmaster out of twenty has ever heard of; and he will also engage to make the progress of his pupils as rapid as if propelled by steam. In England, much longer time is allowed for education than in America. People there cannot afford to pay so much, or so long; and also frequently require the assistance of their children in their own business." This man's remarks I often remembered, when prosecuting my own inquiries in New York.

" Yet," observed I, " they will doubtless shew much respect for teachers who possess extensive acquirements; and this feeling of respect and deference will greatly counterbalance a deficiency of income." " The Americans," he replied, "do not know what respect for learning means. They imagine themselves as well informed in useful knowledge as any nation; and I believe they are so. As to a knowledge of the Greek and Latin, of what advantage is it in life. If a man can understand his own language thoroughly, and be sufficiently acquainted with arithmetic, to keep his own accounts, I do not conceive it possible that any other knowledge, except French, can be necessary." " Is this," said I, " the general opinion of Americans, and do they not value a classical education?" " They give," said he, " a classical education to such as are intended for professions; and any parent can obtain this for his son. But the professions are too much crowded, and are inadequately paid. Those who enter them, are frequently the sons of people who are not wealthy, and their instruction is chiefly derived from charitable funds. Very few, indeed, who can establish their sons in business, would condescend to place them in professions. The profession of the law must be excepted."

" There must," said I, " be frequent openings for foreigners, in a country which increases so rapidly in population. Professions being neither very lucrative, nor very honourable, Americans will not be very eager in striving for them." " In that," said he, " you are completely mistaken.

There is as much contention for such situations there, as in England, and even more. Swarms of scholars pass through the colleges of the New England State every year. These spread themselves over every part of the Union; and, being generally poor, refuse nothing that is offered them. They crowd into every profession, and are ready to become schoolmasters, or doctors, or lawyers, or clergymen, as occasion offers. The Yankees are fond of an easy life. Foreigners are expected to contribute largely towards the improvement of their country. These build their houses, and perform such offices and labours, as the native Americans will not stoop to. The poor English and Irish dig their canals, make and repair their roads, clean out their sewers; in short, do every dirty job. The Americans can supply all the professions from themselves. If any professional foreigner has a chance of succeeding in one, it is the English physician. Gentlemen of either profession had better stay at home."

Similar conversations to the above, I frequently had with this man, which staggered much my confidence of success. Yet, I could not regard the judgment of an unlettered Englishman as sufficient authority on this point. Indeed, I found upon inquiry among the best informed, that his observations were not altogether correct. But yet it will be seen, that much of what he told me was afterwards corroborated by the testimony of others, whose opportunities of accurate information cannot be questioned; and English teachers, before they enter into the service of the States, would do well to deliberate.

Another subject of frequent discussion, was the *superiority of Americans* to Englishmen, in arts and sciences, in steam-boats and steam-engines, in conflicts by land and by sea, in arts of peace and plans of government. The English, " according to the judgment of impartial men," were completely left behind in every thing noble and excellent! This the Americans asserted; and the tallow-chandler assented to it as true. A passenger, a captain in the English navy, observed, " that many of the naval advantages over the English, of which America boasted, had originated from under-rating American courage and skill. Commanders of English ships had held a contemptible opinion of Americans, and had neglected such precautions as are practised against European enemies. Moreover, American vessels are often manned with British seamen, who, being deserters, knew, that if taken, they would be made examples of. Their ships had also more weight of metal than those of the English they encountered, and a greater complement of men." This the Americans denied; and maintained, that Englismen could neither fight, work, nor study, equal to Americans. James's Naval History of Great Britain was sometimes referred to; but, wherever the United States were concerned, it was detected *by Americans* to be one tissue of falsehoods.

One particular, exultingly mentioned by the shipwrecked Captain, and agreed in by all who had been in America, was the skill of American traders in striking bargains. An American, they said, " could twist an Englishman round his finger; could see father into matters hood-winked, than an Englishman with both his eyes open ; could make a fortune, by selling the same merchandize, by which an Englishman would become bankrupt ; and could always gain a living, where an Englishman would starve. In short, it would be a disgrace to his country, should an American, in bargaining, be over-reached by an Englishman, or sell an article below its utmost value." This, as far as my own experience goes, or my inquiries could reach, is perfectly accurate. And the reason of it is self-evident. Americans have rarely much capital; and every dollar they part with, not only lessens it, but their respectability also. An Englishman, with capital, is not likely to gain much from an American, *without any.* Money, if they continue long together, will always change hands; but no inspired prophet is needed to foretell into whose pocket it will go.

My talkative fellow-passenger even asserted, " that American manners are more gentlemanly than those of the English; and that their men and women, of the better sort, are more elegant and refined than our aristocracy." I expressed a doubt of the truth of this statement, and a belief, " that where regular classifications of society are acknowledged, the higher circles must be more refined than elsewhere, in proportion to their greater or less removal from sordid occupations. There are several persons in England, elevated one above another, by gradation of distinction, which cannot exist in a democratic country. I instanced then our English merchants, in general, our East India merchants, our great landed proprietors, our aristocracy, our hierarchy—and considered that the lowest grade of our nobility must be much more refined, than can be found in any country, in which there is an aim at perfect equality." This statement called forth tremendous opposition from all sides. All of the passengers, except one, unanimously concurred in censuring it. They instantly voted themselves, and Americans in general, as good, as highly polished, educated, and informed, as any English nobleman.

That American, who joined in neither absurd exaggeration of the one country and its people, nor invidious depreciation of the other, was a professional gentleman, of New York. In his conduct, during the whole voyage, nothing escaped him unbecoming or improper. "He had," he said, " seen much to charm and delight him, more especially in England. This last country he should ever remember with admiration, since all his anticipations had been unworthy of what he found it." I was quite puzzled to account for his admiration of a country, from which I was hastening into voluntary exile. I once took tea at his house afterwards, and found him there the same gentleman I had observed him to be on shipboard.

There were also on board two gentlemen, proceeding to the British provinces. The one, a physician, a native of New Brunswick, returning to practice with his father, who is in the medical profession also. He had taken his degree in Edinburgh, and walked the hospitals in London. This gentleman told me, that the States would never detain us; and that we, like numbers of disappointed people, would find our way to the Canadas. Indeed, he made himself quite sure of this, and gave me an invitation to his house, should I pass that way. The other gentleman was the son of an officer under the British Government, and was proceeding to join his father at Montreal. He had been studying some of the Eastern languages, in expectation of an appointment to India, but had then given up the pursuit, from want of sufficient encouragement; and intended to pass a few years in the Canadas.

We were thus trained, in some measure, for entering on America, whilst at a distance from her shores. Our servant, also, was equally trained by the observations she heard relative to her own condition, for expecting that the dictinction of master and servant would cease when we landed; and that she would be equal, or nearly so, with her employers. My wife remarked to me, several times on the voyage, that her behaviour was altered. It has subsequently occurred to me, that I have seen some of the Americans in private conversation with her ; and probably preparing her, beforehand, for speedy emancipation from her promises and engagements. I have already told how she acted upon entering the States, and how soon she found her way back to England.

To proceed with my retrospective observations : On our arrival, my books, &c. were conveyed to the custom-house for examination. It cost me six or seven days' attendance before I got them out. This was owing to my claiming them free of duty, on account of their being professional, and not intended for merchandise. At last, after much suspense and trouble, I was permitted to take them to my lodgings, after paying on them, and a few old sheets, &c., about forty dollars. It appeared to me at the time, that the custom-house officers were uncertain and wavering, respecting the duties which ought to be imposed; and that they had no certain rule to go by. Upon stating to the British Consul the sum I had paid, he informed me, that if I had applied to him previous to the payment, my books would have been admitted free of duty. I believe that the revenue-officers, like all persons in trade of that free country, adopt this maxim of their great philosopher: " Get what you can, and what you get, hold."

I could not but remark, that a freedom and ease of address and conversation, not known among the lower orders in England, prevail among these classes in New York and Boston, as well, I was informed, as throughout the Union. The people, even those who are regarded as of the lowest grades (for there *are* grades in society there as well as in England), have no appearance of servility. This arises from the republican form of their government, which regards every man as politically equal to his neighbour. The carters I employed to convey my trunks and boxes to and from our residence, felt as little of obligation to me for employing them as it is possible to conceive. Perhaps there is a greater degree of independence felt by the Americans, than by English people of the same stations? yet I doubt if it be accompanied by greater comfort.

When attending at the custom-house, on the morning after our arrival, to procure the admission of my books, &c., free of duty, some of the principal officers remarked to me, that literature in England was retrograding; that her scholars had exhausted their subjects of inquiry; that America had taken them up at the highest point at which England had left them, and was advancing them to a state not attainable in Europe. "Indeed," added they, " the best English scholars are emigrating to our country to gain instruction." I was then a stranger of half a day, and American literature was unknown to me. On hearing frequently such assertions, I was speechless from wonderment. I had gone with an expectation of employing greater than ordinary acquirements for their improvement; yet, should things prove as they told me, I must be a useless teacher at the first, and must have additional learning to acquire, before I could find employment. I could only reply, that much had been rumoured in England of their astonishing progress, but that I had not been prepared for the fact they related. When I compared the manner of their speaking with the things spoken, I could not help observing a striking incongruity.

The mistress and boarders of the house where we first resided, informed us that the publication of Captain Hall's Travels, had shut the entrance against any future reception of English gentlemen into American society. " No Englishman will hereafter," said they, " be caressed in the States." I did not find this to be absolutely true; yet I have no doubt it is accurate to a great extent. An English gentleman incurs no hazard of entire exclusion from the best society; but I much doubt his success, if he go for the purpose of location. All classes, except the very highest, entertain strong prejudices against his paternal country, and seem to regard it as the duty of a foreigner, to fill inferior, rather than higher situations. Hospitality, in the sense in which it is understood in England, I believe he must not look for to any great extent. Yet he will find instances of it.

There is a singular custom, which prevails in New York, but, I am informed, in no other part of the Union : on New-year's-day, all gentlemen call on their female friends, to renew or perpetuate their friendship. A lawyer, with whom I had contracted an intimacy, introduced me on that day to about thirty ladies. The round of calls we made, occupied our time from nine in the morning till seven at night. In almost every house we entered, we found other gentlemen on the same errand. It would be regarded as unpardonably rude in any lady, to treat with indifference a gentleman, who had honoured her with his call. This is often the commencement of new acquaintances, or the reconciliation of former ones which were before broken off, or discontinued. All the ladies we called on, as is universally the case, had prepared cakes, sweetmeats, wines, cordials, &c. in great profusion, in readiness, to exhilarate and regale their visitors. They were themselves, in general, very elegantly decked out and beautified. All appearance of mercenary business was wholly laid aside, and calculating penury had its annual slumber. Many gentlemen jaunted about in sleighs, a kind of carriage which slides upon the snow, to pay their devotions to the fair recluses; ladies on this day not being permitted, from punctilios of etiquette, to stray from home. The scene to me was as gratifying as it was new. All was animation, cheerfulness, and friendly feeling. The Americans seem, on this occasion, to have light hearts and buoyant spirits, and fulfil as much as any nation, the command, " Take no thought for the morrow." Thus some traits in their character are extremely pleasing to a foreigner. This was the only occasion, on which I saw the bright side of American sociability. In the midst of this joyous and festive gaiety, my fancy whispered, that the Americans are really a pleasant people. But the day, with all its pleasures, passed away, and I was forced to moderate my flattering conclusions!

The 22d day of February is Washington's birthday. Last year, being his centennial birth-day, it was observed with much solemnity ; and the preparations for celebrating it were unusually great. A numerous assemblage of officers, and gentry of different orders, congregated at the Town-hall, and marched thence in procession, attended by soldiers and military music, through some of the principal streets, to the Middle or Reformed Dutch Church, in Nassau-street, to which communion Washington belonged. After a service, well suited to the occasion, the procession returned by another route to the Town-hall, where refreshments had been provided ; some of the public buildings, and the Town-hall among others, were in the evening splendidly illuminated ; the scene was impressive, and its effect was much augmented, by the immense concourse of well-dressed ladies and gentlemen, with whom that large church, the largest in the city, was crowded. It is, perhaps, proper to remark, that this was in commemoration of one of the most extraordinary revolutions that ever took place. I had a full view of the whole, being seated on the platform erected for the clergy and other distinguished members of the procession. The address then delivered, I could not help applying to my own case, and I thought of my doubtful conduct in relinquishing my country without any cause, while Washington, even in violating his fidelity and oath of allegiance, was actuated by evidently patriotic motives. I found that this great republican had sworn allegiance to the King of Great Britain, when he first became a soldier, and had served in the king's troops in his native country. Meditating on this subject, I requested of a clergyman seated near me to be informed if Washington had ever been absolved by the general council of the United States, from his duty and obligations to his king, and received this in answer : " That no public act to that purport had been passed, but that it was tacitly understood." Thus the perfidious conduct of an enterprising man has given birth and freedom to a collossal power, and has transmitted to posterity his own name, enshrined among those of the greatest warriors, statesmen and legislators, that have appeared in the world ; which conduct, had his object been defeated, might have been branded as the crime of a base deserter, and have been followed by degradation and death, according to military law.

I had preceded the procession on the occasion I speak of, and applied at the church door for admittance : it was there I was first informed, that, according to preconcerted regulations, no person could be allowed to enter without the passport of a card. My desire being thus frustrated, I continued walking backwards and forwards in front of the principal entrance, in hopes of finding some one with whom I was acquainted, who might be able to introduce me within the walls. I had not long sighed over my unexpected rejection, before I observed Colonel H., to whom my New-year's-day's ramble had introduced me, mixing with the people scattered around. On recognition of me, he extended his hand, and welcomed me to this annual commemoration of their national independence. I thanked him for his kind welcome, but told him I feared I should not be so fortunate as to obtain admission, since the door-keepers had already excluded me from want of a ticket. He laughed heartily, and replied, " The Americans are much captivated by appearance and show : use only a little confidence and exertion, and your dress will get you in." Admission, thought I, as well as honour, " is like a widow, won by a brisk attempt, and putting on." I could not refrain from moralizing on this merry observation of the Colonel: conclusion led me to imagine, that Americans, equally with others, are the legitimate descendants of *Mother Eve*, whom a superficial and outward comeliness in the apple, had been chiefly instrumental in seducing. The same promptitude which she exhibited, to be fascinated by the adventitious finery of exterior decoration, seems to have been entailed on the generality of her offspring. We find the greater part, not only of women, but of men also, viewing every object with the eyes of Eve, and sacrificing duty and interest to please the eye.

I felt some hesitation in following the Colonel's advice, and sauntered away a few moments longer, in reflecting on the course I should adopt. Presently I descried, among the crowd, Dr. Matthews, a clergyman. Pressing towards him, I made him acquainted with my difficulty. " Thrust your arm, said he, into mine, and allow no person to separate us. I shall find means to introduce you." He accordingly made his way to the outer-door, and was pushing in without ceremony. Having appeared in his canonicals, his profession was visible through his gown, and his person was recognised. By dint of mere impudence a passage was made for the Doctor and me. The procession then passed us, in the train of which we followed, and ascended to the platform. During the service, Dr. M. made a polite remark :—" We derive our principles of freedom," said he, " from the English, whom we regard as our parents and brothers. Those of the best class, who come over, bring with them a spirit of independence, which Americans admire." I felt flattered by this delicate compliment, and expressed the delight which his liberal sentiments gave me. " I hope," I said, " that similar feelings may rapidly spread in America, for they are not yet general." And I then added, " liberty in England is more perfect than in America, and any one can there express his political sentiments more freely, and with less of personal detriment than in New York." He answered, " the late war engendered much bitterness of feeling, and a strong antipathy against the English, but it is fast disappearing from among us." I had heard the same remark more than once before; and I am inclined to believe that there is, among the best informed, a growing disposition for friendly intercourse between the two nations. But there is, in the mass of the people, a deep rooted hostility to England, a malignant envy of her greatness, and an eager wish to witness her decline, by revolution or otherwise.

Dr. M. desired I would inform him what my real opinion was of the American clergy. To which I replied, " I admire them exceedingly, and think highly of their church government; but I believe they are deficient in dignity and sound learning, which the English clergy possess in a greater measure. I perceive also," added I, " that the precarious tenure of their stipend, destroys their feelings of independence."

I have heard Americans assert, that England has no business in the Canadas, which they consider as part and parcel of America. They declare that Upper Canada was first peopled from the States. But they omit to mention, although their mortifications hinder them from forgetting, that those who preferred Canada, were loyalists, lovers of good order, and had an irreconcileable hatred to democratic principles. The Americans feel the present government of that province to be a thorn in their side, and would bestow half the dollars they possess, dearly as they love them, to produce a separation between England and her colonies. I have heard, more than once, natives of New York debating the practicability and desirableness of a democracy of nations, in which all kingdoms and countries might be equal, and England might sink to a level with the rest. What right has she to be greater than other nations? was a question frequently asked.

The pride of the English was often mentioned as intolerable, by the lower classes, both of emigrants and of Americans, who refuse to recognise any superiority in a well-educated above an uneducated foreigner. Whoever hesitates to associate with such people on familiar terms, will be treated by them as proud and haughty, and they will strive to mortify him, by embracing every opportunity of gaining an advantage, and of throwing all imaginable trouble in his way. I went out one day and purchased something, which I requested the vender to deliver. He promised I should have it in a short time; but as it was not brought in time, and we were wanting it, I sent our servant. The answer she brought back was, " your master must take it himself." The article was charcoal, which we were in absolute want of on a cold day. I went to the man to know what the message was he sent back. " I have no person to send with it," he coolly said, " you must take it yourself." " Who must take it ?" said I. " Yourself," he replied. " Who ?" I repeated; looking him steadfastly in the face. " You may send your help," he rudely answered, " or take back your money," at the same time laying down what I had paid him, and turning away. I was finally obliged to go to another store, and pay some additional charge to have it delivered, although the distance of the former was not twenty yards from our door. This was done to evince his independence, and to prove that he was as good a man as myself.

I was told by a lawyer I sometimes called on, that an English nobleman once bought property near New York city, and wishing to expend some money in improvements, engaged a number of

INDEPENDENCE—THE IRISH. 143

workmen to accomplish them. On the first day of their employment, he sent one of his servants, when dinner was ready, to call them in. They went, but not finding the nobleman at table, they demanded to see him, and inquired if they were not to dine with himself. His lordship replied, that he never sat at table with his workmen. Whereupon those people collected their tools, and desired him to find other labourers, for they were accustomed, at all places, to dine with the master of the house. This, and similar stories, were related to prove American independence. The same is never again likely to occur at New York; but I was informed, that a gentleman in country places must submit to such equality.

The Irish are, perhaps, the most useful people in all America, and not only enter the houses as domestics, but perform every drudgery which Americans can impose upon them. I think the natives of our sister island must be a meritorious and warm-hearted race. They certainly appear to advantage abroad, as persons upon whom one may depend with confidence. The one we had in the place of our false English girl, was a faithful and deserving creature. She would have accompanied us into Canada had we been certain of making any stay. I do not wonder that Americans wish to impress them with the notion that they are free and equal, for they obtain in return a voluntary slavery, which these destitute emigrants perform. Yet the Americans, whose country this degraded people is improving, regard and speak of them frequently with the greatest contempt, as unfit for any thing but the most menial offices.

It often appeared surprising that every arrival of vessels from England brought fresh emigrants, who complained of having no vote for members of representation at home, yet crowded to a country which hates them, and dooms them to the disabilities of an alien bill. I could refer it only to that blind fatuity which appears to actuate a considerable portion of the English, and impels them to court and flatter a people, between whom and themselves there exists a mutual repugnance, and whose manners it is impossible for them ever to admire or adopt.

Perhaps the desire in Americans of inducing people to emigrate, and to submit to the low offices, has obliged them to adopt the expediency of impressing refugees with a favourable idea of their great advancement in arts and sciences. They certainly have the most remarkable confidence in their attainments, and the greatest show without reality, that I ever witnessed. Appearance without·reality is almost as useful for America, during the present disturbances of England, as reality itself, and much more easily attainable. The redundancy of talent and industry in England, must find some field for operation, and America expands her arms to receive them. But she holds out privileges in her outstretched hands very different indeed. Her right hand pours into the lap of her own sons every thing which a fruitful country can afford; and her left into the longing souls of *Englishmen*, the tares of disappointment. This is not in itself wonderful. The wonder consists in this, that these Americans should be able to exercise so much delusion over men, whose skill is so superior to their own. Yet those who do not know how to prize the elevation of their own country, ought to bend in subservience to an inferior people. The English mechanics have generally served a long apprenticeship, whereby they become proficients in their business, and this proficiency of theirs dispenses with the necessity of mere shew and pretence. The Americans hate long apprenticeships, and close application to one pursuit, but have discovered an admirable substitute, in rendering subservient to their interest the greater skill of poor emigrants, and thereby gaining public and private wealth from foreign sinews. This forms one of the many good points of the American character.

Another praiseworthy point in it is their attachment and devotion to their country. It is true, that were they to emigrate to Europe, with no more useful qualifications than they possess, they would never find employment, so long as other workmen could be found; so they are obliged, from this circumstance, to remain at home. Yet the Americans are passionately fond of their country ; and esteem it, its government, laws, and institutions, as the best not only in the world, but which human wisdom can devise. In this respect they differ essentially from the English, who often appear to be destitute of every patriotic emotion, and would promote the welfare of a hostile nation to the detriment of their own. There is, however, at this moment, a greater reaction in the European mind, than at any former period since American independence. Tired with transatlantic impositions, and the encouragement which these afford to dishonest dealings, the English at least are beginning to perceive, that their own colonies present more secure and profitable investment, than that partial country, whose freedom has been so greatly enlarged on.

CHAPTER VII.

VISIT TO THE PASSAIC FALLS—CONVERSATIONS ON ENGLISH REFORM—ON THE CONDITION AND DISAPPOINTMENTS OF ENGLISH EMIGRANTS IN THE UNITED STATES—DESCRIPTION OF THE FALLS—THE PROPRIETOR—AMERICAN AND ENGLISH DECORUM—AN ENGLIH CLERGYMAN—MISCELLANEOUS REMARKS.

THERE were some fine days in spring before the frost and snow had entirely disappeared, during two of which I went to the Passaic falls, at Patterson, in the neighbourhood. I passed the Hudson in a steam-boat, from New York to Hoboken, in company with a gentleman, a manufacturer, of extensive information. He kept his carriage, and was in a large way of business. "England," said he, " has committed two great errors in her domestic administration ; the catholic emancipation bill, and a sweeping measure of reform. Her political constitution will be quickly altered from that which all nations and ages have admired, and she will lose her elevation and distinction." This gentleman was not singular in his judgment. The same I heard from others, whose respectability was unquestionable. I hope, however, that such predictions may prove fallacious, and that the prosperity of our country may increase.

A young gardener, from Brighton, overtook me on the road. He had been in New York three winters, and was engaged in Niblo's gardens. As I never failed to obtain all intelligence in my power from the experience of emigrants, I readily entered into conversation with him. His wages, he informed me, were from thirty to forty pounds sterling, and were considered good. Before he left England, he made as much. His friends had endeavoured to dissuade him from going, but to no purpose. His health, from the great extremes and changeableness of weather, was far from good. Money could not purchase the same conveniences there as at Brighton; and he was not so well circumstanced, nor enjoyed so many comforts. He had often thought of returning, but the shame of having lost what he possessed before, and the uncertainty of as good employment, were the obstacles which hindered him

" Do you imagine," I asked, " that emigrants in general are satisfied, and find their change advantageous upon the whole ?" " I am sure," he replied, " the generality of them are not, but find themselves exposed to many hardships and privations, which they never felt in England. They are not admitted to equal privileges with Americans; and many of them, having lost all feelings of decorum and propriety, and finding spirituous liquors cheap, fall sacrifices to intemperance."

" What do you consider amongst the greatest hardships of an emigrant ?" I asked. " The Americans," he replied, regard all who come over with contempt or jealousy. If he is poor, they despise him ; if rich, they are jealous, and envy him. No Englishman, if he enter into business, long retains his money. He always loses it. Before he can succeed, he must acquire an intimate knowledge of American ways, and during this he becomes poor. Almost every one I have heard speak on the subject says this. He must then begin, like an American, without capital; and if he be *smart*, he may save a little. It is almost impossible for a poor man to become rich in this country!"

" Perhaps," said I, " the thing you complain of is the same in all countries; have you any other cause of complaint?" " Yes," he replied. " An Englishman has here no domestic comforts, as at home. He has none of the same cheerfulness nor amusements. The Americans are not sociable with the English, and have their minds constantly upon gaining some advantage. Yet they have always behaved civilly to me. But I do not admire their manners, there is something in them so cold and forbidding." The same I had heard a hundred times before. I inquired, however, once more.

" Do emigrants frequently complain of this?" " Yes," said he; " very few like America, and it is long before they are reconciled to it. But when a poor man comes here, he finds a difficulty of getting back. He has, for the most part, no way left but to submit. An Englishman would never find good employment, could Americans do without him."

I observed an uniformity of statement quite surprising, among persons from England and Ireland. The same difficulties and privations and dislikes had befallen most of them. But, perhaps, where almost every one is complaining of grievances, these become magnified beyond their due proportions. We find this frequently in England.

" I have heard that farmers do well in this country," said I. " So have I heard," he replied ; " and am going to make inquiries respecting some cheap lands in Pennsylvania, for I am tired of New York. I have sometimes thought of Canada; but the cold of New York in winter is very severe, and the heat in summer ; and Americans tell me it is worse there. But many people have told me, that the Canadian government is lighter, and has less of taxation than the American."

" If you are so poor as you speak of, how can you obtain a farm ?" " I am not," said he, entirely destitute. Americans, too, make it very easy for a poor man to go on, for which they secure some advantages. Persons are wanted to cultivate their country, which is yet in many places waste land. If I had a farm of my own, I might work upon it when I had leisure, and at other times be employed for some neighbours."

" Do Americans," I inquired, " employ much time in gardening?" Very little," he replied. " There are some public gardens, as those I am engaged in, kept in good order; but in general, gardens here are not much attended to. The winter is too long, and spring too short to allow of much time being spent in them. Americans are mostly otherwise engaged. Labour here is much higher, in proportion to the value of produce, than in England; and the people less able to purchase it. I do not think the Americans have any taste for such things." This young man's views of the people of America were far from favourable; but some allowances and deductions must be made, on account of his line of business, which is certainly not yet much wanted. Few houses have even so much as a shrub or evergreen to decorate them.

We at last reached the Passaic falls. There is something in the bolder outlines of nature, which awe and astonish. The body of waters at the time I saw them, was considerably augmented by the melting snow. The river flows over a bed of stone, with much descent. All at once, a rent or chasm extends across the bed of the river from one side to the other, which serves as a channel to the waters, and through which they are impetuously hurried down successive precipices, from a perpendicular height of about seventy feet. As this channel is very contracted, when compared with the breadth of the river above, the water acquires an astonishingly hurried motion, and assumes the appearance of cataracts of foam.

There is a handsome footbridge of wood thrown over the chasm, which commands a full view of the water. This bridge is very much above the cataract; and as it is perfectly secure, and well protected by wood work on both sides, it affords the mingled sensation of astonishment, safety, and dreadful apprehension. When we had crossed the bridge, and viewed the natural beauties of the place, we were returning, but were suddenly arrested by the demand of the bridge proprietor, who addressed us, " Two-pence each, gentlemen."

"You take us by surprise," said I, "You have given no intimation by any placard or notice, that you make exactions for crossing; but after you have got us in your power, you have the boldness to demand payment, whether we please or not. Is this the boasted freedom of the Americans?" "Come, come," said he; "it is to no purpose that you make many words. Pay you must. Do you think we put up bridges for every one to pass who chooses, and yet take nothing in return? I possessed much of the land on the other side of the river, on which the factories and town are built; but sold it, when the speculation for making Patteson a manufacturing town was first projected. I got a good price for my lands, and bought these rocks and grounds on speculation; and being a joiner, have erected that bridge myself, and have laid out the ground we stand on as a pleasure ground, which in summer looks beautiful. For all this expense and trouble I only demand two-pence from each visitor. If I made no charge, my purchase and bridge would be a losing speculation." "They would indeed," said I; "and I think your argument a very good one. We shall pay you."

After I had paid him his demand, I asked if his family had come from the old country. "No, thank God," was his answer. "My forefathers of many generations were native Americans. I would not be an Englishman." "Why," said I, "do you entertain so much dislike to English people?" "They are," he replied, "the most beastly people I have seen. I have no wish to encourage them. They come into my gardens, and cut down my young trees, and mutilate my seats and tables and bridge, and get drunk, and curse and swear and use indecent language, and give great offence to the Americans who patronise my gardens. I have forbid the English admittance. I am obliged to have some person to watch them, when they come in."

"Of what English do you speak?" I asked. "Of those," he replied, "who are employed in the mills. They quite demoralise the place. Their conduct and language are utterly abominable." I could well credit the proprietor, and that he found some check necessary, in order to restrain such visitors within due bounds.

The remarks of this gentleman justified some

observations I had heard made in New York, by Americans, who do not wish to see America a manufacturing country. They declared, that the moral conduct of English manufacturers was contagiously contaminating, and infected the very districts where they live. It is unpleasant, it is even exceedingly mortifying, to find so grievous a charge brought against one's countrymen, in a strange place. But yet, when we see American decorum, it is impossible to palliate or explain away the fact. The Americans, in their exterior deportment, are remarkably correct. One cannot but admire it. I never saw in the behaviour, nor heard in the discourse of an American a word or action morally improper. I heard of things done by them in secret; but the report of a tale-bearer has with me no weight, when placed against the demonstration of my senses. Their exterior moral deportment, as far as fell under my observation, is perfectly blameless; if we except their eagerness to obtain dollars, even on the confines of truth and falsehood, of honesty and dishonesty.

" Have you seen many respectable English people here?" I asked the proprietor. "There are," he said, " some manufacturers from England resident here, who brought considerable capital with them, and have built mills of different kinds. They are the leading people in the place. When strangers come into my gardens, and behave themselves properly, I do not know whether they are Americans or Englishmen. There is no difficulty in telling, where ill behaved people come from."

" I suppose," said I, " your gardens are frequented by numerous visitors." " In summer," he answered, " great numbers visit them. They are near enough for residents of New York to leave home in the morning, and after taking refreshments in my gardens, to return in the evening. The Catholic Bishop of New York was here last week, and conversed with me a long time. I think him an obliging and well-informed gentleman." " I am also acquainted with the gentleman you have mentioned," said I " and esteem him highly."

I informed him, that I was an English episcopal clergyman, and had emigrated to the States to examine the country for myself. " If you will remain over Sunday," he observed, " and perform service in our church, I will go and procure you permission. The people will be glad, of an opportunity of hearing an English minister."

" I have not come," I replied, " prepared in any respect for your very kind offer, and must necessarily decline the honour you intend me."

" There was," said he, " an English clergyman living in Patterson two years ago. He remained for some months, and married a lady of the place. He came to America to obtain a situation in some of our churches; but had no interest, and no vacant place presented itself. At last dissatisfied with having nothing to do, and fearing he should never succeed, he returned with his lady to England. He frequently performed duty in our church, and was much liked. Had he continued a year or two longer, he might have had a call to Patterson; for we have now no minister." " Perhaps," said I, " he might have no encouragement to fix his residence here, and the stipend of such a church might not be sufficient for his maintenance." " It is very large," he replied, " for the congregation is numerous. The salary may be between three and five hundred dollars; but it is difficult to mention any exact sum. He might also have had a school."

" I have great respect," he added, " for English clergymen, and request you will step into my house and take a glass of wine." This hospitable offer I accepted, and had the pleasure of drinking wine with the proprietor of the Passaic Falls. From his conversation, I found that Americans, in general, in the vicinity of Patterson have degrading notions of England and its people generally, from the specimen they behold in our weavers and spinners. The monied manufacturers, who have erected mills, they esteem highly. This gentleman and I talked together a long time, and became more and more friendly. He possessed a greater share of liberality than most Americans; and before I parted from him. expressed a wish that I would repeat my visit, and perform service in their episcopal church, of which he was a member.

At the Passaic Falls, the famed Sam Patch performed some of his wonderful leaps. He had been enamoured of a young woman, who rejected his offers, and to drown his love, he strove to drown himself. His intention was only half accomplished; for his love but not his life was annihilated. Although he had lept into the water from a surprising height, yet he rose with animation to the surface. Its chillness which froze his amorous attachments, gave him a distaste for drowning, and the desire of life was rekindled. Having discovered, by a lover's leap, that a fall from even lofty elevations, if upon a substance sufficiently yielding, is unaccompanied with danger, he announced his intention of repeating his leap, and the Passaic Falls were selected. A great multitude assembled, and he descended from a distance of ninety feet into the river below the falls. The event was corroborative of his first experiment. He then betook himself to such exploits, as a profession; and lept in succession several waterfalls of that country. At the Niagara falls, a scaffold was erected, upwards of one hundred feet above the water, sufficiently far over the river to free him from the danger of rocks. The water of the river, at the place he entered, is about one hundred and seventy feet, and a little below two hundred and twenty feet deep. He did not leap the whole depth of these falls, which are one hundred and sixty feet, but more than two-thirds. The Genessee falls at Rochester, were the closing scene of his exhibitions. He had lept them once, and he summoned courage to leap them again; and a crowd assembled to cheer him. But this time the water into which he descended was not twelve feet deep; a space insufficient to neutralize the acquired celerity of his fall, and his increased gravitation. He was also intoxicated, and lost his balance in the descent. His body was not immediately found, but was afterwards taken up greatly bruised, and with some of its limbs broken. Such is the story told of Mr. Patch.

I remained at Patterson all night; and breakfasted next morning at a public table, at which several young men were seated. They were boasting, that their national debt was much reduced, and would soon be paid off. This was a topic of frequent congratulation to Americans, at their social meetings; and is undoubtedly a national freedom from some burdens, although no national advantage. Their public debt is about two millions and a half sterling; of which, in the spring, they anticipate an entire discharge. " What will the English do," they inquired, " when we pay of our debt?" " They cannot then put their money out to interest, and will become bankrupt." I replied; " the American debt is too small to be worth the mention, and can affect England but slightly. There are more individuals than one there, any of whom could have redeemed your debt, at its greatest amount; and many hundreds, who could now singly discharge it." They could not comprehend how this might be, and spoke of two or three hundred dollars as a great sum, and of a person being independent, or nearly so, with a thousand dollars.

Some Americans told me, that poor emigrants complained of their being trodden underfoot by noblemen and bishops; and that they had shown them some pictures of John Bull weighed down by king, nobles, and bishops, standing on his shoulders. I have been asked several times whether, if a rich and a poor man were to meet on the road near a dirty place, the poor man would throw himself down and allow the rich man to walk over him as over a bridge. I only smiled at the simplicity of the question.

At one place on my way back, where I made some inquiry, they asked me what part of England I came from: on my answering, from London, they seemed quite astonished; and said, " Many people from London speak so unintelligibly, that we cannot comprehend them. There is a farmer in the neighbourhood, who came from that place, a decent sort of man. We like him, because he does not run down our country, nor meddle with politics. But he is very poor. He can hardly live. But although you and he have both come from one place, you do not speak alike." " It is very possible," said I, " for London is extensive, and contains many people, but few farmers."

When they mentioned that he did not meddle with politics, I was anxious to learn if the farm he lived on was his own. " Yes," said they, " and he has possessed it many years" " Has he no vote?" said I. " He does not exercise any," was the answer. " If he should be a politician, he would soon find that Americans know how to treat him. We can manage our affairs without English interference." " I perceive," said I, " that the Americans are a free people, and that all who come to them are free and independent." " Yes," said they, " we are the only free people in the world. We do not wish the English people to come to our country; but if they do come, and behave themselves properly, and pay their debts, we permit them to remain unmolested and unnoticed." " You are not only free," said I, " but generous also." They were highly pleased with me; and said, " We like to hear well behaved people."

There were some Irish families along the road, who expressed their pleasure at the sight of a person from the old country. Their kindness and open heartedness was so different from the heartlessness of some I spoke to, that their very conversation, and the inquiries they made, were indescribably gratifying. I was grieved to find that in America the Irish are generally poor. The Americans have much labour to execute, and find in the generous Irish a ready instrument. They have discovered the blind side of that openhearted race; and by copious libations of whiskey, and a little cajoling, have led them completely as they wish. The Americans are truly sharp-sighted.

Great inundations of emigrants from Ireland are continually pouring into America. I do not believe, however, from all I could learn, that their condition generally is much improved. A change of country is to them only a change of masters. They do not feel, indeed, their inferiority so heavily as before, because the higher orders are not so much elevated as in Europe. Our servant had entered the States with the rest of her father's family, which was settled in New York. She informed us, that their emigration arose from flattering statements in some letters, which they had received from acquaintances who had preceded them. They had found, however, no advantage from emigration; for their labour supported them better in Ireland than it did in America.

The Americans are eager to sow dissensions between England and Ireland. The following is an extract from a speech of one of the members of Congress—Mr. Clay. " Of all foreigners, none amalgamate themselves so quickly with our people as the natives of the Emerald Isle. In some of the visions which have passed through my imagination, I have supposed that Ireland was originally part and parcel of this continent, and that by some extraordinary convulsion of nature it was torn from America, and drifting across the Atlantic, was placed in the unfortunate vicinity of Great Britain. The same open-heartedness, the same generous hospitality, the same careless and uncalculating indifference about human life, characterise the inhabitants of both countries. And I have no doubt that, if the current of emigration were reversed, and set from America upon the shores of Europe, instead of bearing from Europe to America, every American emigrant to Ireland would there find, as every Irish emigrant finds here, a hearty welcome and a happy home."

The editor of an American paper, called *The Old Countryman*, made among others, the following observations. " We are aware that there are some men who are always exotics, and never become naturalized. The great mass of persons who arive in the United States from abroad, are allured to it from the feeling, that liberal principles abound, and that they can sit down free and happy, enjoying the rights of humanity. In this they are sometimes disappointed. It is a fact which no one will dispute, that, because they were not born in the United States, they are occasionally treated as if they were not equal with others." Those emigrants, " *sometimes disappointed, and not treated as if equal with others*," will be generally found to be from England; persons not of the lowest orders, of good character and guilty of no misdemeanor. If a man has so acted in his native country, as that his return would be uncomfortable, he must endure patiently his hardships. Many Englishmen would gladly return home, if they could obtain the means; and many more were emigrating from the States into Canada.

The English do not know the happiness and greatness of their own country. It is true that the national debt is a great burden, and that taxes of various kinds are oppressive. Yet the means to meet them are proportionably great. If people, who complain, would tolerate in England the same inconveniences which those must do who live in America, they would all grow rich. It is a very common thing, for three or four families to inhabit one house, because none of them separately can pay for an entire dwelling. This is not confined to the lowest class; respectable professional men, and merchants of good standing, do not esteem it beneath them to be found occupying two or three rooms: some of them only one room. Their mode of life also is much less cleanly and less comfortable, than respectable people in England have any conception of. Yet the better classes live well, and as much as possible after the English style.

CHAPTER VIII.

DEMOCRACY—BRUTAL CONDUCT OF AMERICANS TOWARDS SUCH AS SPEAK LIGHTLY OF THEIR GOVERNMENT—MAY-DAY IN NEW YORK—SILENCE AND HASTE AT MEALS—VANITY AND ILLIBERALITY—AMERICANS FEAR THE REPROACH OF BEING DESCENDANTS OF FELONS—CHANGE OF SURNAMES—FREQUENT FIRES—VALUE OF GROUND LOTS—AMERICAN FRUITS—SERVITUDE—COMPLAINTS OF EMIGRANTS—AMERICAN DISPATCH—JUVENILE DELINQUENTS—WORK-HOUSE—OUTRAGED INDIANS—BOUNDARY LINE BETWEEN THE UNITED STATES AND CANADA.

DEMOCRACY may sound very well in theory; but its practical tendency, I am pursuaded, will never be beneficial, except in a country where population is thinly scattered. There is in America no stability to private or public character. In England,

DEMOCRACY. 171

the conduct of some noblemen was severely censured, for ejecting such of their tenants as voted against them. The same thing will be found to prevail, as far as is practicable, even in America. General Jackson, on being elected President, displaced, I was informed, nearly one thousand public officers, on account of political feelings.

Many of the English have been heard to say that the people of England are oppressed and enslaved, and that there is no perfect liberty in England. This was once my opinion. But it is now manifest to me, that England is the only place where rational and perfect liberty is enjoyed. A person dares not, in America, express his sentiments with half the freedom that he does in England. I once ventured to remark to an American, in the hearing of a person from England, that I did not perceive the Americans, with all their boasted independence, to be really in a more enviable condition than Englishmen: that I began seriously to believe, although of a different opinion formerly, that an hereditary monarch and aristocracy are of vast advantage to a state, and contribute incalculably to its greatness. The Englishman drew me aside, and desired me not to let fall expressions of such import. " The Americans," said he, " have long memories. You are now, from not being employed, independent of them and consequently out their power. Yet should you hereafter have occasion to solicit a favour, and thereby place yourself in dependence on them, you will find that they never forget."

It is evident to any one, at all conversant with the politics of Europe, that France has humbled her hereditary nobility in compliment to American republicanism. France never did any thing so egregiously foolish. She has made herself a laughing-stock to the world, and to well-informed Americans, among others. They heartily despise her politics, which they consider as childish. If England should adopt a similar procedure, she would instantly decline from her greatness. The aristocracy is her strongest bulwark. If any great change takes place in their privileges, or in the privileged classes of the country; or if the elective franchise be extended to the lowest orders; the stability and supremacy and glory of England are at an end. Americans are eager for some great change, or a revolution in England; and anticipate their own aggrandisement from European disasters. Their papers frequently contain fulminations against English principles, against the exaltation of her society, and against the wide extension of her commerce and her sway. This they do, in order to gain converts to their form of government, and citizens to their country. But should any well informed Englishman arrive there, capable of comparing the two forms of government, and of estimating the advantages of his own, they will not encourage his stay.

The best circles in New York disapproved and discountenanced the brutal conduct of their countrymen to Kean and other actors from England, who had spoken lightly of their government. Yet I heard some individuals, whom I had considered as belonging to the higher circles, justify the phrenzy of the mob. A person, to credit and understand the sensitiveness of their body politic, and the electric-like shock and rapidity with which any sensation felt in one part is conveyed by newspapers to every corner of their empire, and vibrates through every chord, must have resided among them, and have witnessed. Woe to the man, whose conduct or expression has provoked their indignation! He will not be expelled from America. He may live there. But he will find himself a marked man whereever he goes; shunned, yet imposed on; and as completely debarred from undertaking any thing, or from succeeding if he should, as if he had his residence with their antipodes. An English captain, with whom I wanted to take a passage home, declared to me that he would rather fall into the hands of any enemy than those of Americans. My opinions on this point are in unison with his. May heaven shield me, from collision with the brutal outrage of a republican mob, and from democratic vengeance!

The first of May is noted among the people of New York for bustle and change. It is almost impossible to rent a house or lodgings longer than for one year; and in any part of a year longer than till May-day next ensuing. We had taken our apartments till that time, at the expiration of which Mrs. F. took other lodgings, during my tour through the States and Canada. She described May-day as affording scenes exceedingly laughable; in every direction were carts and waggons laden with furniture; the streets were literally filled with chairs, tables, drawers, desks, carpets, &c., passing from one house to another, to the great advantage of the carters, who find full employment, and are on that day paid double charges. It is also not a little gratifying to New York gossips, who are allowed a peep into the lodgings of such strangers generally as have not permanent dwellings. As May-day approaches, the landlord proposes to the tenant his terms. The tenant finds, for the most part, an advance of rent, and prefers a change. The landlord annexes to the door-post a written notice, and the tenant commences amusing himself with entering every one's dwelling similarly circumstanced, and exposing his own to the gaze of others. It is almost impossible for a stranger, who has occupied lodgings, and wishes to escape imposition, to avoid such intrusion into his private rooms. We suffered this ourselves, and therefore speak from experience. Many American women, we were told, occupy much of their leisure time about this period in prying into the abodes of foreigners, to see if they are respectable, and have their rooms well furnished. Americans could not have invented any domestic custom more inquisitorial, or which gives a readier access to the privacies of strangers.

Another thing, offensive to English people accustomed at home to the pleasures of a separate table, is, that they cannot find a boarding-house where they may take their meals by themselves. They are obliged to mingle with all promiscuously, whom the mistress of the house admits. It is true, that much conversation need not be kept up, nor many words exchanged. The people, at these houses, sit down to table and rise up again, without thanksgiving and without ceremony. The business of eating is a task, for which a short time only can be spared, and it must be finished with dispatch. The different guests study their own accommodation—in sitting down and rising up—in the duration of their continuance at table—in their entrance into and departure from the eating-room. Sometimes a whole meal is begun and finished, without the utterance of a word. Eating is performed with the same unceasing activity as a walk in the streets, and no intermission can be spared for social converse. Indeed, it is impracticable for an Englishman to indulge himself in talking, as at home, and to acquit himself in eating, as an American. His utmost efforts are required, to keep pace with his neighbours; I never was so much at a loss how to conduct myself properly, as at an American table.

Sometimes a few observations are made, but they always end abruptly, unless rendered palatable by flattery. A physician of some eminence boarded at the same house, and ate at the same table with ourselves; he one day asserted, that literature and scholars in America were infinitely raised above those of Europe, and of England in particular. I mentioned to him my experience in America, and what I had noticed at Boston. He grew rather warm at my narrations and remarks, and said " You must admit, at the least, that American physicians are above those of England, in sound knowledge, and in physic?" " I could hardly conceive," I replied, " that, in a country so recently peopled, and so sparing in pecuniary and honorary recompense to professional talent, any first-rate physicians could be found. Were American institutions on so excellent a plan as to produce attainments of sufficient brilliancy to shine in England, their possessors would never be satisfied with the state of things in their own country, but would emigrate to climates more congenial to their acquired perceptions, where their talents might be appreciated and rewarded." " You have slandered our country," he indignantly exclaimed, " and could never gain a comfortable living in it." " Some of your own clergy and professors were of a different opinion," said I, " and encouraged me to open a school, at respectable terms. I have contented myself with making inquiries respecting professions in general, and my own in particular, and have discovered that America has nothing to confer which could allure my stay." He shortly after left the table, and for three days seated himself at another place, where he could exchange neither words nor looks.

Such is the narrow and illiberal spirit which infuses itself into almost every untravelled republican; and which never can be exterminated under their present system of government, and during the unrequited energies of literary men. A state of things which fosters such a spirit must be prohibitive of American greatness; but it sufficiently accounts for the degrading flattery which prudent emigrants will furnish. The republican ear is never satisfied with praise and adulation; nothing is too fulsome or extravagant. " There is nothing which tyrannic power, equal to the gods, when flattered and extolled, cannot credit of itself." This part of the American character is, I believe, the most offensive to an honourable man. He dares not speak openly his own sentiments; he feels himself in a strange country, where true freedom is unknown, and where unconditional surrender of conscience, and unbounded and unceasing approbation, are rigorously extorted from him. I have no hesitation in affirming, that no gentleman, who can sustain himself with credit in Europe, will reside permanently in the States.

Did this narrowness of spirit arise from mere vanity, it might be more excusable. Its origin is in vanity, blended with deadly hatred to England. America resembles a young girl, just liberated from a severe foster-mother, and introduced into the world : all nations praise and admire her, and she is filled with vanity: all nations persuade her that she has been cruelly treated, and she is filled with animosity and hatred: the refuse of all nations tell her that inveterate rancour is becoming her station, and that her most engaging forms are republican ; and she becomes, as a gentleman of great eminence in Canada told me, more democratic every hour, and neither forgets nor forgives. That she has attained, in some things, almost the lowest depths of absurdity, it is my firm opinion ; and many, even of Americans themselves, are disposed to believe it. She has not yet acquired sufficient insight into other governments and institutions, to perceive their merits, or her own deficiencies. She flatters herself that she has culled all the excellencies of others, without their imperfections; and has extirpated from herself every blemish, and cherished her perfections only ; and that a judicious amalgamation of these perfections and excellencies has rendered her supremely lovely, and supremely great. Had she contented herself with such a vanity, as Dr. Franklin speaks of in his life, she might, with him, have enumerated it among legitimate sources of enjoyment, and have given thanks to providence for the blessing.

Dr. Jones, author of the Greek and English Lexicon, a gentleman with whom I had the honour of an intimate acquaintance, once told me, that he had a strong dislike to that portion of Franklin's works called " Poor Richard ;" " Because," said he, " it has imparted a bias to American principles, and has rendered them too parsimonious and mercenary." I cannot view it in the same light with that gentleman. " Poor Richard," at its first production, was disseminated among a people with whom its maxims were congenial, and did not produce contracted views, but confirmed them. Its precepts are a treasure-house of domestic prudence and economy, to persons in the situation of Americans, but have been acted upon too closely.

Several Americans, with whom I conversed, omitted not to tell me that they are the descendants of those persecuted non-conformists who first took refuge in the wilds of America. It appeared amusing, that they should at this period court and challenge an inquiry into the circumstances of their forefather's emigration, even without any reference being made by myself to subjects connected with it. It is utterly impossible that any considerable number of the present population of America can be the lineal descendants of criminals, transported originally for felony. Yet they seem to be apprehensive that foreigners regard them as if they were, or as if they had fled from England at a subsequent period, for some punishable crime. I have no inclination to charge any of them with a polluted origin, but to consider them all as the offspring and descendants of honourable men.

A professional gentleman from England, who had resided many years in New York, declared to me, that nothing offended Americans more than to inquire after their family ornaments, their necklaces, bracelets, and anklets. That the natives of a country so extensive and flourishing should feel much from a question so impertinently foolish, I could not have believed, had I not observed their eagerness to be considered as descendants from the non-conformists. Were I permitted to pursue the metaphor, I would say, that the Americans have not allowed their ornaments to rust, but have kept them bright and furbished; although the substance of which they were originally fabricated has not, from the alchemy of education and sound principles, been converted into gold.

I was told that a person in the States, who is dissatisfied with his surname, can easily have it changed to another more suitable to his taste and inclinations. It was a subject of discussion sometimes, and the information I obtained was this, that a person on taking up his citizenship, needs only go to a particular office appropriated to this purpose, and having selected another appellation, get it registered as his family cognomen, whereby he and his children may be designated afterwards. This, if true, must render the genealogies of families extremely difficult to trace; yet I must confess that it is very accommodating to persons of dubious character, to whom a change of surname must be a great consideration. I never loved my musical name, and the next time I voyage to the States I may choose to have it altered.

The frequency of "fire! fire!" being called through the streets, at first alarmed us; yet natives, and emigrants of longer residence than we, were but little apprehensive—custom had reconciled them to the hazard of burnings. No day or night, however, appeared to elapse without either a fire, or the rumour of one. I myself was present at several, one of which was a church, which had ignited from a stove-pipe. One regulation respecting fire-engines is, that a person from the house of every citizen is required to attend, the moment a fire-bell rings, in order to work the engines. Foreigners, not naturalized, are exempted. The engines appeared well served, and under proper management, although some of the pipes were sadly out of order.

Fires are chiefly confined to houses built of wood, which, from frequent conflagrations, are fast diminishing. When a wood house, in some districts of the city, has been pulled down or burnt, the city inspectors require that a house of brick, stone, or marble, be erected in its place. I was told that many wood buildings, when favourably situated for business, and let upon long leases, are annually burnt down by some secret incendiary, employed by the landlord. He finds, in such case, that it is his interest to accomplish this ; and his tenant's goods and stores are but slight impediments. The value of ground lots has, in some situations, increased so much as to render a wood tenement a matter of no importance. The wood house once burnt down, the tenant finds himself obliged either to build a fire-proof house, or to evacuate his lease. In either case the landlord is a gainer.

Ground for building is of more value, perhaps, in New York than in London. A space, twenty-five feet in front and one hundred deep, in the best situations, will always realize to the seller from twenty to forty thousand dollars. A small piece of ground, which possessed the advantage of three frontages, was disposed of for no less a sum than nearly one hundred and forty thousand dollars.

During our outward-bound voyage we heard much of the fine fruits of America. Shortly after landing I observed some pine-apples exposed for sale, and purchased four for a dollar. On tasting

I found them destitute of the luscious flavour and sweetness which hot-house pines possess in England. America may boast of natural and indigenous fruits not found in England, except under artificial culture, but they are hardly worth the name. Pines grow in the West Indies only, or in the most southern parts of the States; and although they have a fine scent, yet are not more pleasant to the palate than our garden turnips. It would seem that the original curse denounced on Adam is extended to every region, and verified to every people. Without sweat and labour, inflicted by Heaven for disobedience, nothing in its perfection can be enjoyed by man. His watchfulness and industry must every where second the efforts of nature in bringing her productions to maturity.

No native American, unless from absolute want, will ever engage in the capacity of a servant. Menial offices must all be performed by others. To call a free-born republican a servant, would be degrading him to the level of a slave. Our Irish girl once told us, after hearing us speak of her as our servant, that no other person but herself would allow us to consider her a servant. "But," said she, "you are an English clergyman, and I an Irish girl, and you may, therefore, call me so."

Emigrants from Great Britain and Ireland find practically, that distress in their native country arises more from excess of population than excess of tithes and taxes. Wages in New York a few years ago were double of what they are now; in addition to this, provisions, house-rent, and taxes, were considerably less. Increased population has occasioned this. Personal experience in America is a better refutation of fanciful theories, than rational deductions and cool calculations formed in England. Yet I hope that the public burdens will be alleviated by a moderate and judicious reform.

Americans complain that emigrants have injured them, by causing redundancy of labour, increase of house-rents, poor-rates, and prices of provisions, and depreciation of recompense for industry. Emigrants in America complain that they have been enticed over by flattering statements, which they often find deceptive and fallacious. The English about London make the self-same complaints against the Irish which Americans do against the Irish and them.

The different degrees of perfection with which work is finished in England and America is, as some workmen told me, sufficiently annoying to English mechanics and tradesmen. At home, business and trades must be executed in a workmanlike manner; there, celerity is more regarded than excellence. A skilful workman, and one indifferently so, will find equal employment and equal pay, provided they are equally expert. The British Consul told me, on one occasion, that the Americans can get through more work in a given time than the English. " I employed," said he, " an Englishman to furnish me with a plan and estimate of something I wished to have done. After a period of three weeks he tendered them. Had I employed an American, both the plan and work would have been finished in a shorter time. The American improvement on the English auger is itself an immense saving of time and labour." " Perhaps," said I, " Americans would perform the work more slightly than an Englishman."

" They would do it well enough," was his answer.

The Americans, in person, are generally slender, and very active. They pass through the streets with great agility and haste; if they perform labour with equal dispatch, it must be rapidly accomplished. Americans appear to possess their full share of natural endowments. When their civil institutions shall have been placed on a more liberal footing, and an increase of wealth and independence shall have conferred additional leisure for polite and elegant learning, they will doubtless improve in the embellishments of life, and raise their country to a respectable rank among refined nations. The present generation, however, is far behind, and improvement must be slow.

Some of the public and private buildings of New York are handsome, but none stupendous, far less magnificent. The white marble, which their country furnishes in profusion, is very ornamental, and adds grace and beauty to their city; yet a person acquainted with London finds nothing peculiar in the architecture of the States, except— wood buildings, log-houses, and shanties.

Dr. Word, an eminent physician, and superintendant of the poor-house, called upon us before our departure for Canada, and conveyed us in his carriage to the place assigned for juvenile delinquents. I never saw any place in better order, or more conveniently managed. There is no great severity inflicted on the culprits, the object being rather to guard them from further contamination, by proper instructions, moderate labour, and detention from the sight and hearing of vice or lewdness. The doctor afterwards conducted us to the work-house, and poor-house, in which, during the previous winter, twenty-five hundred paupers had found relief and shelter. After dining with the Doctor we all went, in a boat belonging to the establishment, to the prison on Blackwell's Island, through which we were shown. A plainness, a simplicity, and a cleanliness, pervade all these places, which elicit the admiration of visitors. The plan on which they are conducted is described as admirable, by persons who are more conversant than myself with such institutions.

The poor and outraged Indians were sometimes spoken of as presenting an impediment to national improvements. It was considered as desirable (and *desirable* in American estimation means *right*) to banish these aborigines from the midst of civilization to the western forests. There is something in the logic of Americans so unnatural, and so devoid of generosity, that the mind recoils from contemplating it. I once ventured to question the justice of depriving Indians of their lands, but was answered " They had sold them." I replied that they had parted with them from compulsion, and was answered " They had received an equivalent." I observed, that the Indians had considered the matter differently, and had taken up arms, and was answered " The Americans possessed proof that the Indians had been instigated and encouraged by the Governor of Upper Canada." I replied with warmth that such accusation was unfounded, and was answered by an old American that I had uttered a lie, and reviled their country, and that he consequently regarded me as no better than the dust under his feet.

The rejection by Americans of the awarded boundary line between their country and Canada, was singularly defended by some. The King of

Holland, they said, had not properly decided it, because he wished to secure some favour from England by an unjust decree. He had not settled the question proposed to him, since he was only an arbiter of boundary lines already marked out and claimed, aud had not been authorized to draw another. Had he even decided the question, according to the arbitration he received, yet the State of Maine had never consented to suffer a partition, and would reject any sentence which displeased itself. " I thought," said I, " that the King of Holland had been named as arbiter, by an act of Congress?" " By the President," I was answered, " and the delegates of a few of the States; but those of Maine were not parties to it." " Then an act of Congress," observed I, " is not binding?" " No act of the general legislation," I was answered, " can interfere with the internal regulations, or the boundaries of any separate State, since each State is free and independent."

" It would appear from such reasoning," I rejoined, " that no dependence can be securely placed on the honour of the country, where the interests of any State are concerned or interfered with?"

To which this conclusive answer was returned:—
" If England expects Maine to surrender a portion of its territory, she must make it a compensation." Here ended the argument, and a conviction, from this and other reasoning, rested on my mind, that no treaty will bind any individual State of that country, nor the country generally, where interest suggests a violation.

CHAPTER IX.

JOURNEY TO NIAGARA — ACCIDENT IN A STEAM-BOAT — ALBANY—AMERICAN TRAVELLING—MODE OF LOCATION—INNS—BEAUTIFUL SCENERY—ROADS—TWO FEMALE PASSENGERS—METHODIST PREACHERS—ANCIENT BANKS OF LAKE ONTARIO—NIAGARA FALLS—AN ECCENTRIC ENGLISH GENTLEMAN PRECIPITATED DOWN THE CATARACT—A SOLITARY FEMALE.

With the consul's introduction, my letters of orders, and several testimonials I had lately obtained from England, I embarked on board a steam-boat for Albany, the capital of New York State. This was on the sixteenth of April. Another steam-boat, of greater power and a faster sailer, left New York after us, and overtook us before we had ascended the river many miles. The captain of the steam-boat I was in, boasted manfully, that his was incomparably the speedier vessel, and that he could leave the other at any distance he chose. In short, he was only waiting for her arrival in order to give her a fair trial, by putting on all his steam. As she approached, which, she did with an imposing rapidity, he foolishly and unfairly crossed her course, that he might hinder her from passing. This manœuvre he repeated, until the captain of the other perceiving himself wilfully obstructed without provocation, ordered his helmsman to direct his prow against the broadside of his opposer. The crash that followed was tremendous, and carried away the railwork of half the side, as well as the boat of our vessel. Bars of iron, an inch thickness, were bent and twisted like slender wires. A few reproaches of unfairness on the one hand, and a few threats of action for damages on the other, terminated this foolish rencontre. The passengers of the victorious boat gave utterance to their sense of the bravery of the captain, and the superiority their boat; then passed triumphantly before us, and we saw them no more till our arrival at Albany. Some of the passengers of our vessel encouraged the captain to retaliate; but, from prudence or cowardice, he declined. Similar amusements to those mentioned in my voyage to Boston were resorted to, as soon as darkness covered the landscape. The beauties of the Hudson have often been celebrated, but not above their merit. All ice and snow had disappeared at New York, before I left it; but on our approaching Albany, a distance of one hundred and sixty miles, large masses of both presented themselves.

The consul had mentioned my name to a gentleman of this city, and requested me to call on him; which I did. I found the same disposition to oblige and gratify, which I had observed elsewhere; and am persuaded, that the really respectable are as much in advance, as the other classes are in arrear, of the civil institutions of the country. Among other places, he showed me the capital, the State House. &c. &c. and introduced me to some of the members of the State legislation. The youthful appearance of many of the legislators struck me with surprise. Some of them could not, if one may judge from appearance, be much above twenty years of age. A majority of them are lawyers by profession. A newly invented instrument for ascertaining the purity of oil was placed in one of the windows: it was considered a useful invention, and its accuracy had been proved satisfactorily by successive experiments. Oil being light, the same instrument which would sink in it, would float in other substances of greater specific gravity.

From Albany I travelled to Schenectady, over a rail-road not then finished, but which allowed of steam-carriages going one way at a time; they could not pass each other on the road, as but one set of rails had been laid. This was the easiest and pleasantest part of my land journey, and about seventeen miles. American roads are such, I imagine, as English travellers have seldom seen elsewhere. Their coaches, also, are very inferior vehicles when compared with ours; the sides are not pannelled, but open, and have pieces of leather, like curtains, which serve as weather-screens, and are let down and rolled up at pleasure. There are no outside passengers, except on the rail-road, and these all pay alike.

A young lawyer, a relation to the episcopal

Bishop of New York, was my companion from this place to the Falls of Niagara. He was proceeding to Buffalo, where he purposed to establish himself, unless he should be so fortunate as to discover, at some village or town upon the road, an opening for professional gentlemen like himself. His mode of proceeding, illustrative of the manners of his countrymen, it will be proper to describe.

At every town or village we passed through, where a short interruption took place, he made a hasty call at some of the stores or inns, to inquire how many lawyers were in the place, and how many people inhabited it ; and drew his conclusion thence of the probability of an opening for additional lawyers. At most of the places through which we passed, he declared there were already more lawyers than could gain an honest livelihood ; he must, consequently, move forward. He was making such inquiries, not for himself merely, but for a young friend also, who had not entered on his travels, and to whom he had promised to transmit the result of his inquiries, on his arrival at his final destination. He had once before been

MODE OF LOCATION. 199

to Buffalo, a place he much admired, as it was beautiful, wealthy, improving, and would soon be an extensive city. It afforded openings for lawyers, he said, and he believed for gentlemen of other professions, who might be tempted to try it; and he advised me to accompany him, and try my fortunes Whether he was actually in earnest respecting such inquiries, I will not take upon me to decide; but this is the general practice of American emigrants, as related by others. I declined the trial he suggested, since my immediate object was a visit to Canada, in order to wait upon the Bishop. If unsuccessful in that quarter, my intention was to make an extensive journey through Canada and the States, and then return to England. For my own sake, I may say I felt glad at his successive failures, as he was the most amusing companion I had met with in America, and his society beguiled the tedium of a long journey.

Most of the inns on the road were well supplied with food and fuel, and prevented me from feeling those numerous privations of which travellers in America have often complained. The beds were comfortable—much better than some I met with in Canadian inns—yet not like English beds. The attendance, also, of servants was not much to be complained of; for the American manners were in these inns softened down, by the frequency of travellers. The charges, also, were not extravagant, as in some places of Canada, either for bed or board; and no obsequious waiter came forward to request we would remember him. Coach-hire, and conveyance of every description, is more moderate on the American than on the Canadian side. These praises cannot be denied to Americans; they enjoy, and it is in consequence, probably, of their being more deserving, a greater traffic, and more passengers of respectability, even for Canada, than frequent the British side of the lake. An English gentleman, who returned a cabin passenger in the same ship with us, described the American inns as palaces, and the Canadian as infernal receptacles of plundered travellers. If I should go half his length in praise and condemnation, the picture would be more correct. I am greatly concerned that, although I love Canada and its people, I cannot assert that his description is entirely unfounded. I hope the Canadians will adopt, for their own sakes, at least, better and less expensive regulations ; and evince their desire of pleasing, by improved accommodations, and more moderate charges.

Our journey along the rising grounds above the Mohawk river was exceedingly delightful, from the beauty of the scenery around. The undulations on the face of the country, the mountains, valleys, rivers, plains, and forests, appearing in succession before us, were ever charming, ever new. The Dutch, who are not renowned for taste or elegance, have contrived, wherever they locate themselves, to select and appropriate the most beautiful and fertile places. The lowlands, bordering on this river, were described as belonging principally to Dutch farmers, grown wealthy by the increased value of lands, and their industrious and frugal habits.

The Little Falls, a village on the Mohawk, is one of the most delightful and lovely places I ever saw. The scenery of the surrounding rocks and steeps, its acqueduct, bridge, and waters, and the romantic position of its canal, with the valley below, mock all description.

The worst American road over which I travelled was along the end of Seneca Lake, through Geneva, and to Canandaigua ; the last fifteen miles of which occupied five hours and a half. American roads are always dreadful, at the disappearance of frost. The breaks and holes were so deep in some places, and so frequent, as to threaten destruction to the coach, and dislocation to our limbs. The coach stuck fast several times, and nothing short of the most strenuous exertions and whippings of the driver could have got it out. American coaches are generally constructed with three benches each, every one of which is capable of holding three passengers. There were four passengers in the coach we journied in, which we found too few for comfort. When the coach rocked backwards and forwards in deep places, the passengers were dodged against each other with great violence, and each of us suffered several contusions. I cannot deny that where we had more of jostling we had more of mirth ; for it was quite impossible frequently to refrain from laughter.

There was a kind of road formed, by round logs of wood laid across, over which the coach passed with rapid vaults from one to another. This was the most unpleasant motion I ever felt. Such roads are denominated by the natives, "ribbed or corduroy roads," an appellation not ill chosen.

At Rochester, my companion, after making his usual inquiries about the number of lawyers, accompanied me to the falls. He pointed out the position of the rock, whence *Sam Patch* took his final leap. There is an aqueduct over the river eight hundred feet long.

At Lockport, the frost of the preceding winter, and the thaw and floods before our arrival, had damaged the canal so much that it required great repairs. Many men were employed on it. The American canal, like most of their works not executed by Englishmen altogether, is not so substantial as might he wished, and requires repairing continually.

From Lockport we travelled by coach to Lewiston, on the American side, and thence to Manchester, seven miles farther, and close to the Falls.

On leaving Lockport, two young girls were admitted into the coach, rather singular in their dress and manners. They were also more free in conversation, and with less of reserve, than any American women I had seen before. These Americans alighted at the first inn they came to, for the purpose of warming themselves. My companion, whose curiosity and suspicions were more acute than mine, expressed his sentiments to be, that our female fellow travellers were not of good reputation; and stepped into the inn after them to make inquiries. I felt much at a loss to distinguish any particular criterion from which my amusing friend could have drawn prognostications so unfavourable to their character. Nothing escaped them, which could have excited in me such surmise or conclusion. He soon returned with the information that they were what he expected, and that the neighbourhood abounded with similar characters. This was the only instance, in all my rambles through America, in which female behaviour or language met my observation, betraying a departure from strict reserve; and the departure in this instance was of such a nature, as to awaken no suspicions in a stranger's mind.

A young methodist preacher, from the Eastern States, joined us here. He was on his road to

Canada to buy some land, and was prepared for teaching either religion or politics. He talked a great deal about scripture, of which he really knew nothing, and made so many quotations from the Bible inapplicable to his arguments (if mere rant deserves that name), that were I a perfect novice in revelation, and merely a sceptical inquirer after truth, he might have converted me into an Atheist. After a short conversation with him, and a number of questions relative to the signification of different passages, and one or two requests that he would reconcile some apparent inconsistencies of Scripture, he got such an insight into himself as struck him speechless, and sat fixed up in a corner for a long time. He was far from the only instance of methodistical intrusion and misguided enthusiasm (if crafty selfishness, under the semblance of extraordinary piety, deserves the name), with which I met in America. Many of his misinformed fraternity were uttering unintelligible mysteries, in incoherent language and inapplicable terms, which were shocking and disgusting to men of sober and well informed minds. But I had long before this observed the superficial learning of the best educated among the American population. After any ranter had used an improper expression, or made an inconclusive quotation, I begged him to explain himself, and point out the justness of his inferences. Such incoherent and absurd expressions were hereby instantly suspended; for none I met with could explain himself, or discuss religious subjects without extravagant metaphors. In less than five minutes, in every case, and mostly in less than one, we were all as mute and melancholy as if we had just emerged from the cave of Trophonius.

The only way in which retaliation for such imposed silence was inflicted, was by getting one or two to join in some hymns or sacred songs. These admitted of no argumentative interruptions, and served the interest of the preacher, by cloaking the sterility of his knowledge from vulgar observation. More than once have I been annoyed, and yet laughed heartily, at this skilful manœuvre. In a few minutes, frequently, the silence has ended in obstreperous music, risible yet offensive, from the reason of its adoption and its solemn nature. The young preacher I have mentioned, after having shrunk abashed into muteness of some continuance, collected sufficient courage and self-possession to speak again; and proffered us the option of Wesley's Hymns or Yankee-doodle. My companion and I were amusing ourselves in talking, and were suddenly speechless in our turn, from so singular an offer. He construed our silence into approval, and as there was a poor woman who had just entered, seated on one side, he quickly sounded her feelings, and prevailed on her to join him. These two, and the other females also, esteemed their privilege of singing equally extensive with our right to converse, and made the coach resound and re-echo with songs and hymns. We made a few ineffectual efforts to procure a discontinuance, and then reluctantly submitted, till their humour was gratified, and they thought proper to desist.

This American methodist I discovered to be desirous of being present at some political meetings in Canada, respecting elections, and petitions from the adherents of Mr. M'Kenzie. He was also zealously desirous to preach the Gospel. Most of the methodist preachers in Canada are from the States, and have a double object; they ostensibly minister in sacred offices, but secretly and effectively disseminate principles destructive of the present order of affairs. They are striving to accomplish in the British provinces what American skill and prowess unavailingly essayed. They are concerting schemes for the expulsion of English influence, and the establishment of republican institutions and plans of government. Persons from Ireland, residing in the States, more than once assured me, that much of the money subscribed for the purposes of Mr. O'Connell, was transmitted from America. I was also told that Mr. M'Kenzie, and several others of his political friends, were in the pay of Americans. Yet so deep-rooted is Canadian aversion to American cunning and dishonesty, and so apprehensive are Canadians of Yankee imposture and deception, that republican attempts have hitherto met, and I hope always will meet, with most signal and triumphant opposition. These remarks have arisen from the conduct of our ranting, singing, electioneering preacher, and were justified and corroborated by many further observations in the States and in Canada.

ANCIENT BANKS OF LAKE ONTARIO. 209

We arrived at Lewiston about midnight, a village directly opposite to Queenston in Canada, and located at the foot or termination of the mountain ridge, or alluvial way, and at the head of the navigation on the Niagara river. A ferry is established between this place and Queenston. " This *mountain ridge, or alluvial way*, extends along the south shore (and a corresponding one of similar description along the north, or Canadian shore), of Lake Ontario, from the Genesee river at Rochester to Niagara river, a distance of about eighty miles. The road is handsomely arched in the centre, and is generally from four to eight rods wide. In some places it is elevated one hundred and twenty or thirty feet above the level of the lake, from which it is distant from six to ten miles. The last forty miles of our journey from Rochester to Lewiston, along this natural highway, is broken for a considerable extent by log-roads or causeways, bordered by impervious forests, occasionally relieved by the tempoi iry huts of the recent settlers; but the remaining distance is unusually level, and, with some intermissions, bordered by a line of cultivation. It is generally believed that this was once the southern (and that on the Canadian side the northern) boundary of the lake; and that the ridge was occasioned by the action of the water. The gravel and smooth stones of which the ridge is composed, intermingled with a great variety of shells, leave little room to doubt the correctness of this opinion. It is a great natural curiosity, and should be travelled over by the tourist, in going to or returning from the Falls.

" *Devil's Hole*, three and a half miles from Lewiston," to continue the brief words of the Guide Book, which best expresses my own remarks, " is a most terrific gulph, formed by a chasm in the eastern bank of the Niagara, one hundred and fifty or two hundred feet deep. An angle of this gulph is within a few feet of the road, affording to the passing traveller, without alighting, an opportunity of looking into the yawning abyss beneath. During the French war, a detachment of the British army, while retreating from Schlosser in the night, before a superior force of French and Indians, were destroyed at this place; officers, soldiers, women, and children, with their horses, waggons, baggage, &c., were all precipitated down the gulph. Those who were not drowned in the river, were dashed in pieces on the naked rocks.

" The *Whirlpool*, which is formed by a short turn in the river, is two and a half miles from the Falls ; and a mile nearer there is a *sulphur spring*, used principally for bathing."

We at last reached the Falls. I saw them first on the American side. The mind of Europeans has been stimulated, from descriptions and pictures of Niagara Falls, to anticipations of something wonderful ; and is not disappointed on seeing them. They are utterly beyond any description which can be conveyed by words. I did not, however, weep on first beholding them, as some have done ; but regarded them steadily, and with tearless optics. There was much of snow and ice still around them, although it was the 23rd of April. The young gentleman who had been so long my companion, still accompanied me. He had spent some time here, on his former visit to Buffalo ; and was acquainted with the localities of the place, and the points where the best views may be obtained. We went round Goat Island, to enjoy a view of the rapids above the Falls, which are themselves wonderful, and resemble waves dashing over rocks on the shore of the ocean ; only they are here continuous and uninterrupted.

At Niagara and Rochester Falls, from the sun shining bright when I saw them, were brilliant rainbows. The one at Niagara was more splendid than I ever saw in the clouds ; but very diminutive, its span being not more than forty or fifty yards.

I was told, that an English gentleman of the name of Abbot, most eccentric in his habits, and somewhat deranged in his intellect, and who had escaped from the guardianship of his friends, resided for years by himself in a hut on Goat Island. This hut or hermitage, in which he lived, was pointed out to me. He used frequently to undress himself, and bathe in the rapids above the Falls. He also would often, for a length of time together, walk backwards and forwards on a dangerous bridge thrown over loose rocks in the rapids, with its extreme point, a single beam of timber, projecting over the brink of this tremendous cataract. After having exercised himself in this manner for

ECCENTRIC GENTLEMAN—SOLITARY FEMALE. 213

a while, he would walk to the end of the beam, and having secured himself by his feet, hang with his head downwards, and look steadfastly on the dread abyss beneath him. This solitary, singular, and hazardous existence he long continued. His hat and parts of his other dress, were observed one day deposited on the bank, at a place where he was wont to enter the water for the purpose of bathing; but himself had disappeared. Search was made for him, but in vain. His body was found long afterwards considerably below; and having been identified obtained interment.

At a subsequent period, Mrs. F. and myself, visited this person's hermitage on Goat Island. We found the door open, and we entered. The hut was exceedingly neat,an devery thing in order. But we found a lone and solitary being, a female, the occupant of his cell. Her vacant stare, when we entered, and her precipitate retreat to an inner apartment, excited strongly our curiosity to prosecute inquiries. We followed to the partition door, and knocked; after considerable hesitation and assurances from us that no molestation was intended, she partially re-opened it. Whether from fear at the sight of strangers, or the natural consequence of a secluded life, she appeared in the utmost trepidation, and indistinctly articulated answers to the questions we put to her. We saw no person, of whom to inquire her history, or if she were entirely an isolated being; but left this melancholy and secluded habitation, with sensations not to be described. The recollection, that it had formerly been the shelter of a man, deranged, and afterwards precipitated down the cataract; and that it was now, to all appearances at least, inhabited by a solitary female, almost as deranged as himself, and likely enough to follow him; was sad and mournful. We quitted the spot with impressions of Goat Island never to be forgotten.

BOOK II.

CANADA.

CHAPTER I.

ARRIVAL IN CANADA—IRISH DESERTER FROM THE AMERICAN FORT—RECEPTION IN CANADA—CALLED ON THE GOVERNOR OF YORK—ON THE ARCHDEACON—JOURNEY TO NEWMARKET—WANT OF CLERGY—AN OFFICER—A DEPUTATION—INSURRECTION—MODE OF JUDGING AMONG UNINFORMED MEN—DEMAGOGUES AND REPUBLICANS—JOURNEY TO MONTREAL AND QUEBEC—RETURN TO NEW YORK.

BIDDING adieu to my late companion, I took coach for Youngstown, an American village opposite to the British fort at Niagara. I had scarcely crossed the river before my attention was arrested by a violent outcry, which proceeded from a boat in the middle of the stream. I observed that this boat was pursued by another one, well manned, which proceeded from the American shore, and was gaining rapidly upon it. The outcry was made by an Irish deserter from the American fort, who had scarcely reached the Canadian boundary before his pursuers were close upon him. His vociferations increased, and so affected the Canadians, flocking together from all quarters, that a number of them rushed into the water, and saved the fugitive from further molestation. This poor man declared he had been mis-used, and the Canadians thereupon told the Yankees that unless they instantly desisted and retired within their own jurisdiction, they should be thrown into the water. This little incident, which exibits an occurrence frequent enough there, may shew the animosity still existing.

I called on the missionary of Niagara, who welcomed me in the true British spirit of christian brotherhood, with hearty congratulations on my arrival in Canada. He is a sincerely pious man, greatly esteemed and respected. This gentleman stated the need, felt and lamented, of more ministers than have yet been appointed; and expressed his hope, that some ecclesiastical employment would be offered me.

On my arrival in York the following day, I waited on the governor and stated my object; at the same time frankly acknowledging that my original emigration had been to the States, but that my sentiments were altered. This must account, added I, for my omission, in adducing no letters to gentlemen in Canada, but perhaps my other papers and numerous testimonials may make atonement. His Excellency perused some of these, and returned them with expressions of perfect satisfaction. At his entrance into the audience room, and during the perusal of my papers, I was struck with his gentlemanly appearance and deportment. But a short conversation increased greatly my respect. His Excellency detailed the great deficiency experienced in that province of available means for the maintenance of clergy, and the consequent want of efficient ministers in almost every part. The population was rapidly increasing, the thirst for religious instruction increasing also, and the means for obtaining it in some degree diminishing. He expressed his apprehension to be, that they had no situation to offer worthy of my acceptance, although my labours might be of great utility. His Excellency pointed out the ministerial character which he deemed suitable for Canada, the plan which might be followed with success in building up their infant church, his earnest desire to witness the increase of vital religion, and the appointment of worthy clergymen who would strive to promote it. I had heard from many sources of his Excellency's exemplary moral character, before admission into his presence, but all such notifications were inadequate to convey impressions which a personal interview afforded. After my departure, a card of invitation to dine at the government-house was dispatched to my lodgings, but it arrived too late.

The Bishop of Quebec, whom I had expected to meet with at York, was still in the lower province. The archdeacon resided in York, and I waited on him. He received me most courteously and hospitably, and after a protracted interview furnished me with letters to three gentlemen on

Yonge Street and at Newmarket. He strongly recommended me to examine the country, previous to deciding either on a continuance or return. "After you have seen," said he, "those situations whither my introductions will lead you, I will furnish you with other letters to persons in different directions, by the delivery of which you will become better acquainted with the province. And should you find any inclination to become a Canadian, I will finally furnish you with letters to our bishop. Some clergymen have come out with high recommendations, which they have forwarded to his lordship by post; but their personal appearance and qualifications have not been found corresponding, and they have been afterwards dismissed. Your testimonials are highly satisfactory and creditable, and they will lose nothing of their influence by your presenting them in person. This will occasion you some trouble and expense, for his lordship is in Quebec, but you will see a greater portion of our extensive provinces. I advise you to undertake the journey."

As regular daily coaches had not commenced running so early in the season, I proceeded up the country on foot. The distance from York to Newmarket is thirty miles, but one of the gentlemen resided thirteen miles on the road, on whom I purposed to call, and to take up my residence for the night in the neighbourhood. A lady and two gentlemen overtook me, to whom my arrival had been mentioned, and granted me the privilege of riding in their carriage to the very door.

The gentleman I called on is a person of opulence, and a justice of the peace. My surprise, on entering his house, was great, to find in the wilds of Canada the comforts and even luxuries of civilized life. I was not prepared for expecting the elegance and refinement which appeared around me. A large family, handsomely attired, in apartments well carpeted and furnished, a good library, a blazing fire, and numerous servants. I delivered the introductory letter, and was soon at home and at ease. Here I remained all night, and found more of European information and of true hospitality, than I had done in any part of America. The whole family joined in conversation with an openness and cheerfulness peculiar, I believe, to the English; and I could not help remarking, that it appeared to me as if I were once more in England. The mistress of the house is a very superior lady, in piety as well as intelligence; and this appeared as well in her own conversation, as in the arrangements of her house, and the conduct and appearance of her children. At the regular hour observed by them, the domestics assembled, and family prayers were offered up. I was their chaplain. Accommodations for the night were offered me which I readily accepted, and found every thing most comfortable.

In the morning, after breakfast, they took the key of the church door, and accompanied me thither. The church is delightfully situated on a rising ground above a winding valley, and is built entirely of wood. A house was shewn to me which had lately been purchased for a resident minister, as soon as the bishop should send one; for none had yet been appointed, although the church had been finished three years. Possession of the house had not been obtained, for the title was disputed, and the present occupant could not easily be dislodged. " You will find a residence then," I observed, " for any clergyman whom the bishop may approve." "Certainly," they replied; "but nothing more at present." I then proceeded on my journey, in love with the place and pleased with the family, and wishing for nothing more earnestly than this charming little church. It was the mission I afterwards filled, and which I left with regret.

Newmarket lay seventeen miles further, which I reached also on foot. At a house on the road-side I called at, to make inquiries and to quench my thirst, there was an elderly man seated, who eyed me for some time with a keen and steady look. At last he began questioning me; "You are lately from the old country, I suppose." "Yes," I replied, "although I have not come direct, but spent five months in the States." "Have you come to settle here?" "I left England with intentions of residing in the States; but have grown weary of America, and am now passing through this country to view it for myself, and to form my plans according as it may please me." "You talk mighty fine," he said, "you are a mighty elegant gentleman, and have a noble look; have you seen the governor since you came?" "You pay me more compliments," I replied," than I ever had before; I have, however, seen his Excellency." "Now I thought as much," he instantly rejoined, "I thought by your appearance you were one of those who come into the country and get grants of land. You have obtained five hundred acres, I suppose." I looked at him with astonishment. At last I told him, that I was a perfect stranger, and had never heard of such a thing." "Besides," added I, "I left England a downright radical, and am certainly without the smallest claim to partiality, and without any expectation of such a favour." "You tell us so," said he, "but we know things better. We gave them a sample last winter of what they may expect. We want nothing with governors and bishops, and archdeacons." He left the place soon after; and I was given to understand, that he was a republican, an adherent of Mr. Mackenzie. I had often, whilst in the States, observed the narrow and intolerant spirit of democracy. It occupies the same place in politics, as popery in religion.

On my arrival at Newmarket, I called immediately on a medical gentleman, with whom I lodged all night. My object was to inquire about the state of religious worship, and the probable erection of a church, and provision for a clergyman. The people, he observed, are very desirous of building a church, but there are no funds; and but a small part of the population are of the Established Church; almost all here are either Quakers or Methodists. Many who came from Great Britain Episcopalians, have since become Methodists. The want of clergy in this country is a great evil. I inquired what encouragement would be given to induce a clergyman to settle there. " It would not be possible," he replied, " for any great inducement to be offered: if we should furnish a house for him to live in, that would be the utmost in our power. He must serve other churches at the same time. You have not yet been long in the country, nor come to any determination, and my advice to you is, that you return to England, unless a certain stipend is allowed you.

In the morning, I waited on a gentleman, a member of parliament in Canada, with a letter:

he offered me a horse to ride on, tha I might have a better view of the country round. After a short ride, I returned, and had a hasty conversation with him respecting my object. I soon found his statements to correspond with the former, and forbore further questions,

In my rambles I met with an officer, who had entered Canada the previous Autumn with his family, and from its being late in the season before his arrival, had been under the necessity of wintering in a shanty. He had, like many other officers, accepted of a grant of land from government for his services, and was about to proceed to Lake Simcoe, in the neighbourhood of which his estates were situated. He had obtained his grant nearly two years before, and was one of the last officers to whom this favour was extended ; government not now allowing of similar largesses to any person. Every man is obliged to go into the open market, and purchase such lots as he wishes at a public auction: no favoritism is allowed; the gentleman and the labourer are, in this respect, alike regarded. Indeed, from all I could learn, so great is the desire in the governor of Upper Canada, to remove every impediment out of the way of the laborious and industrious poor man, that he gives an easier admission to such of entering upon farms, than to the more wealthy. One cannot but rejoice at the favour thus conferred upon the indigent; yet I am of opinion, that more liberal offers to persons of greater capital would be sound policy. From the statements of this officer, I perceived the prudence of emigrating in the Spring; as a longer time is thereby afforded, before the approach of winter, for providing every necessary article of food, clothing, and convenience. He and his family had endured many privations from the length and severity of the frost and snow; and had found that winter, like the present government of Canada, is no respecter of persons.

On returning to York, I found a large party of gentlemen exulting at the general expression of public feelings of loyalty and attachment to the throne of Great Britain, and at the discomfiture of those who had endangered public order. These gentlemen formed a deputation from the districts of Coburg, Newcastle, Brockville, &c., and had waited on the governor, to congratulate his Excellency on the restoration of tranquillity, to assure him of their steady adherence, and that of all respectable men in their neighbourhood, to his Excellency's government, and to present an anti-grievance petition, in opposition to Mr. M'Kenzie and his party. I had heard many in New York frequently asserting, that England would do well to leave Canada to itself, before she be expelled by revolt or revolution. "What business has she with Canada? What business has she with the West Indies? We can take them from her when we please;" were sentences frequently uttered by Americans. So warm an interest appeared to be taken by them in the disturbances of England and Canada, that no doubt rests on my mind of systematic arrangements being carried on by them, with democrats in both countries, and perhaps to a still greater extent in Ireland.

During the preceding winter, when Parliament was assembled in York, so great were the crowds of revolutionary rebels and American democrats, and so strenuous their efforts to intimidate the governor, and compel him to surrender up the province to misrule, that apprehensions were entertained in that capital of an overthrow of government. These misguided men, instigated by factious demagogues, or by those supposed to be in American pay, entered York armed for the most part with bludgeons or shilalos, and marched in tumultuous procession, with menaces and threats towards the government house, where the governor resides. His excellency had timely notice of this outrageous insurrection, and, having ordered the riot-act to be read, caused some loaded cannon to be so planted as to command the principal streets which lead to his residence; and the soldiers to be drawn out, and artillery-men with lighted matches to be stationed ready. The factious and tumultuous mob, amounting in numbers to many thousands, pretended, when they saw the reception prepared for them, that their sole object was to present a petition for redress of grievances. Conscious of their guilty and abominable purposes, and shrinking in cowardice and dismay upon detection, they quietly presented their petition, and withdrew. They were overjoyed at escaping merited punishment, and dispersed with all practicable haste; thus permitting his excellency, and, through him the inhabitants of York, to reap the fruits of this firm and decisive measure in recovered tranquillity and order. Such were the facts as related to me.

These disturbances, no doubt, originated in the revolutionary spirit lately displayed in England. That the dependencies of a mighty empire should participate in the convulsions of their parent state, and should travail with corresponding throes, is not difficult to account for, where kindred causes are in active operation. In this case, the body and its members are sympathetic. But where, as in the British provinces of America, there is a cheap and easy government, no tithes, no taxes, no oppression of any kind to complain of, it is no easy matter to trace to their origin, the complaints of grievances among a certain class. It must be referred only to that natural disposition in uninformed men, of yielding their understandings and judgments to the *dictum* of those whom they consider to possess more extensive information.

When once conversing on subjects concerning England, and perceiving that Americans were violent in condemning what they did not understand, I took occasion to remark, that the people of the States appear unaccountably ignorant of the laws and customs of Great Britain, at the same time that they condemn them; and was answered, " If you will consult our lawyers, you will find them better acquainted with your laws and customs than any English judge." When speaking on Scripture subjects with a man of very limited knowledge, who pertinaciously maintained absurd doctrines by absurd arguments, and found himself hard pressed on some points which he could not explain or avoid, he, at last, resolved the difficulty by saying, " If you will consult Dr. Clarke's Commentary, you will find them."

Having once heard an Englishman in Canada assert, that by the laws of England every clergyman is obliged to maintain all the poor of his parish and to keep his church in repair, I demanded his proofs, and was answered that he had forgotten them, but had read them in Cobbett's Register. In like manner, a democrat in Canada I was informed, complaining bitterly of oppressions and grievances, was requested to state what those particulars were by which he felt himself so much aggrieved; to which he answered, " I do not know them myself, but if you will consult Mr. M'Kenzie, you will find him able to inform you." With ignorant people, bold assertions fearlessly defended, have more influence than sober reason. Mr. M'Kenzie has enlisted them in his cause, and and has partially succeeded. He is eager to establish a democracy in the Canadas, and to join them to the States. The Americans, whilst evidently gratified with the disturbances of Canada, and even fomenting them, often told me when in in New York, that they would not accept of the British provinces, if offered to them freely. This was only the old story of the fox and the grapes. I heard republicans in Canada repeat this American boast of prowess and moderation; and smiled in derision on observing, that they had mistaken the fox concealed under eagle's pinions, for the noble and majestic lion, and hearts of pine wood for hearts of oak.

The object aimed at by Mr. M'Kenzie, and for which he endeavoured to excite the rabble, was a seat for himself in the house of legislation. He had been twice or thrice elected a member, but on account of his vile and levelling principles, had as often been expelled. Even the other democratic members of the house considered his proceedings as improper, and either connived or assisted in expelling him. His constituents and political friends were eager to have his election confirmed, and did all in their power to promote it. He relied on their exertions, not only in his nomination, but in his being admitted as a member of the house, if not by right or courtesy, at least by force. They imagined that if he and they should gain their heart's desire, they would speedily behold Upper Canada one of the States of the American Union. No efforts were to be spared. They told him, that a majority of the people saw through his eyes and throbbed with his pulse, and were well prepared to prosecute his views and invigorate his pulsations. He believed all this, and encouraged them to make the trial. It has often happened in other instances, that calculations were made at random; and it proved so in this. They found their numerical strength not more than one-third of the entire population. Their objects were now fully developed; and the loyalists, who had hitherto remained inactive, stepped forward openly. The effect was instantaneous and decisive; and the republican party, disconcerted and dispirited, resigned further contest. Anti-petitions from faithful and loyal subjects, and warm congratulations, were presented to the governor from all quarters; and thus the machinations, which were intended for the overthrow, proved a firmer confirmation of British power and influence.

It was to give assurance to the governor, of the general adherence of people in their neighbourhood to his Excellency's person and administration, that these gentlemen had assembled in York. I had the pleasure of spending part of the evening in their company, and of descending the lake in the same steam-boat, and delivering a sermon before them, I admired the enthusiastic expression of their loyalty and patriotism.

I called on the archdeacon to decline more introductions, for the mere purpose of viewing the country, since I was extremely pleased with what I had already seen; and assured him I could reconcile myself, without violation to my feelings, to a residence in the province and being called a Canadian. " You have not yet," said he, " seen the most beautiful parts about York. Burlington Bay, at the head of the lake, is incomparably finer. But as you seem satisfied with the portion you have seen, I shall furnish you with a letter to our venerable bishop. I can say nothing more at present; but merely request, that you will send me intimation of the result of your visit, on returning to Montreal. This gentleman and his son accompanied me to the steam-boat.

Our voyage down the lake was pleasant. We were never out of sight of land, some parts of which were agreeably variegated by wood and water, by hill and dale. Several villages or mansions on the margin of the water were delightfully located. On passing through the *Lake of a Thousand Islands*, almost forty miles in length, the prospect varied every moment. The number of islands is nearly twelve hundred, of all forms and sizes, almost, but not entirely uninhabited. The innumerable shapes and views, presented to the eye in rapid succession, had a magic and fairy-like effect. Had it been a few weeks later in the season, and the trees been clothed in vernal beauty, a romantic mind might have fancied itself among the Islands of the Blessed. But the atmosphere was too cold to be comfortable, and ice and snow still lingered on the ground.

At Prescot, a town at the eastern end of Lake Ontario, I found I might either go by land, or down the rapids of the St. Lawrence, to Cornwall, a town fifty miles below Prescott. To descend the rapids was recommended in preference, as being speedier and easier than travelling by coach; for roads in Canada, like those in the States, are not always smooth. The rapids also afford a species of navigation, combining rapidity and safety to a degree not known on any other river in the world. The rapid called *Longue Sault*, which is nine miles long, is often passed in from seventeen to twenty minutes time, being at the rate of nearly thirty miles an hour. No accidents, except from gross inattention, ever take place. In two hundred and eighty miles from the commencement of the rapids, the channel of the St. Lawrence has a descent of two hundred and thirty one feet.

Later in the season, it would have been no difficult matter to meet with passage boats, in which to navigate the rapids; but our arrival at this time of the year was rather unpropitious. The river had but recently been freed from hibernal obstructions. No boats had ascended from Montreal; and few of those belonging to Prescott were remaining. There was one, however, about to descend immediately, considerably laden, and with three passengers, previous to our application. One of our party, who was better acquainted than myself with the proper mode of acting, and knew that a small boat could not take us all without incurring danger, went privately and made a bargain with the owner. The rest of us made a later application, and he demanded three dollars each, the regular fare being one. This we hesitated to give, and he refused a more moderate offer. I perceived that this river-tar was already satisfied with his freight, and therefore returned to the inn; but the other unadmitted passengers remained by the boatman, cheapening his fare. Suddenly pushing off his boat, he laughed in their faces, and wished them a pleasant journey. I had not, therefore, the pleasure of floating down.

We, who had been left behind, immediately took

coach, and arrived in Cornwall considerably after dark, where we found our late companions, whose arrival had been four hours earlier. They gave us a tantalizing account of the pleasures of their voyage, which but ill accorded with our uneasy drive. The road in many places was bad; in some places there was no road but what lay over pasture ground sadly cut up; and our fare for such conveyance was even more than his extravagant demand. We were therefore both wearied and laughed at.

In our journey from York to Montreal, we had three several alternations of steam-boats and coaches. The steam-boat we now entered was moored by a ledge of ice, of a thickness so great as to conceal entirely the vessel, till we approached close upon it. We embarked by steps excavated in the ice, for the convenience of passengers. We now found that we were pursuing the retreat of winter, and treading hard up his rear. In our descent, we were evidently coming into a colder climate. The Upper Province, before we left York, had begun to exhibit symptoms of vegetation; but here the ground was sprinkled with snow. In some of the streets of Montreal and Quebec was ice of two or three feet in thickness. The snow grew more dense and the landscape whiter, as we approached Quebec; between which city and the Falls of Montmorenci, this fleecy covering was two feet deep.

The climate, in many parts of the lower province requires a variation from the modes of agriculture in milder regions. Wheat does not succeed well, if sown in autumn. The usual practice is, to prepare the land in the previous autumn, and to sow it in the spring. If wheat is sown in autumn, the frost destroys it; and if land is not prepared till spring, the fittest season for sowing wheat will have passed away, before the plowing has been finished. The frost and snow lighten, mellow, and fertilize the soil, and render the produce more abundant.

The situation of Montreal must in summer be delightful. The waters of the St. Lawrence, both above and below the town, have a great descent and rapidity, which refreshes and purifies the atmosphere. Montreal is considerably elevated; and a mountain seven hundred feet high rises close behind it, studded in its acclivity with several mansions, and having on its summit a charming retreat,

I was told, belonging to the Catholic Clergy. The Roman Catholic is the prevailing religion of Quebec and Montreal. It has a larger revenue than is possessed by any other denomination, and is really wealthy. "Its revenue is derived from grants of land made to it under the ancient régime, and from contributions ordained by the Church. Besides these, another principal source is from the fines for alienation, which amount to about 8 per Cent. paid by the purchaser of real estate, every time the same is sold, and which extends to sales of all real estates in the séignory or Island of Montreal." Their church here is considered the largest, and most elegant and lofty edifice for worship, on the Continent of America. There is a monument near the market place in honour of Nelson. Four of his glorious achievements are recorded on its sides. It appears to be constructed of very perishing materials, for the parts on which his victories were inscribed are crumbling to decay. The splendid career of that hero has little need of such frail memorials.

A Montreal gentleman of great legal eminence, and a member of the legislation, with whom I had a long conversation, was on his way from this place to Quebec. He was hostile to the project of a chartered company in the lower province similar to that of the Canada Company in the upper. One of his reasons was the influence it would confer upon the English above the French Canadians. The enterprize, skill, and capital of English emigrants give them an enviable pre-eminence. This gentleman is a Canadian, and of French descent; yet I could not enter into his views. Experience has since convinced me of the great advantages derived to the upper provinces from the Canada-Company. But I shall advert to this hereafter. He also approved of a tax of one dollar a head to be levied on emigrants, payable by the captain in whose vessel they arrive. This tax, he said, is necessary to indemnify Montreal for expenses incurred in maintaining pauper emigrants, and in administering medicines to the sick. The upper province claimed a drawback for such of the emigrants as found their way into it without expense to the Lower, which was refused. He strongly objected to the introduction of a bill into the legislature for making Montreal the port of entry of the Upper Province. This was greatly desired by many persons in both provinces, as likely to prove extensively beneficial; but it was opposed by many. These two parts of the British provinces have distinct and separate interests, and a jealousy exists between them. Montreal is considered as the wealthiest place, and as possessing the best society of any city of its extent on the continent of America.

I arrived at Quebec on the fourth of May, the day appointed in the Lower Province for a general fast, on account of apprehension of cholera. This dreadful visitation had not then commenced its ravages. The day previous to my arrival, the first vessels of the season from Europe had reached the harbour, and were ordered to the quarantine ground. The Archdeacon of Quebec informed me he would have invited me to dine with him, had not one of his servants been dangerously ill, but of the nature of the illness he did not inform me. Yet I do not imagine it was cholera, for nothing had yet been imported from England. The fast was partially observed in the steam-boat. The same day was not appointed for

M

its observance in the Upper Province. On reaching Quebec, I entered the cathedral church, and heard an affecting discourse delivered by the Archdeacon appropriate to the solemnity. He is popular, and deservedly esteemed for his humane disposition, and the efficient discharge of his duties. He officiates in both the French and English languages. The church was numerously attended, and the discourse impressive.

The Bishop conferred on me the honour of inviting me to dine at his house every day I remained in Quebec, and I availed myself of it in every instance except one. His lordship examined my papers, and approved of them. I was also questioned as to my views of some leading doctrines of our church, which I answered to his lordship's approbation. I was requested to read part of a Greek play, and a few verses of the Hebrew Bible, and thus my examination ended.

His lordship made mention of a gentleman from Oxford University, who had held a mission among the Indians, but who, after some residence in Canada, had resigned it and returned to England. His resignation arose principally from not finding his hearers so tractable and docile as he wished them, and the Bishop expressed the reluctance felt by him in losing so efficient a minister. I believe the mission he held was included in one of greater extent, which his lordship offered to my acceptance. Its length extended from Newmarket to Pentangueshine, a distance of about sixty miles. I stated to his lordship that I had not been on horseback for almost ten years previous to entering Canada, and that my powers of walking were not adequate to such journeys. " I myself," replied his lordship, " have performed much greater journeys than the one proposed to you, on foot and unattended. I was a missionary for thirty-five years, at a period when the country was in a less civilized state, and when greater self-denial than is required of you was unavoidably imposed on the preachers of the gospel. There is no part of my large diocese which I have not visited, and travelled on foot, with a Bible, my sole companion and only solace, under my arm. What therefore is proffered to your acceptance, is not to be compared, in labours and privations, to what has been experienced before you. But since you shrink from the undertaking, I have another offer to make you. The gentleman on Yongestreet, on whom you called, offered you a house. To this provision I will add from my private income one hundred pounds annually; for I do not know that the sum will be refunded me; but the people of that village have often applied to me for a resident minister, and I have never had so favourable an opportunity of gratifying them."

This was the mission which I had earnestly longed for, and I accepted it immediately. But, at the same time, I mentioned that my final acceptance of it must still depend on Mrs. F.'s pleasure, whom I had induced to cross the ocean much against her wish, and who seemed resolute on returning as speedily as possible. " You must write to me from New York," said his lordship, " after your resolves have been concluded ; and if you accept the mission, your stipend will commence from the date of your letter." In this I acquiesced. On the Sunday which I passed in Quebec, I had the extreme pleasure of preaching twice before his lordship, the archdeacon, his lordship's chaplain, &c. &c. in the cathedral church.

At my departure from Quebec, his lordship presented me with a sermon of his own publication, and a report of the society for the propagation of the gospel in foreign parts; and requested I would deliver, in his lordship's name, another copy of the society's report to the Episcopal Bishop of New York. Mutual respect for each other exists in a high degree among the clergy of the States and those in Canada, and reciprocated favours are frequently exchanged. This is very pleasing to contemplate. The Bishop of Quebec has repeatedly been in New York; and is personally known to, and much esteemed by, not only the Bishop, but the clergy generally, of that city. Dr. Milnor, who has occasionally dined with his lordship, mentioned this circumstance.

The banks of the St. Lawrence throughout all its course are in general well peopled and cultivated. The districts bordering on the river are represented as being remarkably fertile. From Montreal to Quebec the margin of the water on both sides is diversified by frequent dwellings, and sometimes clusters of houses, which are represented as forming continuous and almost unbroken streets. Many churches are visible from the water at about six or nine miles distance from each other.

My return from Quebec, after accomplishing my object, and seeing the fortifications and classic spots in and around it, was by Montreal, la Prairie, St. John's, Lake Champlain, Whitehall, Troy, Albany, and the Hudson river. From Montreal I dispatched a letter to the Archdeacon of York, to state the probability of my residence in Canada, and the consequent necessity of a house being provided as soon as possible by the parish.

Part of Lake Champlain belongs to the English, and part to America. I had read, that the borders of it belonging to the States are under better cultivation than the other, and was anxious to examine the correctness of the statement. I could not, however, perceive any truth in the assertion; but I remembered the boast of American superiority in other things to England, and the vauntings of their vanity still tingled in my ears. Along the shores of the Lake, at different places were vestiges of fortifications, which had sustained conspicuous parts in our wars with America. It was on this narrow piece of water, that one of those naval engagements of which that country boasts was fought. The lake is one hundred and forty miles long, and but fourteen (some writers say six) miles broad in its widest part. At the head of the lake is the town of Whitehall, from which I took coach for Albany. Part of this journey lay among mountains of considerable height and beauty. From Albany to New York was passed in a steam boat.

When descending the St. Lawrence I had observed, that the climate grew sensibly colder, and more snow was still on the ground. In returning to New York, my course was almost due south; and every day seemed more grateful, and every degree of decreasing latitude more richly clothed in verdure and vegetation. Along the banks of the Hudson were numerous orchards, with fruit trees covered with blossoms. In short, spring had arrived, and nature was beginning to awake, and to put forth her strength.

This was by far the longest and most delightful excursion I ever made. It was undertaken as well for inquiring after professional employment, as for information and amusement: and was in all respects perfectly successful. Without an introductory letter from England, I enjoyed every advantage which thousands could procure. Without one single previous acquaintance, I was welcomed with hospitality. My previous defection from patriotism was overlooked, and I shared the patronage of those who preside over one of the finest regions of the globe. I had travelled, in less than one month, by means of steam-boats and steam-carriages, of coaches and waggons, of ferry boats and jaunting carts, on horseback, and on foot, a distance of almost eighteen hundred miles. I had seen some of the most beautiful tracts of country, some of the finest rivers, the most astonishing rapids and cataracts, the finest lakes and mountains,—some of the most magnificent works of art, the canals, aqueducts, rail-roads, mills, steam-boats, fortifications, and religious edifices,—which the new World has to present to the eyes of strangers. All this I had accomplished, without one drawback; without more fatigue and weariness than what is necessary to enhance the pleasure of repose; without any loss by pilfering, of which travellers often complain: with hourly increasing intelligence; with recovery of stronger vision, which long and intense study had weakened; with more confirmed health, and a higher flow of spirits; with longer cessation of domestic discord and family cares; than my life had hitherto allowed me. I had passed by or over some places rendered classic and immortal, by deeds of warlike valour, and of private sacrifice for public good ; by victories and defeats; by bloody struggles, both by land and water.

After all, I had the crowning felicity of returning safe to my family, and of finding even that part of it, which was sick at my departure, in renewed health and strength. Flushed with my good fortune, free from sickness and debility, and welcomed by the endearments of my family, I disclosed the issue of my journey. My tale was told in a propitious moment, and imbibed with an approving ear. One only stipulation was proposed and agreed to, that I would resign if required. I wrote the next morning to the bishop, and announced my acceptance of the mission. We packed up the articles we deemed essential, and were on our journey to Canada in the course of a week.

CHAPTER II.

SECOND JOURNEY TO CANADA—SALT WORKS AT SYRACUSE VOYAGE OVER LAKE ONTARIO—A BROW-BEATEN IRISHMAN—FARE ON THE LAKE—ARRIVAL IN YORK—LODGINGS — FELLOW LODGERS — NEW CHURCH—MARKET-HOUSE—PARLIAMENT HOUSES—KINDNESS OF THE ARCHDEACON—OUR PARSONAGE—KINDNESS OF PARISHIONERS—MODE OF LIVING—LANDLADY—YANKEE IMPOSTURES.

After making arrangements for our journey, we embarked on board a steam-boat, for Albany. I again waited on the gentleman from whom I had in my former journey to Canada, received so many kind attentions. He advised me to prosecute my travels this time in a canal boat, since my family and baggage would be found too inconvenient for a coach. I adopted his advice, and went in one boat from Albany to Syracuse. and in another from Syracuse to Oswego; and from this last place to

York, by way of Niagara, in a trading vessel. Many parts of the country through which we passed, appeared extremely fertile. The short interval of one month had produced an astonishing alteration in the aspect of the country, which was now in many places covered with verdure. The flats through which the canal passes, are the richest grounds, but are not cleared from want of drainage. The canal has rendered them more swampy in some places than they were naturally; and this change is visible in the state of the forests, which are rapidly decaying. A vast portion of New York State is yet in its original condition, uninvaded by the axe; and is of itself sufficient to receive and sustain the excess of population in all the kingdoms of Europe, being nearly as large as England. At Syracuse, I entered the evaporating houses of some salt-works; there were in some of them twelve or fourteen pans or kettles, arranged in parallel rows, and heated by fires at one end; the flues of which pass under all the kettles of the same row in succession, and discharge the smoke at the end of the building. The pans nearest the fires are evaporated in from four to six hours, and those at the greatest distance in about twenty or twenty-four. When the water, which is exceedingly saline, is at first admitted into the kettles, an iron vessel, in the shape of a frying-pan, is let down to the bottom, having a perpendicular handle extending above the surface of the water. This vessel is intended to collect particles of lime, or other impure substances contained in the water, and which are always precipitated to the bottom, previous to the formation of salt. The salt does not begin to form until the water has acquired a certain temperature. The proprietor of one of these houses explained the various particulars of his business, and lifted up one of the iron vessels I have mentioned, to show me the quantity of feculent matter contained in the water: it appeared very great. He told me that the daily measure of salt made in his pans, was nearly one hundred bushels. Eight bushels at Syracuse, are worth a dollar; and the duty upon it, which increases the cost to a quarter of a dollar per bushel, belongs not to the Federal Union, but to the State of New York exclusively, and is applied to liquidate the expenses of their public works, of which the Erie canal is one. New York State is the most valuable in the Union; and must, from its natural and artificial advantages, always continue so.

Much chrystalized salt is also procured from solar evaporation: a barrel of this last is considered more valuable than one of salt obtained by boiling, and will bear the expenses of farther transportation. Its superiority consists in its greater strength, a smaller quantity of it being equivalent in virtue to a larger of the other.

On our arrival at Oswego, thirty-eight miles from Syracuse, I proceeded to the harbour in quest of a trading vessel bound for York in Canada, and had the good fortune to find one which would sail in an hour. I agreed with the captain for nine dollars for myself, family, and baggage; and he, on his part, assured me, that he would land us safe in twenty-four hours. Our provisions were included in the fare. Instead of reaching York in one day, we were five days on the lake. He had to call at Youngstown on the American side, at the mouth of the Niagara river, in order to unship part of his freight, and receive payment. There were two passengers, besides ourselves, equally disappointed and impatient; I therefore intimated to the captain, who was a good-natured man, that unless he proceeded immediately to York, I would, when he landed us, oblige him to compensate his passengers for loss of time. He declared to me, that the store-keepers had not been able to pay him, and his stay for the previous two days, had arisen from this circumstance: he soon afterwards hoisted his sails, without being paid, I believe, and we reached York in the evening.

While detained at Youngstown, I witnessed a scene between an American and an Irishman, painful yet ludicrous. The latter had been a servant in the employment of the former, and feeling himself ill-treated and deprived of his wages, left his employer in disgust, with an intimation that he would sue him for the debt. The American followed his servant, "independent, free, and equal," and having overtaken him at this place, was cuffing and shaking him most unmercifully: "You shall go back with me," he said, "and submit to your work." The poor Irishman swore he would not, and the American swore he *should*. I could see, from the first, that all the American wanted, was to dismiss him without payment. A great number of Americans were standing near, enjoying the sight, rapturously applauding their countryman, and encouraging him to pay Paddy his wages to his heart's content. This the scoundrel continued to do, till the brow-beaten Irishman agreed to trouble him no further, and to accept blows for wages. The Irish are frequently wronged and injured in the land of their exile! but they have been long oppressed in their own land, by those very persons on whom they have claims as friends and brothers. I trust in heaven that their long-endured wrongs will ultimately be redressed.

The cabin of the vessel served for the sitting, eating, and sleeping room, of passengers, captain and crew. I expostulated strongly on this usage, but the captain informed me he had no alternative. The place commonly assigned to sailors had not been fitted up. We were forced to tolerate this inconvenience: the sailors slept on the floor, and resigned the berths to the passengers; but not from choice. I frequently perceived, in travelling, the unwillingness with which people in the States give precedence to the English. The two first nights I slept soundly; but in consequence of becoming pained from sleeping on a thin mattrass, spread on boards, I passed the three last nights without much comfort. On the first night, Mrs. F., whose slumbers are generally light, heard the sailors say to each other, that they could see no reason why these Englishers should be better accommodated than they; "We are as good flesh and blood," they muttered aloud, " as these foreigners." Thus, notwithstanding we had promised the captain his full demand, the sailors regarded this privilege, and that of eating before them, with a grudge and jealousy.

The food generally placed before us for dinner, was salt pork, potatoes, bread, water, and salt; tea, bread and butter, and sometimes salt pork, for breakfast and tea; no supper. Some displeasure at this fare was expressed, when the cook informed us that their vessel had a better character than any on the lake for liberal treatment: yet our murmurs obtained for us a quarter of good lamb at Youngstown. At this place the captain advised us to go on shore, and board at some inn till the vessel might sail. "It is quite uncertain," he observed, "when

I shall be at liberty to sail, for I am not yet paid; and it is customary for passengers, under such circumstances, to leave the vessel." This we all refused, and declared he had deceived us; and we would not, therefore, quit the vessel till his arrival at York. On debarking, he told me that he perceived we would suit the country, for we knew how to take care both of ourselves and our money.

Immediately on landing, I went in quest of lodgings; but emigrants had begun to pour in by hundreds daily, and all places where boarders were admitted were already occupied. The Archdeacon's son, on learning my difficulty, accompanied me to two or three houses, at the last of which we obtained lodgings for eight dollars a week—about one third what they had cost us in New York—and remained a fortnight. The Rev. Mr. Bolton, one of the Professors of the College, on hearing of our arrival, called on us with his lady. During the course of their visit, they described the country as abundantly fertile; but added " It is yet more adapted to the prosperity of the labourer, mechanic, and farmer, than of other classes. It may properly be termed, The poor man's country. The prudent, industrious man, finds in it an inexhaustible treasure." My stay was sufficiently protracted to shew me the correctness of the statement.

The house in which we boarded was occupied by an officer and his family, who had resided for some time on a grant of land to which his service had entitled him. They had found a dwelling-place among forests to be unsuitable to their former habits, and were obliged, after making a great sacrifice, to take up their abode in a town. They had, at their first arrival, expected to live with the same ease and embellishments around them as in densely peopled countries; and had, consequently, provided such articles of various kinds as ill accorded with the place. Their clothes were too light, and of too fine a texture, to withstand the cold of a Canadian winter, and were unsuitable to the labours of a rural life. The lady was obliged, during winter, to dress herself in so many gowns and under garments as quickly lessened her wardrobe. The whole family, however, were in good health, although herself was of a delicate and slender figure, and had never before been accustomed to hardship. This lady, I am grieved to add, fell a victim to cholera a short time after.

At this gentleman's house was a barrister lately arrived from London, in hopes of obtaining professional engagement. He had suffered disappointment, in consequence of a prohibition, unknown to him previously, which precludes an English lawyer from practising in Canada till after a five year's apprenticeship in the country. He had fixed on no plan at the time we left the house, and I am ignorant of his subsequent fortunes. I was informed that a law to the same purport exists in the States, although legal proceedings are conducted much after the English mode in both countries. I attended the trial of an action in New York, and heard our great law authorities frequently referred to and quoted. This ought to be well understood, that others may not be similarly tempted to leave their country, and sustain the bitterness of blighted hopes.

There were also at the same house, as boarders, a medical gentleman and his two sons, who had arrived about the same time with us. He had been an army surgeon, and was appointed superintendant of the hospital at York. I had the pleasure of dining with this gentleman at the Governor's: he complained that parliamentary grants were discontinued, and that those who had spent their lives in the service of government were no longer rewarded, as before. The retiring pension of gentlemen employed under government is now paid in money, and they are obliged, like others, to enter the market and encounter fair and open competition. This is certainly just and equitable; but gentlemen so situated no longer obtain the same extent of acres, for land has risen in value. It will be seen from this that great impartiality is exercised. I can bear witness to the fact, that every industrious man who settles in Canada will find a greater degree of freedom, and a smaller weight of taxation, stricter regard to equitable and impartial measures, and a closer assimilation of all ranks, than in any other country, the United States not excepted. He will, in many respects, be more favourably circumstanced than even those whom, in other places, he might be tempted to envy. He will, if really deserving, obtain full employment, ample remuneration, secure investments for his money, and may live with equality of privileges, and perfect independence; without finding that there is one law for the wealthy or the favoured few, and another for the poor or the industrious. He can obtain equally excellent land, and on as favourable terms, as the officers of Government.

Two other gentlemen, brothers, the elder of whom had been employed four years in New York, were inmates of the same house. They were highly respectable, and were employed in an iron-foundry; the steam-engine for a boat on Lake Simcoe, was manufactured under their superintendance. The elder brother spoke favourably of Americans, whom he represented as more enterprising than the people of Canada, or perhaps of any other country; yet he had adopted Canada in preference, and had purchased property in it; and found that, by his industry and talents, his riches were rapidly increasing.

During the fortnight we were in York, the corner stone of an elegant church was laid by the Governor, with the usual solemnity: the Archdeacon delivered an appropriate sermon. In consequence of oversight in the managers, no separate accommodations were prepared for ladies, and they were under the necessity of struggling through the crowd, or of being excluded. This new church is contiguous to a former one of wood, from the belfry of which the place where the corner stone was laid could be distinctly seen. The Archdeacon's lady and daughters, with some other ladies, ascended to the belfry, but the room was already so crowded with spectators, that admission to the windows was impossible, unless some of the others would resign their place. I interceded for the ladies, but those who were already on the vantage-ground refused to resign it, and the ladies were consequently debarred. This proves how strongly the spirit of independence exists in Canada, as well as in the States. A great difference, however, is perceptible between American and Canadian manners. The old church, I imagine, will be removed, when the new one, which is of stone, shall have been completed. It will form one of the ornaments of that capital.

The number of brick and wood buildings in

progress of erection was quite surprising. All over the town were building lots, on which masons and carpenters were busy. The saw, the axe, the chisel, the hammer, and the trowel, resounded on every side. In addition to the numerous private buildings in which workmen were engaged, there were some public edifices, as the church I have mentioned, a capacious market-house of brick, and the houses of parliament. The market-house is a quadrangular building of great extent, fitted for the accommodation of a much larger place, and having a prospective reference to the rapidly increasing population. It stands upon a block of ground of an oblong square, occupying the area contained between four streets, with a dead wall on its two longer sides. At one end, which faces the principal street of the town, a town-hall is erected, through the centre of which is an archway, and a street passing down the middle of the market within, to a similar archway at the opposite end, which faces the waters of the harbour. On the other two sides are parallel streets, passing from side to side, and cutting the former at right angles. The market-stalls are, consequently, all formed to face the interior of the square, and are not observable from without. The convenience of this building, and the building itself, has no equal of the kind even in New York or in the States.

The houses of parliament are beautifully situated on the west end of the town, near the Governor's residence, and not far from the college; they face the water, near the entrance of the harbour. The principal part of these elegant buildings is of brick, but with ornamental stonework around the doors, windows, &c. The extensive plot of ground encircling them has been levelled and beautified. In front of them a spacious and delightful road passes from the chief landing-place in the harbour, along the summit of the banks of the lake, for several miles, and will be one of the most beautiful promenades and drives imaginable, when the improvements now in progress are completed. No building between it and the water is permitted to be raised. Several extensive and imposing mansions and residences line the ulterior margin of this road, on both sides of the parliament houses, and command an extensive view of the lake. York town has a fine appearance as we approach it from the water, and has become much more healthy since the draining of the marshes.

The Archdeacon, with his lady, called on us, and kindly offered me a horse to ride on, whenever I might desire it. To this gentleman I am indebted for more favours than need be mentioned, all of them conferred with the greatest readiness, and without the expectation, or even the possibility of requital. Perhaps I might have imagined myself a particular favourite, had I not found out that his kindness extends to all of every class, whose condition requires his assistance. His disposition is benevolent and open, and Heaven has blessed him with resources which he employs for the benefit of his fellow-men. Of this kindness I failed not to avail myself, and rode on his horse several times to my new church at Thornhill.

The house promised at Thornhill, where my church was situated, could not be procured for us. The gentleman who formerly received me so kindly, informed me that the title was disputed, and possession not yet given, and that for the present I must content myself with lodgings. Lodgings were accordingly provided instead of the house, consisting of five rooms, three above and two below, and comprising one half of a large mansion. The upper rooms were merely lathed, but not plastered ; and consequently could be seen into from the outside. As another family, the owners of the mansion, and the estate it pertained to, resided in the same house, we made no use of them except for our servant.

Had the inside of our residence corresponded with the outside, it might have been counted among the beauties of Canada. It was delightfully situated on the summit of a hill not far from the church, and above a pleasant bend of the valley. A perennial stream, sufficient at all times to give motion to a grist and saw mill, ran through the grounds a little below. In front, but at the distance of three hundred yards, were the expanded waters of a mill pond, forming a small lake, which gave variety to the scenery, and was exceedingly agreeable from the prospect it afforded. Behind this sheet of water was a thick grove of lofty pines, standing on a steep acclivity. The view from the house was extensive, and commanded a sight of Yonge Street for a considerable distance on both sides. The village of Thornhill, a thriving and increasing place, was on nearly the same level, and one third of a mile distant. We were surrounded on all sides by families of great respectability, from whom we received every attention we could wish. The same conveniences, however, could not be obtained as in a larger and more populous place ; and this formed the grievance of which my family afterwards complained.

Mrs. F. was impatient to enter her parsonage house, as she imagined when we left New York, she could speedily do, and was already wearied with confinement to one room in a boarding house. She hastened me to take her from York into the country, even should the house not prove so convenient in all respects as she could wish. I lost no time in making such arrangements as were in my power. We took possession of our lodgings. Dissatisfaction however, soon evinced itself. She grew more and more averse every hour to continue, and her first impressions could never be effaced.

The gentleman who had actively interfered in procuring for us the lodging, had a few things done for our convenience, and omitted nothing in his power to make us comfortable. All the most respectable of our neighbours, and several of them were highly respectable, and very wealthy, and influential, had visited us on our arrival, and welcomed us to Thornhill. When we alluded to our apartments and furniture, they replied invariably, that they had encountered the same inconveniencies to a greater extent; and that a little time, exertion, and expense, would completely remove our disquietudes. The lady of the house, where I remained all night on my first ramble up Yonge Street, accommodated us most obligingly with a good feather bed, which she permitted us to use during our residence at Thornhill.

The manner in which we lived was not very splendid, but sufficiently accorded with the country and our recent arrival. The house had no oven. One had been built, which was fallen to decay.

The bread we eat was consequently either thin cakes or loaves, baked in a pan. We could sometimes, but not regularly, have bread from York; but as we could not depend on such luxury, and as the obligation we seemed to owe to the person who brought it, appeared greater than the favour, we discontinued our orders for its supply.

It was not always possible to obtain joints of fresh meat when wanted. There are no butchers' stalls in country places, at which a constant supply of meat is provided. We were consequently often debarred from such food for several days together, and had only salted pork, and puddings or pies; with fish, when I could find opportunity to go to York. Our usual drink was tea, into which a little whiskey or brandy had been infused, Sometimes a little wine and water. Mrs. F. occasionally procured ale for herself, at the price of eight-pence per quart. Butter, milk, cheese, &c. are attainable, but not at lower prices than in England. Cheshire cheese was between three and four shillings per lb.

Our landlady was a widow, and had come originally from New York. She was one of the United

States Loyalists, and the second or third person who settled at Thornhill. This was at a time when Yonge Street was no better than a continuous forest, and a foot-path, or at most a horse-path, was their only road. At that period, their wheat had to be carried through forests, or by water, fifty or sixty miles, before it could be converted into flour; and letters might remain for six months in the Post Office at York, before they could be forwarded to the proper persons. Our landlady sometimes alluded to the changes she had witnessed in the removal of forests, the cultivation of lands, and inconveniencies of all kinds. But she deplored these changes; since people from England of some capital, who generally prefer to purchase farms partially cleared rather than seclude themselves within almost impervious forests, were hereby induced to take up their residence along the road, and to buy out the original settlers. She had witnessed the departure or death of most of her co-temporary settlers; and began to feel herself among a strange people of another generation, with whom she had little intercourse and less sympathy.

The former husband of our landlady had left

her with a family of sons and daughters, with a highly improved farm, with flocks of sheep and herds of cattle, and with five hundred pounds in money. American republicans have been frequently found prowling up and down Canada, in search of something which they might be able to convert into their own profit, regardless of the character or welfare of their dupes. Our landlady, a handsome widow with a handsome fortune, was not likely to continue undiscovered. One of them, a physician by profession, learned her history, was introduced, gained her heart, and married her. He obtained possession also of her cattle and her money; but not of her land, for this was a grant from government originally conveyed to herself, and she would never part with it. This American, after living with her for some time, and obtaining all she possessed but her farm, found his way back into the States, where he had another wife. The cattle and money obtained by our landlady had previously disappeared.

This is by no means a solitary instance of such tricks. During the year we were there, an American, I was told, found his way to the affections of a young and beautiful Canadian, and to the purse of her father. He married her, and secured her fortune, and then vanished for ever, from the confines of her country.

Americans boast of their skill in money-making; and as it is the only standard of dignity, and nobility, and worth, in that country, they endeavour to obtain it by every possible means. A person in Canada informed me, that he and another gentleman, once overheard two American fathers, arranging a marriage between a son and a daughter. The bridegroom's father had but little fortune to bestow, and the father of the bride would not give his consent to such a degrading union. The other hereupon assured him, that his son was deserving of the wealthiest lady in America, and then recounted numerous instances of successful and clever villany, of which his boy had been guilty, and which the young lady's father admitted as equivalent to a fortune. I heard so many instances of well-accredited cunning and knavery practised by Americans on Canadians, that a volume might be filled with such incidents. Some of the tales are false, no doubt, or at least exaggerated. Yet too many are sufficiently authenticated, and have been *accompanied by so much notoriety, as to prevent the imputation of falsehood or enlargement.*

CHAPTER III.

CHOLERA—OUR PRESERVATION—ITS PREVALENCE IN THE STATES—IN CANADA—CANADIAN PHILANTHROPY—PREVENTIVES OF CHOLERA—EFFECT OF FOREST RAMBLES—REMEDIES FOR CHOLERA—ITS INFECTIOUS NATURE—CASES OF CHOLERA—DEATH OF A MEDICAL GENTLEMAN—OF A YOUNG LADY.

I HAVE often felt how remarkably I and my family have been preserved during all our travels and residencies in America and Canada, when I consider the multiplied instances of sickness and mortality which encompassed us on every side, while we were still spared. We had entered New York at a season of general sickness, and our family did not altogether escape. Yet the temporary illness we endured was followed by better health than we had enjoyed for years. I had been at all the places where cholera raged in its utmost latitude, and had only just departed when it made its appearance. Our two boarding houses in New York, and the one in York, in Canada, had each a visitation of this dreadful scourge. Our landlady's father-in-law and daughter were attacked, and the former died. We lived three months in its more immediate sphere; and there were numberless instances of its fatal virulence on every side, over seven of whom I performed the last sad offices of a minister. Yet we all escaped. We had, indeed, three weeks illness from ordinary cholera—the cholera of the country; but not more than might be looked for from so complete a change of diet and climate, and from the numerous vexations we felt or fancied.

I had hardly departed from Quebec, after my attendance on the bishop, before this plague broke out with violence. Before we left New York for Canada, the papers there were filled with accounts of its ravages at Quebec. It soon extended its desolating progress to Montreal; from whence it branched off in two directions; to Whitehall,

Albany, Troy, and New York, and to all the towns and villages on the Erie canal on one side; and to the Canadian towns on the margin of the lake, and to some towns in the interior of the country, on the other. It fell upon New York with dreadful fury, and so great was the panic it occasioned, that a dispersion and flight from the city took place, hardly to be parallelled for amount and rapidity. One half of the inhabitants were said to be frightened from home, and to take refuge on Long Island, or on the shores of some of the Eastern States. Great numbers of houses and stores were entirely closed. Almost every person, whom business or pecuniary need did not detain in the city, left his dwelling, after securing his doors and windows. Many stores and houses were shut up, even where the owner remained at home, lest any customer or friend should communicate the plague. There was an entire stagnation to trade. The numbers of the dead were so great, that human bodies were conveyed in cart loads to places of interment, and put promiscuously into graves. I believe none of the Episcopal clergy in the city, but one or two on

CHOLERA IN THE STATES. 277

the island, and several medical gentlemen, were among the number of the dead. The authenticated deaths were between six and seven thousand; and many hundreds were imagined to have taken place which were never reported.

If we suppose that nearly one-half of those resident in New York were panic-struck, and put to flight at its first appearance, and that seven thousand of the remaining half fell before it, we should find that about one in sixteen were ushered by it into eternity. This seems an awful mortality; but not equal in comparative extent to what took place in York in Upper Canada. In that ill-fated capital, between six and seven hundred died, although the population is but six or seven thousand;—about one in ten. Yet we must not omit to mention, that a great majority of those who died were recent emigrants. In some parts of the States the poor emigrants were harshly repulsed, as if the occasion of the malady; and were abandoned to their fate along the roads and canals.

Many conjectures were entertained, as to the modes by which cholera found a communication from one place to another. Some affirmed, that it passed along under the surface of the ground; others, that water was a conductor, from observing that the towns situated near lakes or rivers suffered in a conspicuous degree; others again, that it was borne along on the wings of the wind. I read in a New York paper, that Mrs. Taylor's family where we had boarded, caught it from some hides which were deposited in a warehouse adjoining their house. It was also suggested, that the innumerable herds of swine in New York streets, had an active part in spreading the disorder.

The newspapers there expressed a just condemnation against street-going hogs, and recommended the enforcement of a regulation, which imposes a fine of five dollars upon those who allow their hogs to range at large. I had hoped to find, on my return from Canada, that this public nuisance, by means of papers and the strictures of different authors, had been abated; but was disappointed on finding that it was as great as ever. The lawyers and judges dare not inflict any mulct or censure, where many persons have conspired to transgress. They, like gentlemen of other professions, are the creatures of the mob, and have not the hardihood to offend it, by a rigorous adherence to their duty.

This afflictive plague was severely felt in many parts of both America and Canada, and it would be difficult to point out where its prevalence was most extensive. In *one* American paper, I read accounts of the death of four canal-boat captains. There were few boats, to which it did not pay a visit. I was told, that the greatest severity experienced from it in the States, was amongst the soldiers employed against the Indians It might appear, that Heaven regarded with disapprobation the Punic faith of Americans, and afflicted their martial operations with unwonted chastisement. Officers, men, and cattle, died in promiscuous crowds.

In that boundless country, the cholera had not accomplished its rounds before we embarked for England. It was extending its march through the western forests, accompanied by desolating effects. In every place it entered, there was a rapid depopulation. It invaded the town of Cincinnati, rendered memorable by a lady's graphic pen, and occasioned a panic similar to that of New York. The daily number of deaths in that place alone, when we left America, was reported in the papers to be thirty-six, and the numbers were said to be on the increase.

One curious feature in the American character, extremely foreign to an Englishman, is this, that no social bond exists there, sufficiently close to connect the different members of the body politic, so as to insure assistance from one another in seasons of general distress. "Every man for himself," is, perhaps, more fully and regularly acted on in America, than elsewhere. This was strikingly exemplified in New York, and in other places where cholera raged, by the flight of the wealthy, and of such as could conveniently withdraw. Many of the medical profession imitated the flight of their splendid neighbours, and abandoned the less fortunate part of their fellow-citizens in the hour of danger.

I heard of no clergyman of any denomination, who, in this trying season, withdrew from the scene of his sacred ministrations.

In Canadian towns, no such absence of sympathy was betrayed. Scarcely any persons left the places, where its desolating influence was most destructive. In York, and other places of Canada, every available assistance, as well pecuniary as medical, was rendered to the distressed; and the patients received attendance and consolation to the very last. The more opulent part of the population were strenuous in their endeavours to mitigate the sufferings of others, by every means in their power. They exhibited a striking contrast, in this particular, to Americans.

But Canadian benevolence did not rest here. The governor, the archdeacon, and other leading men resident in York, were conspicuously active in providing permanent resources for orphans left destitute by cholera. The gentry and respectable people around, admitted orphans as part of their household, and engaged to feed, clothe, and educate them till a certain age; after the expiration of which they promised to furnish to their foster-children a certain sum of money, and some articles of utility in the business or employment to which they might be trained. They thus became fathers to the fatherless, and abated the miseries entailed on hundreds by this epidemic plague.

Various methods were resorted to, as preventives or remedies of cholera. The best preventives were always declared to be, what can in general be obtained in that country by all, viz. plenty of nutricious food; an adherence as much as possible to long established habits; sufficient repose of mind and body; abstinence from excesses of all kinds; as well as from every sort of fruit, particularly water-melons; and from every thing likely to produce irritation of the gastric nerve, such as excessive and unaccustomed bodily exercise. &c.

With all these preventives I complied as far as possible. During all the summer, whilst cholera raged in York and its neighbourhood, I rarely went so far. It appeared more prudent to avoid every exposure to heat, than to walk a distance of thirteen miles in a warm day; and as my continuance in the country was of uncertain duration, I did not purchase a horse; which I otherwise would have done. The great hospitality and kindness of several gentlemen in the neighbourhood prompted them to offer me their horses, and

I sometimes availed myself of the favour. My most frequent rambles, when pleasure was my only stimulus for exercise, were directed to some neighbour's, to make inquiries respecting the spread of the contagion, and other matters of a similar nature; or to while away an hour in amusing converse. The most amusing gentleman I met with at Thornhill was from Scotland; one who had resided for some years in Boston, and who had married the daughter of the British consul at that place. He was well acquainted wih the American character, and related many humorous anecdotes of the country and its people. Had I taken them down in notes as he related them, and found leisure to grace them with a few embellishments, I might have been qualified to furnish to the public a series of tales, as entertaining, and containing as many truths, as the stories of Boccaccio.

I often strayed through some parts of the forests, the dense and sombre shade of which screened me from the powerful rays of noon-day splendour.

At first I experienced unusual shudderings, from the surrounding solitude, and the uncertainty of my path. But every renewal of such excursions lessened my disagreeable sensations, till at last my mind became quite reconciled to wilderness scenes, and derived a tranquil pleasure from their presence. A longer residence might have ended, as I believe it would, in so firm an attachment to that charming region, that not even my promise to Mrs. F. would have caused a resignation. Nothing was wanting but her acquiescence, a good library of useful and entertaining works, a comfortable residence, and a full missionary stipend, to have rendered me sufficiently contented. The dread of cholera never haunted me in these secluded rambles.

Many remedies for cholera were mentioned, none of which, except calomel, proved of much service. At the commencement of its fatal visit, such immense quantities of opium and brandy were administered in conjunction, as would extinguish life in the most athletic constitution. Scarcely a patient survived such treatment. These were ultimately discontinued, and ten grains of calomel were substituted. The last mentioned prescription was generally attended with beneficial results, unless the constitution had been impaired by intemperance, or the sufferer too much exhausted, and in the last stage of the disease, before it was administered. If the wished for consequence was not derived from one dose of calomel, the same quantity was repeated at a stated interval. After the general adoption of this remedy, cholera soon abated, and had entirely disappeared, or nearly so, from all the Canadian territories, previous to our departure from York. In America, injection into the veins of certain ingredients, which are supposed to bear close affinity to the component parts of the serum, was had recourse to for the purpose of imparting renewed circulation to the blood. This, it was asserted, produced an instantaneous and favourable effect ; and the patient so treated, although before in excruciating torment, or in a state of complete exhaustion, was instantly in perfect ease and animation, and could converse with his wonted cheerfulness and strength, as if nothing had befallen him. Yet none ever eventually survived this operation. Relief thus obtained was momentary and evanescent.

It was a matter of considerable speculation, whether cholera would henceforth become naturalized in America, and be numbered among those constant attendants on its people, which are regularly active in destruction; or its presence was merely a solitary visit, which, like that of comets or blazing metors, was transitory in its nature, yet attended with such appaling aud horrifying circumstances as to impress us with awful sentiments of God, and of his mysterious dealings with the children of men. Most people were apprehensive, that it would take up a permanent residence among them, and lose nothing of its terrors by greater familiarity. Probably neither cholera, nor any other disorder to which the human frame can be long exposed, can visit Europe for any length of time, without its causes and cure being discovered. The progress and diffusion of science and experimental philosophy are so rapid and general, as to leave nothing unexplored which is worthy of the public attention. In America, science is not much advanced; but the people there are disposed to borrow (although unwilling to acknowledge it) whatever is useful in Europe; and we may look forward to a time of greater knowledge and learning in that country. The period of literary splendour has not dawned there; but should it bear hereafter a proportion to their country, its dazzling glories will be unequalled. When that period arrives, neither cholera, nor any other mortal disorder, can escape investigation into its nature and antidote.

The debate of the question as to the infectiousness of cholera was productive, often, of fatal effects; for, from the assertion of some eminent men of its non--contageous nature, many persons were induced to neglect proper precautions. Hundreds, it is my belief, owed their death to this representation. They courted every opportunity of rushing into places where its victims were laid out, and thereby put its malignity to the test. Several such men, thus uselessly fool-hardy, found their constitutions not proof against it, and afforded by their death striking demonstration of their error. I read in an American paper of a dead man having been found in a field, around whose corpse a crowd and an inquest attended. Within two days, eight or nine of the jurymen were themselves precipitated to an untimely exit.

For my own part, I have no doubt that it is

both infectious and contagious. There were six instances of mortality from it, in my immediate neighbourhood, and one at a distance of five miles, over the graves of whom I read the funeral service. The six first were all traceable to the indiscretion of one man, who entered the abode of an acquaintance struggling in the agonies of death. This was at the distance of thirteen miles from his own dwelling. He returned home with the cholera upon him, and died shortly after. His mother and brother met with a similar fate a short time after, having caught the malady from himself. A person on Yonge-street, within a quarter of a mile from the house where we lived, was reported to have come in contact with one of the above, caught the disease, and died; and was followed almost immediately by two more out of the same house. These six cases appeared to me conclusive of the communicative nature of cholera. The introduction of it was, in them, accurately marked, and its progress traced beyond the admission of dispute.

Two of the above persons died very suddenly — in a few hours after their first attack. They had both been seated at the supper table with the other members of the family on the proceding evening, and appeared cheerful and in health; yet were both interred before the morning dawn. I was awaked out of sleep about three o'clock in the morning to attend the grave of the one, and I attended that of the other about two hours after. Great numbers died in three or four hours after their first attack. It was particularly fatal to aged people upon whom it fell, and to the intemperate of all ages. Few of such patients recovered.

Although our compassion cannot but be moved at the recital of miseries, or diseases, endured by others, yet we are more sensibly affected when the suffering objects of compassion are our intimate acquaintances. This was the case of one, a gentleman whom I had regarded as likely to be serviceable, by his talents and experience, to the land of of his adoption ; I mean the medical gentleman, whom I mentioned before as superintendant of the hospital. Dr. M. (for such was the initial of his surname) had purchased three hundred acres within three miles of our residence, and had come with his two eldest sons to take possession. He intended to go to York, on particular days, to practice in the capacity of a consulting physician. My church was the nearest, and he and his sons attended it. As he and his family had, a few months previously, been moving in the higher circles of a fashionable town in England, perhaps a short account of his case may not be unacceptable. Soon after his purchase he attended public service, but previous to doing so he paid us a visit. He expressed his surprise, on entering, at finding the apartments so indifferently finished, whilst the exterior was so beautiful and the position so charming. It resembles, continued he, a shewy brick building on a farm which I was anxious to purchase, but for which the price demanded was too great. The older settlers are more desirous of appearance, than of real comfort; indeed they are ignorant of the signification of comfort. I differed in opinion from him on this point, as I shall state hereafter.

" We are quite ashamed," said I, " to be found in such lodgings, and have been ill from vexation." Your rooms, " replied he," are not such as I had anticipated, from the appearance of the house; but yet they are certainly not such as you need be ashamed of. You live in a palace, compared with the apartment which I and my family occupy." " You greatly astonish me," said I, " you cannot surely be in earnest." " I assure you," he replied, " that my statement is the truth. I repeat it, your rooms are as the apartment, of a palace, when compared with mine." " I shall embrace an early opportunity to return your visit," I said to Dr. M. To this he replied; " a lady in York, the widow of a captain in the army, invited herself to visit me. My reply to her was; I have much reluctance to be found in a lodging so unusual, and shall not be at home when you call. I am now fitting up another house. If you will patiently delay your visit till my arrangements have been completed, I will send you an invitation. You must not call till I invite you. Such," continued he, " was the warning I delivered to the lady; and such it must be to you. I cannot at present be found at home."

This visit of Dr. M., and his prohibition, instead of repressing, excited my curiosity to the highest pitch. But as he had laid so strong an emphasis on not being found at home, I did not venture to intrude within his liberties till a specious pretext was afforded. I had established a Sunday-school, and was eager to procure books for its use. For this end I delivered an appropriate sermon, and made a collection in the church. I also took upon myself the business of calling on such of the more respectable inhabitants as appeared likely to feel an interest in the matter.

Among others I called on Dr. M. His house was surrounded by lofty forests. On two sides, the trees were at some distance, and two or three farm-houses, with considerable clearances to each, were within the same opening. On the remaining sides, the native forests were untouched, and extended close to his doors. I set out one sultry morning, and proceeded through dense forests to his house. It was with difficulty I found my way, and my perspiration was excessive. From the heat, and the confined atmosphere of the woods, I felt a slight lassitude; and as my handkerchief was become so saturated with perspiration as to be of no further use, I rinsed it in a rivulet, and spread it out to dry on a fallen log.

I soon felt myself recruited, and approached with eagerness to his door. There I quickly learned, that my arrival was extremely unpropitious to myself. Dr. M. was in the cholera, extended on a bed in the corner of the room which served for their cooking, eating, and sleeping room, for they had but one apartment. During my stay, he made uninterrupted moanings. He was in such excruciating tortures as to be unable to converse. Round his bed were curtains, suspended in such a manner as to form a small state-room. I knelt down within these curtains, and rested my head on my hand by his bedside. I had been previously heated with walking. Fear, and the heat of the room, increased my predisposition to perspire, and drops of sweat fell from me in great profusion.

After prayers had been offered up, I retired from that scene of sorrow to my own house, and related the circumstance to Mrs. F. As every day brought tidings of the death of some acquaintance, and as I myself had now been more immediately implicated in cholera atmosphere, I deemed it prudent to make such arrangements as might leave my family, in case of my death, without much embarrassment. I had made up my mind for the worst. The first tidings I heard in the morning was Dr. M.'s decease.

Dr. M. could not be said to have died very suddenly. My call was made on a Monday, and he was first indisposed on the Saturday previous. There appeared to be some negligence on his part in procuring advice and assistance, for no medical gentleman had been called in at the time I was there. His son approached the bed, and requested permission to proceed immediately to York for medical assistance. The same request had been made several times before, but had been treated with inattention. The early stages of cholera were frequently so gentle, as to furnish no forebodings of its fatal termination. A slight indisposition or sickness was often its precursor, which in ordinary seasons would occasion no disquietude. But when the animal frame had been thus prepared, and no precautions been adopted to arrest its progress, the rapidity of its strides was most awfully alarming. In many instances, the short interval of from five to twenty minutes would entirely alter the condition of the patient. His pulse would suddenly become languid, and almost cease to beat; his extremities would grow cold; his strength and spirits would forsake him; his powers of utterance and motion would be nearly suspended; he would feel an entire prostration of all his energies, and a certain anticipation of almost immediate death, in a shorter time than it would require to describe them. Dr. M.'s declining state was, his sons informed me, now more perceptible every moment. He now gave permission, in my hearing, for a doctor to be called. Nature had, however, been exhausted and overpowered before medical skill could be rendered available. He was not indeed actually lifeless at the time the physician arrived, but he was beyond the limits of human succour. His spirit, already flickering on the confines of eternity, soon took its flight from its dilapidated tenement to the mansions of the dead.

Dr. M.'s death did not take place till some hours after I had left him. At my departure, I gently grasped his hand, and expressed a hope that I should again have the pleasure of seeing him in a more favourable state. "Never, never," was his answer; "there is no hope."

I was credibly informed that something unfeelingly callous and devoid of generous sensibility, and even of delicacy, was exhibited by the medical gentleman who came to administer advice. He thus announced the inevitable death of Dr. M. to the afflicted sons: "Your father is a dying man; there is no hope; and now where am I to obtain my fee? I must be paid immediately."

The farm which Dr. M. had purchased was not immediately on Yonge-street, but between two and three miles in the forest. Speedy assistance could not be procured, and it was Tuesday evening before he was taken from the house; his corpse, therefore, was permitted to remain uninterred during the greater part of a day. As he had been attached to the army, his remains were deposited in the military burial-ground at York, and had to be conveyed a distance of fourteen miles. It was almost midnight before his interment took place; which, notwithstanding the prevalence of cholera, was accompanied with military honours. The archdeacon, whose time was almost unceasingly occupied in administering cordials or medicines, in prayer with the sick, or in burying the dead, was called upon to perform the last solemn offices over Dr. M. The soldiers who attended the funeral, had peremptory orders not to approach the coffin, lest they might introduce the plague within the confines of the garrison. It was probably owing to such scrupulous proceedings, on this and other occasions, that the garrison of York escaped without any considerable loss. From this proceeding, however, much more of toil and danger fell to the lot of the archdeacon than was his proper share. He was himself obliged to assist in removing the coffin from the waggon to the grave, and also to procure the assistance of his own son; a sufficiency of help, independent of the soldiers, not having attended. Both the archdeacon and Dr. M.'s son complained of this paucity of attendance.

On one occasion, the archdeacon informed me that the greatest number of authenticated deaths by cholera in Yorktown in one day, was twenty-three, and that Dr. M. was the only professional gentleman in Upper Canada who died of this disorder. The number in York itself was sometimes reported to be between thirty and forty; but the archdeacon must have had many opportunities of actual information. Dr. M.'s estates were situated in the township of York. The circumstance of this gentleman's family being well known in England must form my apology for so minute an account.

From Dr. M.'s case I learned this lesson of instruction, that no person ought to place himself in such a situation as excludes the enjoyment of his wonted comforts, nor should he too suddenly or extensively change his diet. Dr. M. exchanged the comforts of civilized life for the privations of a forest residence. He did not indulge in such generous sustenance as his age and habits required. He subsisted almost entirely on salted provisions, without a sufficiency of fresh eatables to correct their unwholesome tendency. His friends in Canada did not exculpate him from the charge of inconsiderate and imprudent rashness. His purchase was judicious; but he should not have abandoned the conveniences of a town till his country residence had been suitably provided. He was censured by some as too parsimonious, but perhaps the charge was unfounded. I returned from his residence with many apprehensions, but with heartfelt gratitude. I had not till then found out that our condition was more comfortable than that of many, and that we had less reason than we supposed for vexations and complaints.

I have already stated my persuasion that from all I could learn cholera is highly communicative. My own case, however, may be adduced as evidence to the contrary; may I therefore trespass further on the patience of the reader, by inserting a few observations illustrative of my ideas on the subject.

The fact appears to be, that we are placed in the midst of innumerable natural agents, either in active operation, or only waiting a proper occasion to spring into activity. In cases of earthquakes, plagues, and pestilences, those dreadful visitations which sometimes depopulate a province or a city, who can tell how far they depend on the negligence or the agency of man? Since the invention of metal conductors, which were first employed by the American philosopher as a protection against lightning, fewer fatal accidents have occurred from electricity; and scarcely any where that precaution was adopted. It may be reserved for some future philosopher to discover, by what means earthquakes may be prevented, and the countries now subject to that dreadful scourge preserved from desolation. Should such discovery be made, any nation, province, or city, neglecting to adopt it, and afterwards visited by an earthquake, might properly be considered its own destroyer. In like manner, should a person suffer calamity from lightning, or from any other natural agent, when antidotes are provided which he has omitted to employ, the calamity may justly be attributed to himself. When in Quebec, I observed a boy almost blind; and on making inquiries respecting him, was informed, that it had been occasioned by the action of the sun beams on the snow, and their reflexion on the vision of the boy. Should loss of sight be the consequence, the parents must be considered as having occasioned it, by neglecting to furnish their son with shades and glasses. In Lapland and Greenland, I was told, the inhabitants from similar causes are frequently blind at an early age. Such are guilty of suicidal blindness, in proportion to their knowledge of an antidote, and their ability to obtain it. Whatever dangerous or fatal consequences happen to mankind, from want of caution in avoiding or guarding against their causes, must be regarded as self-inflicted. In the instance of that dreadful pestilence inflicted on the Israelites, after David's foolish numbering of the people, we may reasonably suppose that those who fell before it, had debilitated or injured their bodily constitutions, or were in some respects more liable than others to disease and dissolution. The same observation may be extended to that dreadful visitation the cholera; since it was observed to be confined more especially to those whose mode of life, generally speaking, was detrimental to health. I do not mean to insinuate, that this was universally the case, or that many good and temperate people were not its victims. But it was more fatally prevalent among such as had lived intemperately, or had subsisted upon unwholesome food, or had not sufficient proper nourishment, or had exposed themselves to situations dangerous to health. It was almost invariably found to take up its quarters in the earthly tenement of those, who had prepared their constitutions for its reception. Now, just in proportion to this preparation for disease, may every one invaded by cholera be viewed as having welcomed it, and his own blood as resting on himself.

In all ages, at intervals, various plagues and epidemic disorders have raged in every climate. Against the virulence of these, mankind are furnished with numerous antidotes, which are generally efficacious if habitually used. These consist in strict temperance; in using such exercise and medicines as keep the body in a proper frame, and rectify the unwholesomeness or impurities of meats and drinks; in avoiding all needless communication with persons or places of doubtful character, or reported to be infected; in keeping the mind unruffled and composed, free from such turbulent emotions as endanger the corporeal faculties. I do not say, that these antidotes are always a safeguard from infection or contagion; but they are so generally. In places where such plagues, as have committed the greatest ravages, and have been the most circumstantially related—in London, for instance—persons of temperate habits have been more frequently spared, and survived the visitation. And after the plague has abated, less of sickness has for some time been felt in reference to the population, than in previous years. This can only be accounted for, by imagining that all whose constitution had been previously impaired being taken off, none but those of sound health were suffered to escape; the antecedent state of the body, as the case may be, repelling or courting the contagion.

Many of those who were attacked by cholera in the vigour of youth or manhood, and not enfeebled by intemperance or other causes, sustained its shock without experiencing its fatality. Yet it sometimes happened that a person of delicate and slender form, even without any previously debility, who had survived the cholera, relapsed into some fever, and expired in a state of mere exhaustion. This was the case of a young lady, whose nuptials I had solemnized a short time previous, and who requested, on her death-bed, that the same clergyman who married her might perform her funeral service. She resided about five miles from Thornhill, and although my services were requested on these two occasions, yet she and her family did not attend my church, but frequented another nearer their house, at which one of the professors of York College officiated.

The burial service over her grave, from her recent marriage and dying request, was more affecting than any office I performed in Canada. Her interment took place in the midst of a violent and tremendous thunder storm, during which the gleams of lightning and peals of thunder were awful. Large hailstones fell mingled with the rain, some of which, driving with great velocity against the church windows, shattered the squares of glass in pieces. The rain fell in torrents, and inundated the grave, out of which two of the men were employed in emptying the water. I had walked from our house to the burial-ground, and had become parched and thirsty. Whilst these men were lifting the water from the grave, I employed the time in collecting hailstones off the hillocks which surrounded me, and which covered the ashes of departed mortals, and with them I quenched my thirst,

It is customary in Canada for ministers to make short extemporaneous addresses at funerals, and episcopal ministers frequently adopt the same practice. My Lord Bishop of Quebec advised all his clergy to accustom themselves to extemporary preaching and prayer; since so many sudden calls might be made, for which no preparation could be given. The friends of the young lady entreated me to conform to the general custom; and as in cases of cholera I never allowed the corpse to be carried into the church, I expressed my acquiescence, and desired the people to attend me. We entered the consecrated temple, and after a brief interval of prayer and meditation, I delivered my first unpremeditated sermon, if any subject can be called unpremeditated which daily and extraordinary sickness forces on our notice, and places continually in our view.

The friends of the departed bride invited me to their house, which my engagements obliged me to decline. They offered me pecuniary recompense which I also refused. One of them then insisted on my taking his horse, and riding to a neighbouring inn, where another should be provided for me. This was not refused, and I thus received that peculiar kind of requital, which so captivates and pleases,—namely, the grateful feelings of those we serve, and such ready accommodation as suits our circumstances. This I often experienced on other occasions; and I assert with confidence, that no deserving clergyman will fail to receive it in that generous and hospitable land.

CHAPTER IV.

DESIRE FOR MINISTERS—CANADIANS FITTED FOR CLERICAL ORDERS—COLLEGE AND UNIVERSITY—BISHOP OF QUEBEC—CLERGY AND CONGREGATIONS—FUNERAL—PROSPECTS OF CLERGY—METHODISTS—A REFORMED PRESBYTERIAN—ROMAN CATHOLICS—PRESBYTERIANS—SHAKING QUAKERS—MEDICAL PROFESSION—EDUCATION—DEFINITION OF COMFORT.

I was occasionally invited to perform sacred duties in other places also, not immediately under my own church. In every such case, an offer was made me of pecuniary recompense, which I invariably waived. Also for burials, baptisms, &c. money was similarly tendered and refused. I am persuaded, that the people of that country would not object to pay fees for clerical duties, as in England, and to subscribe for pew-rents. I never accepted any fee except for marriages. These I considered as reasonably taxable. If the parties can afford to keep house and maintain a family, they will never object to a moderate fee for the performance of important offices.

I had not long been at Thornhill, before I was requested by a gentleman, resident more than thirty miles distant, to travel thither at stated periods and preach, for which service the people there were not only ready to pay all expenses, but also to reward me handsomely. The same gentleman afterwards called on me, and personally repeated the request and the offer. Yet as I perceived from the very first, that my return was unavoidable, from my hasty promise, which frequency of mention permitted me not to forget, I felt little inclination to comply. This was not the only invitation of the kind; and evinces the desire of the people for religious instruction, and their readiness to contribute to the maintenance of clergy. There are so many families from England, both wealthy and intelligent, scattered over the face of the country, and willing as well as able to afford remuneration to worthy ministers, that I am confident I speak within bounds, when I state that there is ample field in Canada for the additional labours of fifty pious clergymen. In some districts, even where population is rapidly filling up, there is no clergyman for a distance of sixty miles.

The present Bishop of Canada, when in England, made inquiries, I was told, for some gentleman of sound classical, and biblical learning; and having been successful in meeting with one eminent in both respects, induced him by a liberal offer to emigrate to that country for the sole purpose of preparing young gentlemen in Canada for becoming catechists or clergymen. The result has answered the original design, and several Canadians have been qualified in their own country. Still, however, English clergymen are preferred; not so much perhaps, for their more extensive reading, as for their greater experience, and their more intimate knowledge of life and character.

I believe several Canadians have already been admitted to clerical orders, and the facilities for obtaining a much sounder education than what is attainable in the States are becoming every day greater. There are better teachers, and a more methodical and efficient plan, I am told, in the college in Upper Canada, than in any college in the Union. What forms as striking a contrast as any thing between the Canadian and American colleges is, that in Canada strict discipline and suitable correction are admitted, whereas in America they are unknown.

Some American youths were placed by their friends in the Canadian college; and were so astounded at finding enforcement of neglected duties by castigation, that they fled home in utter dismay. The flourish of the professor's rod had upon them as terrific an effect, as the brandishing of the sword had on their countrymen when engaged in direful conflict with Canadians. I must, however, do justice to the professors in New York college, by stating, that they were beginning to adopt castigation, as the only sure remedy for confirmed offenders. Some parents objected to the strict discipline of York College, as being unnecessary in a new country. They supposed, that extensive acquirements are not needful. My judgment and theirs are widely different.

If the same unparalleled progress in education and improvement continue in Canada, which has been developed during the last three years, she will set a luminous example to the States which they will be proud to imitate. A university will soon be in progress of erection in Upper Canada, which it is supposed will be completed in two or three years. A large extent of the finest lands has been granted as an endowment, which in time will be sufficient to place the establishment on so liberal a scale, as will attract professors of the greatest literary eminence. Government is doing much for the moral and intellectual improvement of that charming region.

The first visitation held in York by the present Bishop of Quebec, was attended by three or four clergymen only. But so great have been the augmented numbers of the established church, that twenty-six were present at the last visitation. I appeared among them, but did not count the number. The circumstance was told to me by a neighbouring clergyman, who has been present at every visitation. The bishop is much beloved by his clergy, and does every thing in his power to render them comfortable and respected. They regard his lordship, from his simplicity of manners and unaffected piety, and also from his long missionary labours, as a truly apostolic bishop.

His lordship may be properly considered as the father and founder of the church in Upper Canada. He has nursed and reared it up. His only solicitude is the prosperity and increase of his diocese, in ministers and congregations abounding in every christian virtue. His lordship's own life is one of the best models which any clergyman could imitate. Every person, of whatever denomination, acknowledges his exemplary pattern, and admires his purity of life and mildness of deportment.

On the day of his lordship's visitation, a dinner was provided at his private expense for the clergy who attended. It was pleasing to witness the assemblage of so respectable a body of men engaged in ministerial labours in our church, in the midst of a country lately redeemed from a state of nature. Their appearance was highly creditable to the country, and to the church of which they are ministers.

The reverend gentlemen, the professors of York college, frequently employ their Sundays and their long vacations, in journeying to country places and performing clerical duties. This they do, without any other recompense than that of an approving conscience. The Rev. Mr. Bolton called on us at Thornhill, in returning from a long missionary ramble of forty or fifty miles, to describe the numerous congregations he had been able to collect on a very short notice. In two hours after his arrival at some places, he was surrounded by a congregation of three or four hundred people. To look at the forests, one would almost imagine that they form impenetrable barriers to the settler, and are the confines of population. But by following any road or track for a little way, we are quickly introduced into other cleared and open spots, before hidden from our sight, where sometimes one or two, and sometimes many families, are embosomed in the woods.

I could hardly credit Mr. Bolton's statement of so many hearers assembling in one or two hours, nor conceive the circumstance practicable, until the statement was confirmed by ocular demonstration. One day just before leaving Thornhill, a respectable farmer called on me, and informed me that his son was laid in a coffin in his house at the distance of eight miles, and that he had invited his friends and neighbours to attend the funeral, which he had hoped would take place on the same afternoon. He had been to York to procure a clergyman, but found all the professors so much engaged, that none could attend. He had consequently been obliged to countermand the invitation. Hearing, however, that I never refused to render my services to any person who applied, he had come to solicit them. I informed him, that I was engaged in packing up my clothes and books, and purposed to leave Thornhill on the following morning. Upon hearing this, he modestly observed, that my acquiescence might be a greater inconvenience to me, than the delay could be to himself, and he would not press me to accompany him.

I was delighted with this forbearance on the stranger's part, and immediately prepared myself for the journey, determining that his forbearance should meet a proper recompense. He had left his pony at the end of a field near our house, and conducted me to it. Then taking off his coat, he

A FUNERAL. 315

fastened it behind the saddle, and desired me to mount. He ran before me through the woods all the way home. At one house we passed, he called aloud to the people, and desired they would inform another neighbour that his son would be buried immediately. A person also passed us on horseback, whom he desired to convey the same intelligence to such as he might meet. The moment he reached home, he dispatched messengers up and down with tidings that a clergyman had arrived. In a short time a considerable number of his friends and neighbours were assembled, and the coffin was screwed down and placed in a waggon. Before we reached the burial ground, a mile and a quarter from his house, the congregated multitude amounted to between one and two hundred people. I delivered a short address, in which I mentioned my speedy departure from Canada; but assured them, that my praises of the country should not be silent, nor of the hospitality and benevolence of its inhabitants. On returning from the burial ground, the father offered me money; and on finding that I would not receive it, he procured me a horse, and sent another son to conduct me through the forest to that part of the road with which I was well acquainted.

The behaviour of the Canadians at Church, and during religious ceremonies, is, as far as I observed, quite becoming and proper. They always appeared to me to discharge their sacred duties with great devotion. There was no interruption of the most profound attention, by coughing, spitting, &c. Our medical neighbour assured me, that this arose from the excellence of the climate, the air of which is much drier and purer than with us. I think the atmosphere of Canada preferable to that of England, and my experience is the criterion. I could see more clearly, and at a much greater distance; there was less of clouds and more of sunshine; my sight, and general health grew stronger, than when in England.

When it was known that I was about to return, some very respectable emigrants expressed their regret, that any clergyman whose labours might be useful, should return to England; particularly when he had a provision in the church, and liked the country. 1 replied, that although I felt myself obliged to return, the necessity did not originate with myself, for I liked the country much, and the people more. But since my return could not be averted, I would, on my arrival in England, mention publicly what I had seen and heard. And that I would state it to be my firm opinion, that any Clergyman not provided for in England, nor possessing friends to procure his promotion, would assuredly advance the interests of his family by emigration. Yet I must state, upon the strength of what I have heard the Bishop and the Archdeacon mention, that no clergyman of dubious character, or of inferior talents as a preacher, shall ever have in his power to lay to my charge, the disappointments he may meet with in emigrating. Such clergymen are best at home. When the arrangements now in progress are more matured, I am persuaded the clergy there will be better circumstanced than those in England; and persons every way qualified for the office of parish priest, will be not only willing but glad to remove thither with their families. Any other description of clergymen than the truly pious and deserving, will, I am confident, be regard by the rulers and dignitaries there, with no favourable aspect.

The Methodists are very numerous throughout all the country, and use every possible exertion to thwart the views of the established Church. I was informed by an episcopal minister, of some years residence in Canada, that nothing gives greater annoyance to the Methodists, than the establishment in any district of a new mission, and the appointment of an efficient minister. Where this takes place, their efforts are redoubled. This indeed is naturally to be looked for. They derive, I was told, a small stipend from the United States' Methodist Society, but in itself inadequate to their maintenance. This, however, was denied by some. They are consequently dependent in some measure on the voluntary contributions, which those of their congregation who are able, chose to give them. Where a church establishment has been formed, the Methodists gain no respectable converts. In extensive districts, where are no churches, they bear unlimited sway. I do not deny that good is produced by them in several ways. They prevent the people from being altogether without religious instruction; they establish Sunday Schools in different places; they stimulate clergymen of the established Church to greater exertions; and they point out the good effects of well-concerted measures unanimously pursued. There is, perhaps, no body of ministers so systematic as those of the Methodist persuasion, as well in their modes of declamation, as in their plans of church government. They are the same in every place, and with the same hostility to establishments of all kinds. The salaries of their ministers are small; yet I was told, that wherever they go they have houses always ready to furnish food and lodgings for them and their cattle. The expenses of their maintenance are very small, because they mostly live at other people's tables. They are therefore as well paid as ministers of our own Church; and much better, if we have respect to their inferior education, and the trifling expense it costs them in acquiring.

A gentleman of great influence, on Yonge Street, related an anecdote characteristic of the preachers and denomination as a body. He had often seen a carter who drove the waggons of a farmer along the road, and admired his steady and sober habits. Having missed him for some time, the gentleman inquired of his master what had become of him;

and was answered, that he had turned preacher.
" Preacher !" said the gentleman, " what qualifications had he for the office ?" " He is sober and moral, and can read his Bible," said the master, " and is very well qualified I assure you."

Another preacher of the same denomination was a cobbler, a little distance from Thornhill. A gentleman, whose residence was close to the cobbler's, went once to hear him, and found his sermon to consist of texts of Scripture quoted at random, without any connexion, method, or order. Perhaps such sermons, addressed to very ignorant people, may be quite as edifying as more elaborate discourses.

Perhaps as ignorant Methodist preachers, and class-leaders could be found in England, as in that country. Two well-authenticated anecdotes were told me, when filling the situation of parish priest, in a part of Yorkshire; the former illustrative of the ignorance, the latter of the daring metaphors, prevalent among them. At a class, or prayer-meeting, one person when praying, uttered this petition; " Make us, good Lord, like Sodom and Gomorrow." All present, except one, cried amen.

The one who refused, raised his voice, and declared his unwillingness to say amen. On being demanded his reason, he replied, " Sodom and Gomorrow were two very wicked men." The other anecdote was of a ranter, who when preaching informed his hearers. " We'll make the Devil a bankrupt in this place." " We'll sell him up," vociferated one of the company. " Yes," replied the modest preacher, " we'll sell him up, pots and pans and all." The above anecdotes were told me by persons who declared they were present and heard them.

Yet the above denomination, although very numerous in Canada, and withal most inveterate against the established Church, are not the only enemies which oppose its increase. I was one day walking to a brother clergyman's, and met on the road an elderly man, of whom I inquired the way. After directing me how to proceed, he became very inquisitive and communicative. He inquired my profession, which I told him. He then proceeded to inform me of his own. " The Church of Rome," he said, " is the whore of Babylon, and the Church of England is her daughter, and the Kirk of Scotland is no purer than either, but is equally depraved and corrupt. I belong to the reformed Presbyterian Church, which is the only religion truly apostolic."

This gentleman is a preacher from Scotland. Being very poor, his congregation presented him with a piece of land, which he cultivates himself, and goes up and down at intervals to diffuse religious instruction among his neighbours, whom he strives to convince of the purity of his church above all others on the earth. He is exceedingly liberal of abuse against Episcopalians; and never concludes a sermon, without condemning them with his heartiest maledictions.

Our landlady was one of his hearers, and informed us that he was a great favourite, because he was a plain man, and had no pride or finery about him, but was just like one of themselves. This standard of judging among the uninformed is as general in one place as in another. A clergyman in England, of strict moral rectitude, and of great piety, succeeded one, whose mode of living and acting was the reverse. His predecessor had been accustomed to associate on the most familiar terms with his flock, and to eat, drink, and play at cards with any person; and in consequence was quite a favourite in the place. The sober and pious minister gave general dissatisfaction, by declining the footsteps of his predecessor. He set his face against cards and dram-drinking, and against every thing of immoral tendency; so his parishioners set their faces against him, and petitioned the Bishop to remove him; alleging that he was haughty, austere, and unsocial.

There are numerous bodies of Roman Catholics in the Canadas. The ministers of this denomination are second, in point of sound learning, to Episcopal Clergymen alone. Indeed, in the Lower Province, where they possess large resources, and form the prevailing religious denomination, their schools and colleges are of considerable eminence and merit. The impression left on my mind, from every inquiry I could make, was, that in Montreal and Quebec sound education is carried to a greater extent than in any other cities of the New world, York, in Upper Canada, excepted. No person, settling in the larger towns of Canada, need fear that places of public instruction are not provided for his children.

There are great numbers of Presbyterians in the country: this denomination is almost universally well instructed in all useful knowledge. In Upper Canada they have lately founded a college, which will add much to their respectability. I have heard the episcopal clergy of Canada speak of them in terms of great respect, and also of the Wesleyan Methodists. Every denomination, except the common Methodists, appear to have found out, that the officiating ministers of their order, are more respected by being more learned. Nothing tends so effectually to secure to teachers the deference of their flocks, as a good education, unless the moral character be tainted. Of this truth, Canadian Presbyterians are sensible; and having perceived its essential requirement in the present enlightened age, they have founded a college to promote it.

There is a Quaker establishment at Newmarket, bearing some affinity to the Shaking Quakers, yet with striking peculiarities which distinguish them. Their superintendent is an old man, styled King David; but why graced with regal appellation I could never learn. He assumes the entire control of both their temporal and spiritual affairs. I am disposed to believe, that where large concerns are under the direction of one person, competent to manage them, there is greater uniformity of operations, and more success, than where the direction is conducted by the multitude individually. This society has all along been, and is now, in a flourishing condition. King David has erected a sumptuous temple, of great extent and elegance. He has his singing men and singing women, all obedient to his nod. The women of his establishment assemble previous to entering the temple, and march thither for public worship, two abreast, with as much regularity as a file of soldiers.

King David frequently goes to a great distance, in order to edify the people of other townships by his music and eloquence. I have often seen him passing along the road, with two waggons in his train : he proceeded in a third waggon. He never performs such religious errantry, without being accompanied by his virgins, six in number, selected from among the females of his household, for their superior voices. These virgins are conveyed in the same waggon with himself, over which there is an awning, to shelter them from the inclemency of weather, and from sultry rays. In one of the other waggons follow as many youths, who form an accompaniment to the damsels, and swell the anthems and hosannahs by vocal and instrumental music. In the remaining waggon are transported from place to place, their musical instruments, and apparatus of various kinds. These two last waggons have no covering. He never fails to attract a large assemblage of people, wherever his royal presence is announced. The music of his sacred band is considered curious; and the oddity of his manner, and his condemnation of the Established Church, and of the government, are approved of by many. He never concludes a sermon, in which bitter anathemas have not been fulminated against bishops and governors.

Some medical gentlemen emigrate from the States into Canada; but I believe they are never employed, where one from Great Britain or Ireland can be procured. American physicians do not commonly place themselves in any situation in which competition with Europeans is hazarded.

If any professional gentleman from the States be found in such neighbourhood, he forms an exception from the general rule. There was one such at Thornhill, but his skill was not considered as entitling him to much patronage. His practice was very limited, and confined chiefly to the lower orders.

A medical man, who cannot ride much on horseback, ought not to go into that country. So highly are doctors paid in some places densely peopled, that towns and villages are generally well supplied. Medical men from the States are often found wandering up and down; and where European physicians or surgeons are not found, take possession of the practice. In more remote places, a doctor has frequently to ride fifteen or twenty miles to many of his patients. The English medical gentleman near us, was often sent for to the above distance. His charge for an ordinary journey was a dollar a mile. He was making a rapid fortune, and becoming one of the wealthiest gentlemen in the neighbourhood. There are many places upon Yonge Street, and in the districts around, and, I believe, in every district of the country, which are very populous, and where any respectable medical practitioner might settle his family in certain affluence.

A medical gentleman, who emigrated last spring, and whom all persons who know him unite in esteeming, purchased a farm near the Falls of Niagara, and located his family upon it. He immediately resumed his professional duties, and found the most flattering reception and encouragement. I passed a week at the Falls with my family, and had frequent opportunities of hearing of, and seeing his prosperity and success. He took me in his carriage, for a little excursion, to a patient's house, along the Chippawa Creek, and during the drive, assured me that he had fallen into practice, which would realize for him eleven hundred pounds a year. This is almost as large an income as any medical man, except one or two of the most eminent, can obtain in New York. He did not expect to be paid altogether in money; but this occasioned him no inconvenience. A farmer, whose son he had attended, offered to discharge his obligation by a present in produce from his land. The doctor readily complied, and a cart-load of wheat and oats was speedily laid at his door. " These articles," said the medical gentleman, " I was in need of at the time. The farmer felt himself obliged by my acceptance of them, and I felt obliged to him for the handsome remuneration he afforded me, and his handsome manner of delivering them, when he knew they would be taken."

This gentleman, and every person I conversed with, who had recently arrived, and located himself, praised the unbounded kindness and hospitality of the Canadians. He gave me the address of his brother, a gentleman in the law, who resides in London; and desired I would communicate to him the prosperity and welfare of his Canadian brother, whom Canada and its people had captivated, and who had enrolled himself and his family among them for ever, to spend his time and exertions for their benefit and his own, to receive and communicate reciprocated kindness, with them to live and to die. His advice to his brother would have been to go and join him, had not a prohibitory law existed, to the exclusion of English lawyers.

Education in country places is not so far advanced as in towns, nor are facilities of imparting it so general or effective: Yet I am greatly mistaken, if there are many persons in Canada who cannot read and write, if we except poor emigrants from Europe. General instruction of the poor, although not equal to what it is in England, or in the United States, is far from despicable, and is making rapid strides in every part. There are a few government schools in some districts, the masters of which receive one hundred pounds annually; but these are not numerous. The teachers of other schools derive no assistance from government, unless the number of their pupils average twenty-five for six months; in which case a gratuity is given of ten pounds, in addition to the pay of their scholars.

I have already mentioned, that a sunday school was commenced under my superintendence, at Thornhill. Similar sunday schools are in operation throughout all the country. Each denomination has its own, except in districts where population is thin, and where one school receives children of all persuasions. Great endeavours are making to facilitate the enlightening of the population. Yet one thing I felt grieved at observing, that books in Canada are much dearer and scarcer than in the States. Perhaps this is unavoidable, but it certainly impedes information. Many books of instruction used in Canada, are reprints of English authors, imported from America. There are some popular works reprinted in Canada, but they are not numerous.

While we were in New York, an elderly female called on us monthly, to leave a small publication edited by the African Tract Society. She informed us, that a similar tract to the one she left us, was left with every family in New York once a month. We never gave her any compensation for her tract or trouble, yet she omitted not to call on us in her rounds. This was a pleasant mode of obtaining books, although they conveyed no information to one like myself, nor were much wanted in so large a city, where I had my books. But when I had arrived in Canada, they would have afforded a periodical gratification, could they have been procured, since I carried no religious publications with me, but bibles and books of prayer.

Publications of all kinds are more numerous in the States than in Canada. There is one American literary work, which has no parallel publication, as to general interest or utility to farmers, in the British provinces;—I mean the Genesee Farmer. It details the most approved discoveries and plans, for rendering agricultural pursuits more easy and profitable. I read some numbers of it, which cantained several useful observations. Canada is perhaps too young a country for the encouragement, or even the production of such communications: yet there are agricultural societies, formed with a view to stimulate settlers to greater exertions in improved husbandry.

There had been no literary society established in Upper Canada till last summer. The Archdeacon of York, actuated by a laudable desire of advancing literature and science generally, bestowed a valuable piece of ground on which to erect an edifice for a literary club. A number of gentlemen in and around York formed a committee for the prosecuting of it. The Archdeacon, who is a zealous encourager of knowledge and instruction, was the chairman, and delivered an inaugural lecture, which he was about to publish when I left the place. The members will be required to contribute their portion towards the circulation of knowledge; each being bound to deliver a lecture in turn. Physical science comes more immediately under the proposed plan; but philosophy, and other interesting branches of literature, will be admitted.

A splendid instance of large endowments of colleges presented itself while we resided in the States, made by a gentleman who had amassed an immense fortune in business. The late Mr. Girard, of Philadelphia, bequeathed possessions equal to almost two millions sterling, for the purpose of affording education to the poorer classes. The colleges which his property will found, are not confined to any class; but they have principally the education of the poor for their object. He did not leave all his property to one establishment, nor to one State: the greatest portion of it was left, however, for the establishment of a college in Philadelphia, from which classical learning will be excluded. English, and I believe some other living languages, and all things connected with ordinary and every-day business, and with the usual pursuits of life,—such as history, mathematics, geography, chemistry, and many other branches of instruction, are directed to be taught. If it be carried into effect, according to the will of its founder, it will be the most extensive establishment of the kind in the new world, and perhaps without a parallel even in the old.

No clergyman is permitted to be a professor, nor to be concerned in the management of its affairs. Mr. Girard, like many Americans, was under the impression, that religion and its ministers, with professional men of eminence generally, have in all countries been the enslavers of the people ; and therefore founded such an institution, as cannot from its nature, qualify persons for professional employments. I could wish that some such patriotic and public-spirited men were to be found in Canada. There is great need there of similar establishments for education. Information has a tendency to give a man respect for himself and his character, which always elevates him in the chain of rational beings, and which Americans generally possess.

The Americans are certainly better instructed in the history of their own country, than the peo-

ple of any other country are in theirs. General
information to a certain extent is more widely diffused there, than in any country on the globe. It
is not, however, profound even in the best educated. To this general information, their newspapers and journals, their expeditious travelling,
their books of all kinds, and their places of education, generally tend. The Canadians are as
patriotic as Americans, but have not the same facility of acquiring knowledge. They were left for
many years without any nurturing attention from
the parent country; and had many difficulties to
surmount, which the States had surmounted above
a century. Yet; notwithstanding this, the Canadians are making astonishing improvements. Their
newspapers are almost as numerous, comparatively
speaking, as in America. Their schools have multiplied abundantly within the last two or three
years, although not publicly endowed, nor supported by government. It is true, that teachers
are, in country places, not liberally paid; but the
same thing takes place in the States to as great an
extent. This, indeed, must be the condition of
every recently settled country, and is unavoidably

the case. It would, in my judgment, be a prudent measure, for the people of every township to secure a portion of land sufficient for the endowment of parish or district schools throughout the country, whilst land is plentiful, and of easy acquirement.

A mathematical professor in one of the American colleges, originally from England, the son of one of the most eminent English mathematical teachers of his day, applied for a similar situation in the college at York, but was rejected. He had grown weary of, or at least did not admire the manners of Americans, and the republican conduct of his pupils. His rejection was proper; since gentlemen of equal talents, who have not debased themselves by accepting employment among an inferior class of scholars, can always be found to fill such honourable situations.

A gentleman who had emigrated to the States from Great Britain before ordination, and been admitted to ordination in America, and who had also become dissatisfied with his adopted country, applied to the dignitaries of the Canadian church for admission into its service. His qualifications, which were of sufficient extent to fit him very well for America, would not sanction his acceptance there, and he met with a similar repulse to that of the mathematical teacher. Indeed, there are prohibitory clauses, I was told, in the ecclesiastical law, which exclude an American-ordained clergyman from a mission of Canada.

The medical gentleman whom I have mentioned as having emigrated last year, and having settled near the Falls of Niagara, a person of great experience in life, and sufficiently advanced in age to form cool and deliberate views, told me, when about to leave the Falls, that his observations led him to believe that no professional gentleman should enter Canada, whose sole dependence is his pursuit in life. He imagined a few hundred pounds desirable, not only to provide necessaries till his practice becomes extensive, but also to ensure respectability. I regard this gentleman as possessed of sound judgment; yet my observations shewed me, that a medical practitioner without much capital, may readily succeed, if possessed of exertion and activity. Such gentlemen are greatly needed, and meet with a cordial welcome.

I will add a little advice of my own, which may not be unseasonable. I would recommend no professional gentleman to emigrate to Canada without letters of introduction to the governor. For although I felt not the slightest inconvenience from want of introductions, yet I would by no means recommend the same course to others. I was received in the most gracious manner; but my case was novel, and a repetition of such omission might experience the coolness of a twice-told tale.

I will venture to affirm, that there is a greater uniformity of speech throughout the United States, than through any other region of similar extent and population. This is produced, from using school-books with written accents, and made to guide the pronunciation. Walker's Dictionary is regarded as the standard, and every American is taught to conform himself to its rules. I do not mean to say, that Americans pronounce as Mr. Walker pronounced. Their mode of speaking is not with the same modulations and tones, which we hear in the better circles of London. Yet they have fewer idoms and provincialisms than an Englishman has any conception of; which is the result of their accented school books. In Canada we find all the dialects of England in full force. There is not the same system of teaching as in the States, nor the same extent of travelling. Yet I think it quite probable, that the Canadians will eventually lose the different dialects, in the same manner as is felt in America, and, perhaps, by similar means.

I heard persons in America and Canada frequently expressing how comfortable they were, when the appearance of things around them would not warrant the same conclusion in a stranger. Yet I am quite sure they were so. Mrs. F. felt uncomfortable, and so frequently and loudly complained, that I often participated in her feelings, when otherwise I should have experienced the reverse. The word *comfort* should be understood in its relative signification. We must consider it as the fruition of every thing necessary to our position in society, and our acquired habits. Considering the phrase in this light, *comfort* cannot mean the same thing in all countries. In point of fact it does not. Probably a Laplander and a Hottentot would feel more uncomfortable, if placed in elegant apartments in London, than a Londoner would feel if transported to their filthy dwellings.

I perceived, that a sudden transition from the indulgencies and luxuries of civilized life was offensive to the feelings of most people, and that a ready acquiescence in the change was not to be expected. Elegancies and social pleasures, when wanting, seemed to haunt the imagination, and embitter a condition which might otherwise have been fraught with enjoyment. I confess that the want of these things did not trouble me much, but I was not at liberty to adopt my own plans.

I looked around me, and saw that I was better lodged, fed, and clothed, than many others; that was comfort. I found myself sufficiently respected among those whose respect was desirable or gratifying; that was comfort. I found my church well attended, and increasing in numbers daily; that was comfort, and even something more. I found, when I declared my unwillingness to stay, unless I were made equal to other missionares, an immediate offer from one individual of fifty pounds annually, and of a subscription from the parish of perhaps an equal amount; that surely was comfort. I found on every occasion, in which I was requested to perform any extra duty, that those more immediately concerned strove in all things to consult and even anticipate my wishes and convenience, and proferred pecuniary recompense, and expressed their feelings of obligation in terms impossible to be counterfeit; that was comfort in an exalted sense. I found it possible to have established a school of great respectability, from which a handsome income would have been derived, and some were ready to place their sons with me; this was most comfortable, and flattering to my testimonials as a teacher. I found numbers of those around me sincerely religious, constant and devout in their attendance at church, and thirsting for spiritual knowledge and edification; and will leave it for others to idealize, for I cannot express that source of comfort.

There were some things however which I did not consider sufficiently palatable, as, our lodgings and furniture, the difficulty of procuring some articles, and the exorbitant price of others; the envy and ill-will expressed and exercised by some I spoke to against our church, and against the salary enjoyed by its ministers. Yet these unpalatable circumstances may more justly be referred to our neglect of proper exertions and inquiries, and to the want of adapting ourselves to our new situation.

I frankly acknowledge that I had no just cause of complaint. For although I sometimes fancied that there were some whose kindness was fictitious, and based in selfish motives, yet in the calmness of reflection I cannot lay this to their charge. I experienced great and general hospitality, attention and respect, where nothing could be looked for in return; and must admit, that the kindness I enjoyed was far beyond my merits. It is my persuasion, that no clergyman, if at all what he ought be, will, on entering Canada, meet with a less generous reception and cordial welcome.

CHAPTER V.

EMIGRATION—FARMING—FOREST TREES—FERTILITY OF CANADA—ITS INDUCEMENT FOR AMERICAN DEMOCRATS—LIBERALITY OF GOVERNMENT—CANADA BETTER FOR ENGLISHMEN THAN THE UNITED STATES—DISTRESS OF EMIGRANTS—ADVANTAGES OF EMIGRATION—WHO OUGHT NOT TO GO—PRICE OF LABOUR—EMIGRANTS' FONDNESS FOR CANADA.

WHEN I first waited on the archdeacon, he informed me that 160,000 emigrants were expected in the course of the summer. If I remember rightly, the governor also expressed a similar expectation. In consequence of the cholera, a much smaller number arrived than was anticipated—about 60,000. During the two or three last seasons a different class of emigrants have settled in Canada from what had gone out in previous years. Many of these were either wealthy farmers, or merchants and traders, with large capital. Several clergymen and medical gentlemen were also among the number. With four of these I was personally acquainted, and can speak from experience of their finding employment and encouragement. A gentleman who should go out with the intention of embarking all his capital in farming, would not, from what I could learn, be so likely to do well as by putting his money into the bank in York, for which he would draw from eight to twelve per cent. annually.

Some informed me, that unless a farmer can take an active part himself, his money will be uselessly squandered, without producing to himself or others any beneficial consequences. "He will find it extremely difficult," said they, "to obtain persons competent to superintend his farm so trusworthy as he might find in England, and will consequently injure himself." To this statement, however, I will oppose that of Wm. Cruikshanks, Esq., who possesses two estates on Yonge Street, upon one of which he resides, and manages the other by a bailiff. He declared to me, that from the latter estate, of which about 110 acres are cleared, he netted, in the preceding year, one hundred and fifty pounds, after paying all expenses.

The only thing during our Canadian residence with which Mrs. F. seemed to be amused, was the frequent visits which the cows and sheep of our landlady made into the forests and pastures of other people, and which her neighbours cows and sheep made into hers. Almost every week the landlady mounted her pony, and rode into the forests in quest of her live stock. Sometimes she continued seeking them for two or three days together, before she found them. It occasionally happened, in consequence, that we passed a day without cream to our tea. This wandering of her cows and sheep arose from neglect in travellers or neighbours. These, in passing through her groves, omitted frequently to replace the rails of her fences, and her cattle, &c., found their way through the opening. There are in Canada, as in the States, few fences of stone or earth—scarcely any thing but loose rails are used for fencing.

Whether gregarious animals have any instinct which induces them to reciprocate the visits of other cattle, I will not take upon me to decide, but of this I am certain, that the cattle and sheep of others were as frequently in our landlady's grounds, as hers were in those of others. And this did not happen peculiarly to one person, but was a common occurrence to all farmers in the country. This reciprocated intercourse of cattle brought to my recollection an incident which happened to us on our first commencement of house-keeping. The lady who had occupied the same dwelling antecedent to ourselves, had left a cat on the premises, which must have been famished during the nine months the house was empty, unless it had found a hospitable welcome among its kindred of the neighbourhood. The moment it perceived the house to be retenanted, it returned, and such numbers of cats followed it into our kitchen and pantry, that nothing eatable could be left open for a moment without being dicovered by them and carried off. It is most probable that this congregation of cats on the premises was nothing more or less than the repayment of friendship. So the cattle of Canada frequently exchange mutual visits, to the great annoyance of their owners. They are as little ceremonious in this respect as American servants.

When milch cows stray from home, it must be

injurious to themselves as well as to their masters. Not only do they give less milk, but also their udders, from too long distension, are liable to inflame. My father had a cow which could draw her own milk. She was no doubt delighted with the flavour of it, for she practised the sucking of herself every day. She grew quite plump, and was a subject of wonder, at the small quantity of milk she yielded, and at her sleek appearance. She was detected one day in the very act, after which a wood collar was suspended round her neck, which prevented her continuing it. She afterwards gave more milk, but decreased in fatness. Such cows are best fitted for Canadian pastures, when disposed to take holiday in the woods. It is customary to give salt to sheep and cattle, and indeed to every domesticated animal. Our landlady sprinkled a few handfulls, three or four times a week, for her sheep, upon some wood, which they almost regularly came for, when not on a sylvan tour. Animals, in that country, would not thrive without it. The air is too fresh and arid, and too far from the ocean.

Horses are not, at first, of much use to settlers,

except for riding, as they cannot be safely used among the stumps of trees. Being quicker in their movements than oxen, and not so steady or tractable, they are less adapted to the exigencies of Canadian husbandry. After the stumps have entirely decayed, which takes place in from six to ten years, except where pines have stood, horses can be used with the same advantages as in other countries. The price of a good horse, is from twelve to twenty pounds sterling; of a yoke of oxen, from twelve to fifteen; of a cow, from two to four; of a full-grown fat hog, one pound. In winter, I was told, good beef, venison, &c., can be purchased at two pence per lb. In summer, no venison can be obtained, and other kinds of meat is from three pence to four pence per lb. Fish was very cheap and good :—a large salmon for a shilling English; and sixteen white fish, each weighing from one to three pounds, for a dollar.

Many of the horses used in Canada are imported from the States. The old Canadian horse is of a smaller breed, and although well adapted to the forests, yet not so strong, nor so calculated for a cleared farm. The breed of both horses and cows is greatly improving in that country, by intermixture. Dangers, and frequent exposures to fatal accidents, appear to quicken the instinct of animals, as well as the invention of man. Several farmers informed me, that at the approach of a thunder storm, and during violent gusts of wind, all cattle remove from that part of a pasture where many trees are standing, to that spot most unencumbered with them. They are, therefore, sensible of danger from girdled pines. Yet notwithstanding this natural instinct, it frequently happens that animals are killed by trees uprooted or snapped asunder by wind. Sometimes a tree, from radical decay, comes to the ground without any apparent external agency, and crushes whatever is in its way. A neighbouring farmer told me, that he was once standing in a field near his house, and a beautiful horse by his side, for which, in the previous week, he had refused a hundred dollars, when a tree suddenly fell upon the back of the horse and struck it instantaneously dead. This occurred when there was not a breath of air. The falling trees are most frequent in spring. The long frost and the succeeding thaw loosens the ground, even to the very roots. The trees have not so deep a root in the forests as in more open places, and are so continually thrown down, that no person can flatter himself with being able to pass along the same track two successive days, without encountering fresh obstructions from such contingencies.

The whole surface of Upper Canada is laid out in lots of equal divisions, and on a uniform plan. The country is intersected throughout by roads at a mile and a quarter distance from each other, already either formed or marked out. Parallel roads, at that distance, are cut at right angles by other parallel roads, at the same distance from each other. The one set of parallel roads run east and west, the other run north and south. They therefore form blocks of land, perfectly square, containing a thousand acres, and each side of which is a mile and a quarter long. The block is next divided into five farms, of two hundred acres each, being a quarter of a mile broad, and a mile and a quarter long, and abutting upon two roads; whilst two lots out of every five have a road on three sides.

FARMING. 351

The value of land in Canada is increasing regularly and rapidly. For instance, Yonge Street was first settled thirty-seven years ago. At that time land on it was given to any person who applied. A few years after, a lot was worth from fifty to a hundred dollars. A lot now is worth from one to two thousand pounds on many parts of Yonge Street. In the beautiful township of Oro, lately settled, land, a short time ago, was one dollar per acre. It is now from two to five, and increases in value from half a dollar to a dollar every year. On the Huron tract, it is now selling at from one to two dollars. Emigration is setting in that way, and the probable consequence will be, that land there, in two or three years, will be double that sum. Land has generally been found to double itself every three or four years. A person of capital, possessing prudence, is sure to improve his pecuniary condition by emigration. He makes a sacrifice of the refinements of a highly polished life, but I consider his gain as much more than an equivalent.

One day, when dining at the archdeacon's, there were present the chief justice of York, and another gentlemen of great legal eminence. These considered the value of land in Canada as fictitious, and not according to its intrinsic worth, but a capricious standard. Yet we may justly ask, " what is the worth of any thing, but as much money as it will bring!" In the towns of Kingston, Brockville, &c., it is almost as high as in many parts of England; whilst at a small distance from these towns, it can be purchased, equally good, at two or three dollars. In York town, an acre is sometimes worth ten or twelve hundred pounds. A little remove from this, uncleared land is worth six or eight dollars, and a few miles farther off, not perhaps above two. If rail-roads be formed, plans for which have been laid before the legislature, and acts passed to legalise them, the land now selling at two dollars would soon be worth ten pounds.

Nothing can furnish a finer proof of the strength and fertility of the soil, than the number and largeness of the trees. They are magnificent, and afford a subject of admiration. These trees stand so close together in many parts, as to prevent any brushwood from appearing. The surface is beautifully open, and a person may walk for miles up and down, in the very heart of the woods without other obstruction than the mouldering giants of the forest, which lie prostrate on the ground. In most places, no boughs branch off from the trees till forty or sixty feet from the ground. The trunk is perfectly free, generally, from such excrescences. No room being left for them to spread, such redundancy is hindered. I was informed, that the timber of forest trees is not so close and firm, as of trees which have been planted. The reason assigned was, that to the formation of the finest timber free admission of sun and air is necessary. Consequently the density of forest shades, excluding too much the necessary influence of solar and atmospheric agency, prevent the requisite co-incidents.

In grounds which have been planted, the trees are regularly so thinned, as to afford free admission to sun and air. I have often been delighted, on a hot day, after walking through cleared grounds, at being suddenly admitted into umbriferous retreats where noon-day sun-beams never enter. The mind has full scope for contemplation in these fields of nature, and finds sources of astonishment in her productions. Some of the fallen trees are four feet in diameter; and where they are extended over ground with a few inequalities, they form fences which a man can pass neither under nor over. The tops of the trees are often bushy, and form a lofty canopy to the traveller beneath.

I do not wonder, that poets in every age have sighed for groves and secluded forests, where their ardent and wild imaginations might roam for images. It is impossible to have tasted the solace, the calm tranquility, the lofty inspirations they supply, without feeling that scenes like these are the genuine birth-place of poetic raptures. Yet so frequently scattered up and down in the woods are the huts of emigrants, that it would now be difficult for a poet to realize the aspiration of Cowper, at least in Canada :—

" O for a lodge in some vast wilderness, some boundless contiguity of shade, where rumour of oppression and deceit, of unsuccessful or successful war, might never reach me more."

In addition to the numerous settlements and

clearances, which serve as loop-holes for Æolus and Phœbus, and as gardens for the happy emigrants within, a poet would have found, last year at least, the harsh dissonance of cholera reports, of execrations of plundered Englishmen flocking from the States, and of the heart-rending shrieks of helpless Indians, whom American duplicity had robbed of their heritage, and driven from their homes.

So fertile is the soil of Canada, at its first cultivation after clearing, that an acre, upon which no more than one bushel is sown, will produce almost always between thirty and forty bushels. The first crop, with proper management, generally repays the purchase-money, the expense of clearing and fencing, the cost of seed, sowing, and harrowing, and the expense of reaping, thrashing, and carrying to the mill. In short, a prudent and industrious farmer may always calculate on being able to call the land he clears his own, by the first crop alone. The second crop is generally hay, which is reckoned worth from eight to ten dollars per acre. This is obtained without any other expense than that incurred by mowing and carting to the hay-loft. The expense of hay-making in Canada is very trifling ; the fineness of the climate renders no great labour necessary, beyond the cutting of the grass. If a farmer has a family to work his land, three or four years of labour will generally render him independent.

The fertility of Canada is a powerful inducement, not only for Europeans, but for Americans also, to prefer it to many parts of the States. No year passes without witnessing the emigration into Canada of great numbers of Yankees, as well as of great numbers of persons from the united kingdom of great Britain and Ireland, who had resided for years in the States. It was often to me a subject of deep reflection, to have learned that large numbers of English people quit their country in disgust, and swell the ranks of the Americans, whilst Americans go in swarms into Canada, preferring its richness, yet hating its government. The oath which the United States impose on aliens, before they can enjoy the rights of citizenship, is much stricter and more rigid than what is imposed on emigrants to Canada. Persons are not unfrequently found, who being citizens of the States, and possessing property therein, go into Canada, and become proprietors of land under the British government also. If such an oath were administered to persons holding land in the British territories, as is administered in the States, which contains an abjuration of every country and every government but their own, we should find less disturbance in that province. It is impossible for Americans to be loyal subjects of Great Britain, and at the same time republicans.

It appeared to me, that the government of Canada is too liberal in this respect. It ought not to be so strict as to exclude Americans from becoming loyalists, but it ought to be such as would require every subject to abjure every government but the one he had adopted. The stability of the present administration there depends more upon some such regulation, than upon any efforts which its internal or external enemies can use to shake it. A late American eulogist, who scarcely entered Canada, and that only to gratify his wish to obtain favour with Americans, passes a condemnation on the system pursued by our colonial administration, as too illiberal, and throwing too many obstructions in the way of emigrants from the States. I cannot see how an oath similarly framed to the one which prevails in America could be illiberal. America prospers by such an oath, and secures a population devoted to her interests; and I am of opinion that the same results would accrue to Canada, from a similarity of acting. If an American chooses to locate on the fertile soil of the British province, let him become in earnest a Canadian, and he will not object to such an oath.

Several families, whom we knew in New York, and who complained of American usage to Englishmen, went up into Canada last Spring, as soon as the canals were open. On our return, we called on some of their relations who had remained in New York, and found that letters had been received from Canada, which intimated that those who had left New York were, even in so short a time, in a state of greater prosperity than they had enjoyed in America. It must be borne in mind, that this occurred even in the immediate sphere of cholera, in a town more severely visited by it than any other. This will speak for the superior advantages to be gained by emigrating to Canada than to the States.

If many Englishmen, who are divided in their judgment respecting what country to adopt, could be placed on the shores of Lake Ontario, and hear the execrations of scores who arrive with their families daily from America into Canada, after having lost all their property; and then could hear the account of others, who, after having left the States in a ruined condition, have entered Canada and realized a handsome independence, they would require nothing more to fix their choice. But I am sorry to observe, that there are not wanting those who will prostitute their talents, and lend their names, to promote the purposes of an enemy. Mr. Stuart, for one, mentions some prairies in the States as more desirable to emigrants than any other. I take upon me to question the correctness of his assertion, and venture to affirm, upon the testimony of every English farmer I conversed with in Canada, that there is not one industrious farmer in Canada whose prosperity is not greater, from the same labour and capital, than those prairie-farmers of whom Mr.

Stuart speaks. It is also my belief, that, should twenty-five farmers enter Canada, and the same number enter the lands he praises, at the same time, with the same capital, and the same industry, twenty-four out of the twenty-five Canadian emigrants would be in a more prosperous condition, in the course of five years, than any one of the others; and also that twenty out of the twenty-five American emigrants would repent of their choice, and, should they have opportunity of comparing their state with the more favourable condition of the other, would lament their credulity in his statement, and deplore the day on which they read his book.

Every poor emigrant is allowed fifty acres from Government, upon such easy terms as are available to all. In fact, the liberality of Government is proverbial in respect to settlers upon land. If any person chooses to rent a lot of land for a term of years, he will always have the option of renewing his lease, or of purchasing the estate, in preference to a stranger. Government never takes advantage of the improvements which such farmer may have made, without awarding a recompense;

and, as the lands so improved are always offered to the improver at an undeviating mode of estimate, he is liable to no imposition. The good faith of government has never been violated or disputed, and is relied upon with the most unbounded confidence.

Yet it sometimes happens, when persons without capital take such leases, or receive grants from Government, situated at a distance from former settlements, and having no immediate neighbour for whom they can labour, and thus earn something, that they suffer considerable distress. Government, although most liberal in its dealings, does not furnish provisions or implements; these the settler must procure for himself. If he be entirely destitute, and yet cannot find employment near his own farm, he must be badly circumstanced.

Some women, from a back settlement, on their way to the Government-office, called on us at Thornhill, and detailed the sufferings they had undergone from this circumstance. I occasionally met with wanderers on the road craving charity; but they were, in general, only just arrived from

Europe. Industrious people, be they ever so poor, are soon raised above the necessity of aid. The Americans boast that they have no beggars in their country; but it is, like all their boasts, unsubstantial and incorrect. Mrs. F., as well as myself, relieved several importunate beggars in New York. I mentioned this to Americans, who declared they must be English people. We were induced to believe, from what we saw and heard, that pecuniary distress, as I have before observed, was as severe in New York during the time we were there, and felt by as great numbers in proportion to the population, as in London. The numbers in England appear to be greater, because many there betake themselves to mendicity as a calling, who could actually subsist without it. Whereas in America, its unfrequency is a source of shame to any beggar; and no person craves assistance who can possibly live without it. In Canada, as I have already stated, assistance was occasionally solicited, but it was invariably by those who had not been long enough there to establish themselves.

Some of the advantages which emigrants of a

ADVANTAGES OF EMIGRATION.

lower order derive from change of country, is the comparative ease of mind which they possess. They are not tantalized by the presence of luxury from which they are excluded; and they find that labour is a capital which yields then numerous and daily increasing comfort. They cannot indeed obtain, nor can they reasonably look for, sudden wealth. There is no region in the world, however fertile or well governed, which offers this to the generality of settlers; but they are soon raised above indigence. They see their flocks and herds yearly increasing. They behold their families and houses supplied with more conveniences every day, and better furnished. They are not excluded, even at first, from the rights of citizenship, as in the States; nor from possessing real property, which immediately confers every political advantage, and which in most places can be cheaply purchased. They find most of the necessaries of life easily procurable, and some of the luxuries much more reasonable than at home, from absence of heavy duties. They look forward to age and sickness without any apprehension of want, or rather with the absolute certainty of not being destitute when these arrive. They find that their children are more easily provided for than in England, and will fill a higher place in the grades of society. Indeed, I was told by most of those I spoke with, that the sons of frugal and industrious parents, who had arrived poor, were more frequently found in higher situations and easy circumstances, than of others who appeared to emigrate under better auspices, but destitute of these personal recommendations, or possessing them in an inferior degree. But there is one circumstance of more weight in directing men's choice in emigrating than any of the above. In the States, they are among a people of different habits and different sentiments from themselves, in Canada they are among their own countrymen, and find kindred sentiments with their own, and a fraternal welcome.

Persons of idle and indolent habits, of no regular trade or business, of weak or delicate constitutions, of wavering or unstable minds, and such as are addicted to intemperance, or unable to accommodate themselves to privations, or to modes of living and exertion differing in nature and degree from those in densely populated countries, ought never to enter Canada. Nor should persons go who, if married, cannot take with them dutiful and obedient wives, disposed like themselves to submit to temporary difficulties and self-denials for an ultimate and certain benefit. The country having to be cleared, before it can be rendered capable of yielding produce, more labour is imposed at first upon the cultivators than in an old-settled country. Indeed, where every respectable person is employed, there is no place for idleness, nor for men disposed to practice it. They will not be encouraged, nor succeed in any way.

I have heard it often complained of that labour is higher there than in England. I doubt this extremely as a general rule. The best wages are, for a husbandman, about twelve dollars a month; and the lowest about eight dollars. A good servant in Cumberland would generally obtain twenty-five pounds a year when times are good, which is as much as the average price of labour in Canada. Labour is higher there in proportion to the price of produce. A bushel of wheat is there at the price of a dollar, but in England at two or three dollars, and other kinds of produce in proportion.

I am confident that not only the farmer, but the labourer also, improves his condition by emigration. A careful labourer may save as much as will purchase him six acres of land every month in the back settlements. But I conceive that masons, painters, carpenters, blacksmiths, &c. may speedily accumulate property if they are such as can be relied on. Blacksmiths frequently earn about two dollars a day for the greater part of the year.

Almost every person I spoke to liked the country, who had passed two years in it. They told me that at their first entrance on a change of life and habits, they felt so sensibly the want of their accustomed pleasures as to make them wish themselves in their native country and among their former acquaintances; but this feeling soon wore off by the attraction of new habits, and the formation of new acquaintances. They discovered, by degrees, fresh inlets and springs of pleasure. I must add, that I did not meet with one industrious person, a short time settled in the country, who did not assure me that he was not only reconciled to, but even liked it; and that he would not live in England, even if any gentleman would give him an estate, or a house to live in. My own repugnance to our mode of life had, before I left Canada, merged into indifference; and would soon, probably, had I availed myself of the means in my power to command greater comfort, have been followed by an acquired relish, which almost nothing could have induced me to abandon.

CHAPTER VI.

FARMING—GARDENS AND ORCHARDS—CHEAP GOVERNMENT—BADNESS OF ROADS—PRICE OF VARIOUS ARTICLES—FUEL—NEGROES—AMERICAN IMPROVEMENT—A MACHINE—CANADIAN IMPROVEMENT—THUNDER STORM—TEMRERANCE SOCIETIES—CHARACTER OF CANADIANS—CANADIAN HOUSES—CANADA COMPANY—EMIGRATION OUGHT TO BE ENCOURAGED.

THE business of farming is becoming better every year. From the communications opened by means of canals, produce can be readily exported from any part of Canada, and merchandize imported thither at a trifling expense. A few years ago the farmer laboured under great disadvantages, he was obliged to dispose of his produce to storekeepers for about one half of the present prices, and to pay twice the price he now does for shop-goods. Times are evidently altered for the better to them. Every farmer, if industrious, becomes wealthy. Store-keepers are also much better circumstanced than formerly, from the more extensive sale and readier payment they now experience.

The mode of conducting husbandry, both in America and Canada, is rapidly improving. It is beginning to be conducted after the English fashion, as far as husbandmen can afford to do so. The original farmers had no conception of the most useful and profitable systems. They took as many crops as possible from the ground without manuring it. I observed in some farm yards, and more especially in our landlady's, an immense quantity of manure, which had been allowed to accumulate from year to year without being used, till at last it had became so great as almost to preclude the possibility of entering the stable, barn, or piggery. This was universally the case with the first settlers, but the value of manure is now pretty well understood among Canadian farmers.

Gardening is, in Canada as in the States, but little cared for; and garden produce, when purchased, is very dear. We paid five pence English for single cabbage-heads. Much time cannot be devoted to horticultural pursuits, and a little time is not sufficient to keep a garden in order. The people also are not so industrious as in England. Many orchards, however, appear attached to farm-houses, some of them of great extent, and generally well stocked with fruit-trees. I have seen some orchards in that country several acres in extent. Peaches are in abundance on the south western parts of the province, but not on the northern part. As we were returning from Yonge-street, in October, and coming along the country bordering on the Niagara river, nothing could present a more pleasing sight than the numerous well-stocked orchards, the trees of which were bent to the earth with fruit. I had never before seen any trees so completely laden. Cider, near the Niagara falls, was little more than a dollar a barrel; it was brought on the table in jugs-full, as water would be brought in England, and of an excellent quality. Honey also, was, during our stay at the Falls, placed on the table every day, generally both morning and evening, and could be purchased in any quantity at about 12lbs. for a dollar.

The best cider I ever tasted was on Yonge-street. A gentleman had been turning his apples into cider; after he barrelled it, the casks were left so exposed as to be reached by the frost, which congealed the aqueous part of the liquid.. The strength of the cider, the very essence, and spirituous portion of it, was detached thereby from the water. He bored holes in the barrels and drew off the unfrozen part into bottles; this was the cider of which I am speaking, which in strength and goodness more resembled wine than cider.

In the midst of the forests are gooseberries and raspberries, not indeed comparable to similar fruit in England, but which might soon become so by cultivation. I also observed some wild vines with clusters of grapes. Wild apple-trees, yielding fruit much superior in size and flavour to our crab-apples, are frequently found in the woods, which yield excellent fruit when transplanted. There are moreover wild plums of an excellent quality. These fruit-trees will bear removing from one place to another without any injury, and with evident improvement.

There are various sorts of shrubs in some situations, which are beautiful and ornamental; but which, when taken from their natural shelter, cannot bear the heat of summer nor the cold of winter; they quickly fade. A gentleman, near us at Thornhill, had brought some young shrubs from the midst of the forest, and planted them in his grounds, but they all died in the course of the year.

The government of Canada is perhaps the cheapest and least oppressive in the world. Its pressure is not felt in the least. The people of the United States are sensible of this, and admit the excellence of its administration in many respects; but still they maintain that England has no business there and should leave it to itself. They are eager to see Canada disunited from the mother-country, under a republican form of government, and attached to the federal union. The Americans seemed jealous of the easy taxation of the British provinces.

I am, however, far from imagining that the extent of taxation is an accurate criterion of good government. The energy of the States is much invigorated by rates and taxes, which I imagine are higher in proportion to their wealth than in England. A gentleman of New York informed me that the annual rates and taxes of various kinds on his store amounted to forty dollars, and on his dwelling-house to thirty. In country places of America they are more moderate; but even in the most lightly taxed parts of America they are between four and five times as much as in Canada. This was uniformly told me by Canadians, and admitted by Americans. The public works in America are upon a larger scale than in Canada, and are defrayed by imposts of various kinds. Those in Canada are also not defrayed by the provincial government, but by England.

I much question whether the Canadians would allow themselves to be assessed for any improvements, from which, even to themselves, great advantages would immediately result. Their roads are in a bad condition, but yet they are unwilling to pay rates or establish turnpikes. Their roads are at present made and repaired by statute labour, except in places where they are laid out and formed by the Canada Company. Canadians would rather tolerate the inconveniencies of roads, impassable at some seasons, than pay a dollar a year for im proving them. The extra wear and tear of their horses, carts, harness, clothes, &c. cost them ten times more than would be requisite to make their roads and keep them in order; but rates and taxes sound like tyranny to Canadians. There is no country taxed like England, yet there is no country so well able to pay taxation.

An awkward, but yet laughable, accident took place near Thornhill before I left it, occasioned by the badness of the roads. I have mentioned, that the church stood on an elevated rise above a winding valley. The sides of this valley are very steep, and Yonge-street, on the steeper side, ascends the hill in a direct line. Part of the hill has been levelled, but not so as to render the ascent or descent safe or easy. I have no hesitation in saying, that the roads in Canada are the greatest drawbacks from rural comfort. This slope, which is remarkably steep, is famous for the many accidents which annually take place. A gentleman, who had been in the East India trade, had just arrived from England, with his lady and a numerous family accompanied by a young gentleman, who was reported as about to be united to the eldest daughter of the East India captain. They had purchased a valuable and well-situated estate close by, and had taken lodgings on the opposite side of the valley to that where the church was erected. Their house also, and farm, which they had purchased, were on the same side as the church, and their lodgings were only a temporary residence, till such times as their new mansion could be made ready for receiving them. The Sunday morning, on which they first made their appearance at Thornhill church, was exceedingly rainy; and they rode in a jaunting-cart to the gate. The ascent up the hill, for horses in wet weather, is not so difficult as the descent; and their journey to the place of worship was attended by no accident. Perhaps also the uninterrupted rain, which fell during divine service, contributed towards making their return more unpleasant than their previous drive.

I must here explain further that the roads, in many parts of Canada, are composed entirely of earth,—of a rich soil, among which no stones or gravel is intermingled. Many farms along Yonge-street, of two hundred acres in extent, have not so much stone on them as would serve to lay the foundation of a house. This is a proof of the fineness of the land; but also of the paucity of materials for making solid and substantial turnpikes. Of such a nature is the road at Thornhill, and the difficulty of descending a steep hill in wet weather may be imagined. The heavy rains had made it a complete puddle, which afforded no sure footing to man or beast. In returning from church, the ladies and gentlemen I speak of had this steep hill to descend. The jaunting-cart, being well filled with people, was too heavy to be kept back, and pressed hard upon the horses. The intended youthful bride-groom was, I was told, the charioteer. His utmost skill, was ineffectually tried to prevent a general overturn The horses became less managable every moment. But yet the ladies and gentlemen in the vehicle were unapprehensive of danger, and their mirth and jocularity betrayed the inward pleasure they derived from his increasing struggles. At last the horses, growing impatient of control, and finding themselves their own masters, jerked the carriage against the parapet of the road, and disengaged themselves from it. The carriage instantly turned over on its side; and as instantly all the ladies and gentlemen trundled out of it like rolling-pins. Nobody was hurt in the least ; for the mire was so deep, that they fell very soft, and were quite imbedded in it. What apologies the gentleman made I am unable to tell, but the mirth was perfectly suspended. I overtook the party at the bottom of the hill, the ladies walking homewards from the church, and making no very elegant appearance.

We found some imported articles very reasonable. Good brandy could be obtained, for about 6s. 6d. a gallon ; and the best for a little more than two dollars. Sugar and tea were better for the money, than in England ; and about as good as in the States. Whisky is 1s. 8d. per gallon. Yet candles, soap, and other such articles, are dearer in Canada by 2d. or 3d. per lb. than in London. Many of the farmers make their own ; and consequently the chandlers and soap-boilers, not having so extensive a sale for their manufactures, are obliged to have better prices. As population advances, and the demand and consumption increase, competition will reduce the prices, and render every thing easier of attainment than at present.

Yet there often appeared to be an exhorbitant price put upon some articles of consumption, whether imported from Europe, or manufactured in the country. I was told, that shop-keepers in Canada often gain from one to two hundred per cent upon English articles. If more facilities were opened for commerce, and greater inducements to consumers by a fair and moderate remuneration, it would assuredly be advantageous for all parties. There would be closer bonds of union between England and Canada, from greater consumption without greater cost. Retail dealers there would have increased demands for every useful article, which a too high price places out of the reach of some, and out of the desire of others; and without which, many contrive to manage, rather than purchase at the price demanded. Yet notwithstanding the high price of some things, above what they are in England, they are much cheaper than in America. An American can take an excursion from New York to Canada, travel down to Montreal and Quebec, and return by the same manner that I did; and save as much, by purchasing two suits of clothes in Canada, as will defray the expenses of his journey. Yet perhaps a modification of the tariff, which was spoken of in America, may render this impossible in future.

We found fuel much more reasonable in Canada than in the States. In New York, the winter we were there, we were told it was fourteen dollars a cord; but we burnt no wood ourselves whilst there. In Canada we paid one dollar a cord, when laid at our door. A person who is settled on a farm of his own, which every prudent person in country places takes care to be as speedily as possible, obtains his fuel at small cost. If he were to hire a wood-cutter to clear him an acre of land, he would pay twelve dollars; consequently an acre and a half would be cleared for eighteen dollars Supposing the same acre and a half to contain one hundred cords of wood, the cutting of it up for fuel, if the wood-cutter boarded at the house of his employer, would be a quarter of a dollar a cord,—twenty five dollars for the whole. The difference of clearing the ground in the ordinary way, and of cutting it up for fire-wood, is not more than five or six dollars an acre. The expense of carting it home devoles in this case upon the owner, who must find horses and men; but as all residents upon land have horses or oxen, and also men hired as servants, the expense is not felt. When in New York, we often used charcoal mixed with hard coal; and for the charcoal we paid about 10$d.$ a bushel English. Charcoal in Canada would have been brought to our door at 2$d.$ per bushel.

During our residence in New York, an insurrection took place in the West Indies. The slaves had been instigated, by what they heard respecting liberty, to rise up against their masters. We found some of those from Europe, who had been resident in the West Indies for years, to have emigrated to Canada with their families. Independent of a greater degree of civil order, they gain thereby a climate highly favourable to European constitutions, and abounding in the necessaries of life. Some Americans declared to me, that the propensities and dispositions of negroes are not altered by civilization; that they are still blood-thirsty; and would rob or murder when in their power.

In New York no white person will sit down to

eat at the same table with a coloured person, nor associate in the same company. I cannot conceive, why there should be any such antipathy or repugnance. I talked with several coloured people, and always found them, in conversation, rational and sensible. At Thornhill in Canada, there was a black man and his wife, but they were not so treated as in the States. With the woman I had several opportunities of talking. She spoke as properly, and as much to the purpose, on every question proposed to her, as any person, who could neither read nor write, could be expected to do. I encouraged her to join our Sunday school, which she did a few times; but had not acquired ability to read, before she left the neighbourhood. Her husband had been a slave in the States, and had made a premature liberation of himself by crossing the boundary line. Yet he could not gain a living by his skill and labour. He was a helpless and dependent creature. I perceived the necessity of conveying useful instruction to people inured to slavery, before emancipation and the rights of freedom are bestowed. Liberty to the captive is assuredly no blessing, where this has not been previously provided.

I had been much impressed with the activity of Americans in New York; and with their contrivances in rendering subservient to their interest and to their country's welfare, not only their own energies, but those of all who approach them. The consequence of this is visible, in their shipping, their buildings, and their improvements of all kinds. But I had not, till after residing in Canada, a full idea of their national greatness and enterprize. The extent of country they have cleared, their inland traffic, their public works, their increasing manufactures, aud their mechanical inventions, are worthy of unbounded admiration. The forests are made to disappear by the edge of the axe, a four-inch piece of steel; and our astonishment cannot but be called forth, on witnessing such wonderful results, from an instrument apparently so inadequate. Natives are much more expert in felling trees, than recent emigrants; and no one, till after some months residence, can equal them. The logging of trees is also rendered more easy by practice. Some settlers I conversed with informed me that the piling of logs for burning is the most difficult exercise they have experienced in Canada.

It appeared surprising, that among the many inventions for rendering manual labour more expeditious and less oppressive, none has yet been found for clearing the forests. The same process is now pursued, without any variation, which the settlers of three hundred years ago adopted; and perhaps the very same as was followed in the time of Homer. It seemed to me quite possible, to adopt a portable steam engine to this purpose; which might perform the labour more expediently, and which would also tear up trees by the roots, whereby the ground would be cleared at once. I think also, that steam-engines might be usefully applied to plowing and harrowing.

A little before we left Canada, a machine was introduced from the States, of great mechanical powers. A gentleman accompanied me to see it in operation. The usual way of clearing land is by cutting down the trees about a yard from the ground. The stumps and roots are thus left standing, which form great impediments to cultivation. All such impediments, except where pines have stood, die away in ten years at the longest. Pine stumps, from the turpentine and resin contained in them which preserves them for corruption, will stand in the ground forty or fifty years. The farmers uniformly said, that the land produced as much with the stumps in, as with them out; and that the only detriment they occasion arises from their hinderance to agriculture. As all but pine-stumps quickly decompose, the expense and trouble of removing them would not be counterbalanced by any convenience in husbandry. The machine, therefore, which I have mentioned, was to remove pine-stumps from the grounds. It was wonderful, to witness the ease and certainty with which it drew them out. Two oxen were required, to turn the axle on which the chain which dragged the stumps was wound. On the roots of one tree a log was lying, which could not be less than fifty feet in length. This log was entirely raised from the ground and the root turned up, by the power of the machine. The States are much in advance of Canada in mechanical arts, but this one might naturally look for in a country so much longer settled. A gentleman present observed, that should a dentist in London be able to invent so efficacious a stump-drawer, he might soon make his fortune.

The smaller degree of enterprise and mechanical skill existing in Canada, arises from its more recent settlement, and less extent of capital. There have also, till lately, been fewer facilities for transportation of merchandise. A greater activity is, however, now springing up both in the government and the people; and ten years more, I am confident, will make greater changes there, than the last twenty years have produced in the States. Let England do her duty by her colonies, and their attachment and prosperity will be unparalleled. The last year was unexampled for the number of emigrants, notwithstanding the unfavourableness of the season from cholera. This year is expected to be still more so, not only from greater numbers about to leave England, but also from greater numbers about to leave the States. The country is so exceedingly productive, and so well-suited to European constitutions, that but few will enter the States as settlers, if the colonial government pursue liberal measures.

Thunderstorms in Canada are sometimes fearful, and occasion considerable alarm. Yet I believe, that they are rarely attended by any disasterous issue. The lightning which, from falling downwards, might in other places create disasters, is generally attracted by the lofty trees which remain standing on the farms. One sunday evening, between six and eight o'clock, and during divine service, a tremendous thunder-storm took place. It appeared so immediately above us, and the flashes and roar so continuous, as to be really awful. I frequently could not hear my own voice, and was persuaded in my own mind that the congregation could not hear it; so I curtailed my sermon. I had never before seen so much water fall in so short a time. On returning home, I found our landlady looking from the balcony at a burning tree, which she had a little before observed struck with lightning, and thereby set on fire. This often takes place; and I have heard several affirm, that they saw the descent of the electric stream which had kindled trees in a similar manner.

Sometimes a tree so ignited will continue burning for a considerable time. The trees thus struck are generally girdled pines, left standing in partially cleared grounds; and which have become dry, and burn easily.

Temperance societies are represented to have produced much good in America, in reclaiming not only such as were occasional tipplers, but also confirmed hard drinkers. I believe it is to the United States, that temperance societies owe their origin. The number of members of such societies are estimated to be nearly two hundred thousand in New York State. Many grocers, who had previous to their establishment, been in the habit of retailing spirits, have been prevailed on to discontinue such traffic, and confine themselves to other branches of their trade. The numbers of drunkards have been decreasing there for the last two or three years. During my residence in America, I saw but one person drunk, and he was a young Englishman returning to England. I heard a good deal respecting intemperance in the States; but one instance only, and that a fellow-countryman, met my observation, which I am sorry to admit, is much more than I could affirm of Canada. I devoutly wish, that the Canadians were inspired with more self-respect; as also the English. To prove that intemperance, however, exists to a frightful extent in America, I will insert two extracts from the " New York State Temperance Society's Report for 1832." The society held its annual meeting in New York, during my first visit to Canada; but a copy of the report was presented to me by —— Goodhue, Esq. on my return.

The first extract, is part of a letter addressed by the chaplain of the State prison at Auburn, to the chairman; and is as follows: " The male convicts remaining in prison on the 1st. day of January, 1832, may be classed, with reference to their former habits of drinking, in the following manner:—grossly intemperate, 209. Moderately intemperate, 257. Temperate drinkers, 132. Total abstinents, or nearly so, 19. Of this number of convicts, 346 were under the influence of ardent spirits at the time of the commission of their crimes. The number discharged by pardon and expiration of sentence, during the past year, was 133. Of these, 95 had been drunkards."

The second extract, is from the report of Cherry-Valley, in Otsego; as follows:

"Within the last year, we have distributed 6,000 pages of temperance addresses, &c. and 500 State circulars; and since the formation of our three societies, we have distributed 27,100 pages. The effect of this reading matter upon the community appears from the fact, that when our societies were first formed, 30,000 gallons of ardent spirits were consumed in the town the preceding year, and that, from January 1831, to January 1832, there were sold only 8,028 gallons, 6,000 gallons of which were sold to the inhabitants of this town; 976 gallons of this was brandy, gin, and rum; the remainder whiskey. It has been ascertained, that 4,000 gallons have been retailed out in small measure, which, at the rate of two dollars per gallon, makes 8,000 dollars; to which, add the 2,000 gallons at thirty-one and a quarter cents per gallon, and we have 8,625 dollars, paid by the inhabitants of this town for ardent spirits the past year. 1,310 dollars were expended in this town for common schools; last winter, four districts were *unable* to have any school, and this winter five districts have none yet; there was paid for ardent spirits, 8,625 dollars. The whole amount of our town and county taxes is 2,177 dollars, and our rum and whiskey tax is 8,625 dollars. The consumption of spirits, the past is greater than the previous year, for the reason, that two groceries and a tavern have gone into operation and sold 3,000 gallons, and because too, many who were *temperate* drinkers, have now become *intemperate* drinkers. We have seventeen places where spirits are vended. Number of members 230, increase 100."

Intemperance exists to a great extent in Canada; and the cheapness of intoxicating liquors, which, when retailed, are more moderate in price than in America, is an irresistible inducement for the continuance of intemperance among such as had formed the habit previous to emigration. A person of such habits will never succeed in Canada, or in America. He generally becomes worse than before from increased temptations, and descends into the grave from premature decay.

There is no temperance society in Canada, I believe. Should the final result of such societies in the States be successful, Canada has sufficient emulation and modesty to adopt them, and to acknowledge her obligations to America. The national vanity betrayed in Chancellor Walworth's anniversary address to the society is allowable, and perhaps commendable, on this subject: " Recollect, that a ray of light from this country has already shot across the Atlantic, and that the nations of the Old World are now looking to America for an example of wisdom and prudence in conducting this great moral reformation, as well as to witness the benign effects of our free institutions upon the temporal happiness of man."

The Canadians who, as the English loyalists, had preferred Canada to the States, were sometimes represented as of doubtful principles, and as disposed to be unjust or knavish. I must protest against the sentence. I found many of them persons of excellent character, honourable in their dealings, and studious of peace with their neighbours. Their conduct appeared remarkably inoffensive. I do not now speak of Americans of recent settlement, but of those who first emigrated in the time of the war. I heard other clergymen make the same remark that I am doing; who considered these loyalists as often traduced and imposed on by settlers from Europe, whose greater information and skill, enable them to take advantage. The person, in whose house we had lodgings, was originally from the States. Many predicted that we should never be able to continue in the same house, but should soon inquire for other lodgings. Yet we had never a single difference with her for four months. She had met with many losses and impostures, and had become timorous and distrustful; and her neighbours construed this disposition into quarrelsomeness and ill-nature.

Many persons in New York made complaints to this meaning: we work four months of the year for our landlords, and four more for clothing and fuel, and the remaining four are little enough to procure food and to be idle. It often appeared to me, that although many seemed to obtain greater wages, yet, the persons really benefited by them, were coal-merchants and landlords. Also in Canada, house-rents are high. Capital not being so abundant, such as possess money lay it out to greater interest. Houses being property, produce greater interest from investments than with us. Most houses in many parts of Canada are built of wood, and pass under different appellations, according to their size or mode of construction. A *shanty* has a roof sloping one way only, and contains but one apartment. It is very commonly the only residence of officers and other gentlemen, on their first retiring to the forests, and is built of rough logs with notches in the end, into which transverse logs similarly notched are in a measure dovetailed. The interstices between the logs are filled with lime or clay, to exclude the free admission of air. Shanties are never any thing more than temporary dwellings, till part of the estates are cleared, and log or frame houses erected. *Log houses* are built in a similar manner to shanties, but are larger and with roofs shelving towards both sides, and generally containing sleeping apartments on an upper floor. Sometimes the logs are squared before being used in building, which renders the houses much warmer as well as more substantial, and adds greatly to their beauty. *Frame houses* are constructed of boards of timber nailed to upright frame-works. They are generally boarded both inside and outside. Frame houses have a neat appearance, when well finished and painted white. Shanties and log-houses are erected at small expense; but frame-houses, are considerably expensive, often costing from one to three thousand dollars. Brick buildings are rarely seen in remote places.

Some gentlemen asserted strenuously, that Mr. MacKenzie has done good in Canada, by exposing the abuses or negligences of government, and by exciting the people to investigation and inquiry. If he has produced any beneficial result, or if his object is that of an honourable man, I hope he will ultimately reap his reward. Many are persuaded, that he is in the pay of the Americans, and eager to establish a democracy. This would prove advantageous, neither to the province nor to England. His ruling passion is considered to be ambition, and the desire of ascent to power by misleading the people.

I met with some from England, who censured

the Canada Company in unmeasured terms. They regarded the increased price laid on the company's lands as an imposition on the public, and as detrimental to the general interests of the province. They imagined, that some emigrants were deterred thereby from settling on them, and were induced to proceed to the States. I do not believe, that a respectable emigrant who had once entered Canada would be deterred by such increased price from purchasing. I am persuaded, that land in Canada at five dollars an acre, is cheaper ultimately, than land in the States at one dollar. This arises from the superior quality of soil and healthiness of the climate, and from the better and readier market under the British government. But the Canada Company is capable of justification, according to the established usage of all trading bodies, in demanding more for a commodity which has risen in value. If we investigate the cause of this increase in value of the Company's territories, we shall find it closely interwoven with the Company's existence. The Company, by opening roads, has given greater facilities to the more remote districts. It incurred a large expenditure in doing this; and it was reasonable it should reimburse itself, by imposing a higher price for possessions which had been rendered more valuable from the outlay. The Company also contributed to render the country better known in England. It employed agents to survey the extensive tracts it had purchased, and to report their general character and capabilities. Certainly nothing could be more reasonable, than that it should obtain some equivalent from territories, which had been explored by the agents it employed, and improved by the capital it expended. The Company, notwithstanding, has been strongly condemned for advancing the price of lands. The price is extremely moderate, if we consider that the lands are in themselves invaluable, from the fertility of the soil, the abundance of excellent water, the ready market now found in every part of the province, and the facilities for commerce which are every day increasing The English appear not yet sensible, either of the exuberance of its productions, or their immense utility to the crown of Great Britain.

Yet whatever claims the Canada Company may

have to liberal remuneration, it ought to be suggested, that the real interest of the British nation requires all imaginable facility to be given to persons disposed to emigrate into Upper Canada. The public lands, as well as those of the Company, ought to be disposed of at the lowest price, consistent with justice, and the proper administration of government. If there exists any real cause of dissatisfaction, or if there be even an imaginary one, which throws a stumbling-block or shadow of offence in the way of any emigrant, however humble, it ought to be removed immediately. The Canadians are still proud of their connexion with England. A vast majority are staunch loyalists, and glory in their privileges as English subjects; and nothing should be omitted to prove to them, that England is proud of their loyal adherence. Many even of those most warmly attached to the British government imagined that a cheaper sale of lands would be good policy. Many emigrants are divided in their choice, who would never have felt such hesitation, had not unfavourable statements of the government, and of the unsettled condition of the country, been industriously circulated.

These reports, however unfounded in the general they may be, have considerable influence with many, who perhaps enter the States, and squander their property, and afterwards find that their most prudent plan would have been to go direct to Canada by way of Quebec and Montreal. Hundreds of such families enter Canada every year, after a previous residence in the States, and make the most valuable settlers. Yet one cannot but grieve to find them purchase their experience at a price so great, from unfavourable statements of the province.

The following is an extract from a volume of American anecdotes, and deserves the attention of the British government and the Canadian Company. It is spoken of an American revolutionist. " Mr. Henry proceeded to shew, in a very forcible manner, the policy of using every possible means of augmenting the population of a country as yet so thinly inhabited as America, whose future greatness he thus prophetically depicted : ' Encourage emigration, encourage the husbandmen, the mechanics, the merchants of the old world, to come and settle in this land of promise. Make it the home of the skilful, the industrious, and the happy, as well as the asylum of the distressed. Fill up the measure of your population as speedily as you you can, by the means which heaven hath placed in your power: and I venture to prophecy that there are those now living who will see this favoured land among the most powerful on earth. They will see her great in arts and in arms, and her golden harvests waving over an immeasurable extent.' "

Let the same be supposed as spoken of Canada, and the same means taken to increase its population, and it will be found that the richness of its soil and the stability of its government will immediately attract greater numbers of emigrants than ever entered America. The country has hitherto been little known and less regarded. Those who flocked to it, until the last three years, were generally persons without capital; a paucity of men and money prevented the same rapidity of improvement as characterised the rival country. But now, when its resources are beginning to be appreciated and unfolded, and the tide of emigration to be setting into its territories in unprecedented numbers, and with greater wealth, the reproach of its enemies that it is poor and unimportant will be quickly done away. It is beginning to furnish proof of this important truth, which those who have visited the continent of America can easily comprehend, that it is population which imparts value to the soil, and not the *soil* to population.

CHAPTER VII.

CLERICAL EMIGRANTS—A GERMAN MISSIONARY—REMOVAL TO THE FALLS—A PROJECTED CITY—LAW-SUIT—REPUBLICAN REVENGE—THE INDIANS—SPREAD OF CHRISTIANITY—CHARACTER OF THE ENGLISH EMIGRANTS—CUSTOM-HOUSE OFFICERS—AMERICAN INTEGRITY—A MICHIGAN LADY — BUFFALO — AMERICAN JUDGMENT OF MRS. TROLLOPE—EPISCOPAL SYNOD OF AMERICA—POLITICAL ABSORPTION—CHURCH OF ENGLAND AND AMERICA—RETURN TO ENGLAND.

DURING the visitation-dinner, my Lord Bishop stated to his clergy present, that he had received intimation of four clergymen from England and Ireland, whose arrival in Canada might be expected daily. One of these shortly afterwards made his appearance, and succeeded me at Thornhill; and another of them arrived about the same time, and accepted the mission of New-Market, which I had declined at my first interview with his lordship. The gentleman who succeeded me had three sons, whom he had apprenticed to different trades and businesses. The youngest of these was twelve years of age. Children are in Canada no encumbrance to parents, being soon able to obtain a subsistence for themselves. The youngest of his boys was lodged, boarded, clothed, I believe, and received one shilling a week, at the very first, and he would receive an augmentation of salary every year. My successor assured me, that he conceived himself immensely benefited by emigration. His lady, with three daughters, were still in England, waiting till he should have prepared a residence to receive them. This is the most advisable method to pursue. He expected that she and her daughters would join him in the spring.

Before we departed from Thornhill, we received a farewell visit from some of our neighbours, and among the rest from a clergyman who officiated in both German and English. He had formerly been a Roman Catholic clergyman; but on becoming convinced of the errors of popery, he abandoned the Roman church, and emigrated to America. The present Bishop of Quebec heard of him when he was engaged in a college in the States; and as there were many Germans settled in Canada, over whom no episcopal minister was appointed, his lordship induced him to enter the Canadian church, and superintend their spiritual instruction. His stipend, at first, was nominally fifty pounds; but he was obliged to allow a retiring pension to his superannuated predecessor of thirty pounds. The second year, his stipend was raised to eighty pounds, but subject to the same deduction as before. His income was therefore but twenty pounds for the first, and fifty for every subsequent year. His parishioners promised a subscription equal in amount to the pension he advanced to the superannuated clergyman, but never paid it. This gentleman complained, and I think with great reason, that while he was discharging the duties of two clergymen, and in two languages, he did not receive a remuneration equal to any other. He had walked twelve miles on Sundays during twelve months between morning and evening service, being too indigent to purchase a horse. The Bishop presented him with money to purchase one, on which he afterwards rode. This clergyman had memorialized the Archbishop of Canterbury in a Latin letter, but had received no answer. He had once entertained the intention of presenting another; but having learned, from the Bishop's visitation sermon, that the church of Canada must henceforth depend on its own resources, he abandoned the design. He has a very numerous family. It can never be to the interest of any establishment that its zealous and faithful servants should be overlooked. This was a meritorious pastor, and highly deserving of more generous treatment.

A gentleman on Yonge-street, who had frequently lent me a horse, sent his jaunting-cart and waggon to convey my family, servant, and baggage to the steam-boat at York. The brother of this gentleman drove the jaunting-cart, his servant the waggon, and I rode before to prepare for their arrival. I could not have desired more hospitality and kindness than I and my family experienced during our Canadian sojourn. We proceeded from York to Niagara in a steam-boat, and from Niagara to the Falls in a waggon. Here we spent the pleasantest week passed by us on the other side of the Atlantic. The stupendous cataract, and the scenery around it, delighted us greatly, and made us forget the inconveniencies of Thornhill.

It is in contemplation to build a city near the cataract of Niagara, to be called *The City of the Falls*. The property on the Canadian side adjoining the cataract is in the hands of a few individuals, of whom the principal are Messrs. Clarke and Street. The ground lots for building were offered at 500 dollars each. Part of the land on the American side was claimed by Mr. Clarke; but on what grounds I do not know. His claim was disputed by an American, and a law suit was the consequence. As might be expected from an American judge and jury, the American was declared the rightful owner.

This action was attended with expense to both parties, and the American thirsted for revenge. The only ferry over the river at the Falls is through Mr. Clarke's grounds on the one side, and through the successful American claimant's on the other. There is yet no ferry, except for foot passengers. The American proposed to Mr. Clarke, that if he would cut a road down the Canadian bank for horses, wagons, carts, &c. he, the former, would cut a corresponding road down the American bank; but that Mr. Clarke's should be first done. The latter agreed, and commenced the work immediately. At an immense expense he prosecuted and completed it. When the Canadian road had been executed, the American informed Mr. Clarke that he would not fulfil his part of the agreement. "You caused me," said he, "to expend some money in the law suit, and now I have my revenge." It would be greatly to the advantage of the American to form his road, but his revenge would thereby cease to be gratified. Mr. Clarke's road has been executed some years. This revengeful feeling prevails to an astonishing extent in almost every republican bosom.

The place where we lodged, near Lundy's-lane, was at nearly equal distances from two churches, served by one missionary. In the one he performs morning, and in the other evening service. In these two churches I had the pleasure of performing one Sunday's duties. The congregations were highly respectable, and very well dressed, and also pretty numerous. I must say, that during all the time of my residence in the States and

Canada, I never witnessed any thing approaching to impropriety in any church. The missionary offered to take me in his carriage to the Indian settlement at the head of the lake, which 1 should have readily complied with had our stay been longer.

The Indians were uniformly described as indolent, and as difficult to be roused to activity. But yet the rising generation were willing to be instructed. They would not, however, suffer themselves to be driven to any thing, even for their own benefit. They have to be led, and that gently. The older Indians express a great contempt for learning, but yet encourage the education of their children. The mild spirit of benevolence and christian principles are, however, not fruitlessly bestowed on them. They have, in many places, large farms of cultivated lands, and are beginning to betake themselves to the forms and habits of civilized life. There are missionaries among them, and also schoolmasters; and their improvement, I am told, is perceptibly advancing. Portions of scripture have been translated into most of the Indian languages and dialects; and even the

Indian chiefs have sometimes aided in translating.

That the Indians believed in some great and powerful spirit, prior to the introduction of christianity, we have frequently been told; but I believe they had no places of worship devoted to his service. It used to be urged as an argument of the existence of the deity, that the rational part of creation almost universally refer the derivation of their comforts and enjoyments to the supreme God, and express their feelings of gratitude in hosannahs and thanksgivings; that, whether their lot has been cast in the howling wilderness or the crowded city—on the icy plains of northern latitudes, or the scorching sands of Africa and Asia— on the rugged tops of mountains almost destitute of verdure, or on fertile plains, their souls, impressed with religious veneration, turn instinctively to their Maker; that on whatever land we enter, we find the temple and the altar, and the sacred incense of prayer and praise ascending up to heaven; that when wandering through forests or over mountains, by cascades or foaming cataracts, among savage or civilized man, we meet every where with instances of the bended knee, and hear the language of adoration. With the Indians of America, that part of this description which refers to temples and public worship, is not strictly correct.

If, however, the traveller of former days, before the introduction of christianity, found in every region he explored instances of prayer, and praise, and adoration, he will find these religious feelings and expressions more rational, pure, and fervent where the doctrines and precepts of the christian faith have been promulgated and embraced. The christian missionaries who, in pagan countries, were long impeded in their labours by deep-rooted prejudices, and by the princes of the people, are now triumphantly succeeding in their object, and are spreading the knowledge of Christ and his salvation from pole to pole. The kings of the earth who stood up, and the rulers who took counsel together against the Lord and against his anointed, have, in many instances, desisted from opposing, and have become nursing fathers and guardians of the religion of the cross.

This great reformation in the moral world has, under providence, been principally achieved by the English nation, and cannot but be contemplated, by every traveller possessing British feelings, with peculiar interest and pleasure. He will find, in every place he visits, multitudes of fellow-countrymen who have emigrated thither, and introduced with themselves a portion of the arts and sciences of their paternal land. He will find them, wherever they locate, converting the barren wilderness and the almost impervious forest, into smiling and fertile regions, producing supplies for their own necessities, and enabling them to contribute, by the channels thus opened to trade and commerce, to the employment, and consequently to the comfort and happiness of tens of thousands.

The English, by their enterprise and skill, and by unwearied perseverance, impart energy and life to those around them, and serve as an example to the whole world of what, under providence, may be accomplished by a nation influenced in an eminent degree by the principles of honour, integrity, and virtue, and giving expression to those principles by unparalleled exertions, and by widening the sphere of their utility. Wherever they advance, the rigours of despotism cease, the savage loses the ferocity of his nature, and adopts the habits of civilized man. They have discovered that the pure religion of the gospel is too spiritual to be comprehended by men whose minds are swayed by ignorance and superstition, and have founded seminaries of instruction in all countries over which their empire is extended. In short, they appear to have been placed as lights in the world, as a centre from which the whole earth might be irradiated, and have been chiefly instrumental in producing a moral and religious reformation in pagan countries. Those, in every country, who speak their language, and have access to their literature, imbibe, more extensively than others, the spirit of civil and religious freedom, and are distinguished in dignity of sentiment and action above the rest of mankind. The nearer any nation approaches to the laws, the constitution, and the customs of England, the nearer it approaches to perfect freedom; and every deviation from these is, in general, a deviation from dignity and greatness.

We recrossed from Canada to the States at Black Rock, seventeen miles from the Falls, and three from Buffalo. Many writers have asserted, that no American will accept a present, whether a waiter at an inn, a custom-house officer, or in any other capacity; but that he would consider himself affronted if money were offered to him. *Credat Judæus, non ego.* If gentlemen are the same all the world over, so are others. I offered money to persons connected with the custom-house, both at Black Rock and new York, which was accepted at both places. A person, also, employed in the custom-house at New York stole my umbrella; and had I not persevered in calling at the place, and making considerable stir about it, I should have lost it finally. As it was, the rogue retained it a week. They may perhaps assert, that all these were Englishmen. I do not blame Americans for accepting presents; but to hear them extolled for qualities not possessed by them, is intolerable. I presented some Eastern books to a gentleman in Boston, from whom I had received many kind attentions; but he made no acknowledgments. An American will accept; but feels, or at least expresses, no obligation.

Mr. Green, an English gentleman, accompanied

us from Canada into the States. I mentioned to him during the journey, that I had heard several recount the robberies they had suffered whilst passing through America. He expressed his disbelief of such stories. The first thing presented to our notice, on entering the Eagle tavern at Buffalo, was a piece of paper in a conspicuous place, describing some lost property which had been found, and which the owner would obtain on application. " Behold," he observed, " an incontestible proof of American integrity !" I shall also add, that we could not charge Americans with having taken any thing, except the umbrella, surreptitiously. We had stored our books and furniture at New York, and after five months, found them there exactly as we left them.

We paid in that inn, for one day, a dollar and a half each. There were some sitting in the room, who paid but half a dollar each, and yet made loud complaints at the enormous charge. A young American lady, who had just arrived from the Michigan territory, offered to sell to Mrs. F. her ear-rings and other trinkets. The expenses she had incurred, she said, were so great that she was quite impoverished; and she was consequently compelled to dispose of them to pay her way. She was very desirous to persuade us they were pure gold. Mrs. F. recommended her to compare them with those she wore, which the young lady did, and seemed surprised at the difference of colour; after which she left the room, and we saw her no more.

Nothing afforded me so great pleasure, as the sight of improvements both in Canada and the States. Those in progress at Buffalo justify the belief, that it will at no distant day be an important place. Great numbers of workmen were employed in levelling hills, and filling up the lower parts of the ground bordering the canal.

From Buffalo we returned down the canal. A young Englishman took a place in the same boat, who had resided four years in America; but who had afterwards been induced, from multiplied statements made to him of the advantages of Canada, to change his country once more. He had been nine months in Canada, and declared his opinion to be that it is incomparably preferable, as a residence for Englishmen, to the States. He had received intimation, that some of his relations were expected from England at the place of his former residence, with a large sum of money; and had taken the journey with no other view, than to hinder them from settling in America.

On arriving at Albany, I again called on the gentleman whose kindness I had twice before experienced, and enjoyed as warm a reception as before. His lady was seated by him. Mrs. Trollope's work had made its appearance in America, subsequent to my previous call, and was the subject of a few remarks. He admitted the general correctness of her statements; and added, " I have often told my friends the same thing, and that Mrs. T. is a benefactress to our country ; in return for which they call me an Englishman." His lady had no gracious yearnings towards the authoress. She corroborated, notwithstanding her dislike, the truth of some of the statements contained in the book ; the account of Dorcas societies, for instance, which she said was minutely accurate. This gentleman accompanied me to the steam-boat.

I called on one of the professors of Columbia college, previous to embarking for England, to take my leave. He was from home; but I had a long conversation with his lady. I inquired of every lady I conversed with in the States, if she had read Mrs. T.'s book. The same question was asked here. The professor's lady was the only female in America, who made the acknowledgment of having read it; although I am persuaded, that it is generally read by Americans from one extremity of their country to the other. "Can you believe, Mr. F.," she inquired, "that any clergyman would act as Mrs. Trollope has described?" "I have not witnessed," I replied, "any thing approaching to it; yet as every thing described by her, of which I could form a judgment, is circumstantially correct, I have no reason to disbelieve her on that point." "We can generally tell," she then said, "from what class those we converse with have come. The best informed from England always speak of us in the same way. But it is very hard, that we can admit no respectable English person into our houses, without running the hazard of being exposed or caricatured." "You will shortly have an opportunity," I replied, "of reading another work on America;

since it is my intention to publish my remarks, on my arrival in England."

In the preface to the American edition of Mrs. T.'s work, the writer mentions the probability of Mrs. Trollope and Captain Hall being one and the same person. This opinion was entertained by almost every American I spoke to on the subject. The real ignorance there, as respects literary subjects, is quite surprising. Scarcely any are able to distinguish one style of writing from another. If an American editor should assert that all the English books he edits were the productions of one author, let them be ever so dissimilar in composition or argumentation, he would be believed by almost every reader from Maine to New Orleans.

"What a foolish preface that is," I observed to the professor's lady, "which some editor has prefixed to her book!" "Pray, Mr. F." said she, "make no more observations. The writer of it is a particular friend of ours." "Pardon me, Madam," said I, "for my freedom in proposing one question. Could the author of it really persuade himself, that Mrs. Trollope and Captain Hall are one and the same person? The styles are so different that it is impossible to mistake them as identical." "The truth is," she replied, "that Mrs. T. had an introductory letter to us; and was introduced to the writer of that preface, and to some others of our acquaintances. She was personally known to several in New York, but not generally known. The great fault of Mrs. Trollope," she proceeded, " is this, She resided in a remote part of our country; and has described the manners of the people there, as the manners of Americans in general." To this I replied, "that in those circles in which I had the honour to move, during my stay in New York and Boston, I observed no correspondence with her Cincinnati delineations. But Mrs. Trollope herself, admits the same thing."

We had again taken up our residence at the lodgings which Mrs. F. had formerly selected during my first Canadian tour. The medical gentleman, who, when I disputed the superiority of American to English physicians, told me I should never be able to gain a respectable living in their country, boarded at the same house. He and some other Americans declared Mrs. T.'s book a *fabrication* of falsehoods. In that land they always denounce as false whatever truth offends them. Her statements were always expressed, said they, in illiberal and vulgar language, and arose from disappointment. " If you can shew me," I observed, " one statement in her book, which you can prove false or illiberal, I pledge myself to do penance for my fair countrywoman, and will eat her book." The book was procured, and I have no doubt examined with great attention. On the following morning, I desired them to tell me if they had succeeded in detecting one. The further mention of her name was immediately interdicted. At the shop of a bookseller, from whom Mrs. F. and myself had received many kindnesses, I inquired for Mrs. T.'s work. He replied, " I would not keep it in my store."

Mrs. T.'s book is producing, and will produce incalculable good in America, and a wonderful alteration in the manners of the people. Their great removal from other nations more advanced in refinement and civilization, debars them from possessing the same facilities with other countries, of divesting themselves of national foibles and partialities. The poor emigrants also, who flock from other countries to their shores, are really behind them in some kinds of information; and they hence infer that all those of the same countries are also behind them. The highest class alone have abandoned this opinion. When, however, they have perceived that no really respectable and well-informed European will continue in their country, longer than his business, or the purposes of travelling and making observations may require, they must find out that something not entirely attractive pervades their national character. They possess a high degree of native talent, and of emulation as far as commerce is concerned. When they find leisure for emulation in polite literature, and foster with greater patronage the arts and sciences, and the embellishments of life, then European emigrants of a higher class may continue in their country, and find a comfortable home. Till that period, many a Captain Hall, and Mrs. Trollope will be found among the number of their visitors.

The Archdeacon of Upper Canada had just published " *The Life and Character of Bishop Hobert, in a Letter to Dr. Chalmers,*" of which he presented me with a copy on my departure from Canada. The Archdeacon spoke of a journey to New York, that he might be present at the convention of the clergy. This convention is triennial; and is composed of all the American episcopal bishops, who form the the upper house; and of four clerical and as many lay deputies, from every State which has joined the church, who form the lower. These two separate bodies, enact such regulations, in their triennial conventions, as are deemed expedient for their church, and which are made obligatory on every minister and every congregation of the episcopal establishment throughout the Union. Sometimes a congregation solicits the convention, for a private regulation for itself alone. The Archdeacon did not attend this synod, which was considered as unusually interesting from the resignation of Dr. Chase.

Dr. Chase, the bishop of Ohio, had, while in England solicited subscriptions for a college which he was desirous of founding in his diocese. He obtained, by this means, a very considerable sum, and applied it to its purposed object. A college was erected. Dr. Chase claimed unlimited control over the establishment; which produced a collision between himself and the faculty of the college he had instituted. Party spirit ran high against him, and a deposition from his episcopal dignity was meditated, on account of the alleged tyranny and arbitrary measures he had ventured to pursue. This was the sole reason stated to me of his intended deposition. I heard no other. When he perceived his deposition meditated, he offered to resign, and his resignation was refused. The question respecting him, discussed in the convention, was whether any bishop under a contemplated deposition, had the power of resigning. After a protracted discussion of some days, the convention nominated Dr. M'Lvane his successor, without deciding the question. As the convention had been sitting a week before our arrival in New York from Canada, the debates on this question had been closed, and I consequently did not hear them.

At this convention, there were four clergymen, consecrated bishops, among whom were Dr. M'Lvane, now bishop of Ohio, and Dr. Smith, bishop of Kentucky. It is an unwonted occurrence, for four bishops to be consecrated at once. Dr. Milnor and Dr. Wainright invited me to be present at the consecration, but I found this impracticable, The ship in which we returned, left the place of lading on the afternoon of the same day.

The time we spent in New York, on our return, was between four and five days; the greater part of which was employed in inquiries for a vessel, and in making preparation for our voyage. I found time one day to enter St. John's church, in which the convention was held. The ecclesiastical business was nearly ended. One of the subjects I heard discussed, was the admission of the church of Michigan into connexion with the general episcopal church of the United States, and to a participation of its privileges. No State is obliged to accede, on the first instance, to the regulations of the episcopal church. It may voluntarily join, or it may constitute a church of its own. But the continued adherence of any State, which has once united itself to the general episcopal church, is no longer optional. It must regularly send its deputies, lay and clerical, to the convention, and conform itself to the rules prescribed. This observation extends only to the episcopal portion of the inhabitants. This was the first proposition from the Michigan territory of joining the church, and its final admission could not be ratified till the following convention.

The postures of body—when to stand, when to sit, and when to kneel, during the communion service—were also regulated in the convention during my presence. Thus a uniformity in the conduct of all episcopal congregations, throughout the Union, is preserved in every church. In England there may be observed a great diversity, in this respect, in different churches. If any stranger, from a distant part of England, should enter a church in or near London, he will often feel embarrassed by some customs with which he is unacquainted: he will have to watch when others stand, or sit, or kneel, that he may imitate them. This observation holds more forcibly true, when applied to different country churches. By the regulations of the episcopal synod of America, such discrepancies and embarrassments are prevented; every episcopal congregation being required to comply with the rubric of their church.

In England, and, till lately, in America, the new version of psalms has been appended to the common prayer book. This portion of the common prayer book will, in future, be exchanged in America for a selection of psalms and hymns, to be prepared under the superintendance of the bishops. This selection will be printed uniform with their books of common prayer, and bound up with it, and must be used in all American episcopal churches. In England, each congregation may make and publish selections of such psalms and hymns as may please its taste, without any reference to a synod. In America such selection is not, I believe, permitted. This appears very judicious, and a great advantage. It produces uniformity in psalmody, as other regulations produce uniformity of exterior posture, in episcopal churches there, and prevents a book of psalms and hymns used in one church from being useless in another. The episcopalians of America have long had a selection of hymns for public worship, but they were hitherto separate from the prayer-book. This regulation I also witnessed.

I had many opportunities of observing how

entirely the public mind in America is engrossed by political questions. New York was in a ferment respecting the election of a President; and I believe, notwithstanding the vote by ballot, there was as much bribery, corruption, venality, and personal danger in that city, as is ever witnessed in any town in England. I can, of course, only judge by what I heard, and what the papers stated. Some of the clergy deprecated very much the political confusion it occasioned. I was eager to make inquiries among the people, what were the charges made against Bishop Chase, but scarcely any person knew. Many were ignorant in what church the synod was held, and several had not even heard of it. The discussion of politics had uncontrolled possession of their thoughts. I had conversations with several gentlemen, native Americans, who declared to me that they had never voted on any political subject. The reason they assigned for this omission was the unbounded and tyrannical despotism of the democratic influence, which rendered nugatory the voting of the more respectable classes.

Many of the episcopal ministers of Canada

think favourably of the American church, and imagine that if their own were made to approximate more nearly to it in church government, they would find it become more flourishing, and interest more warmly the lay members of its body. More energy would, they thought, be thereby infused into it, and its measures invigorated.

The Archdeacon of York, in Upper Canada, was of opinion that the system of church government, which connects church and state so closely together as to admit of no trifling alterations being made without the intervention of parliament, is untenable by scripture, and hurtful to the interests of the church itself. The church of England, he remarked, is the only religious community which does not possess inherent right to regulate its internal affairs. There are no synods of its clergy, no unity of counsels and proceedings, like what were possessed originally by the christian church, or like what are adopted by other denominations of the present day. The national church ought to be so modelled, as to be able to conform itself, in its outward ceremonies, to the improvements of the age.

I shall conclude my observations on America with some extracts from the Archdeacon's letter to Dr. Chalmers, on "The Life and Character of Bishop Hobert." The letter is well written, and merits general perusal. Bishop Hobert had published a sermon, on his return to America after a tour through Europe, in which he condemns the church establishments of England, and extols those of his own country. I introduce them, for the sole purpose of conveying some idea of the difficulties under which the American church labours, and the progress it has made notwithstanding: —

"I dined with Bishop Hobert," says the Archdeacon, "on my way to England, in March, 1826, and the conversation, long and animated, turned on the sermon, which had not long been published. As the comparison, I observed, is between England and the United States, I shall confine myself to these two countries; but in shewing the necessity of the ecclesiastical establishment of England for the religious instruction of the nation, I seek not to vindicate abuses, for such may be removed, and leave the establishment more efficient than ever. The Church of England is commensurate with the natural boundaries of the country, which consists of about 55,000 square miles, containing fourteen millions of inhabitants, and divided into about 11,000 parishes. The number of clergymen actually employed in parochial duties are not fewer than 16,000. The parishes may be reckoned to contain five square miles each, a space not by any means too great for all the residenters to attend regularly the service of the church; and the average population not quite 900 souls, or about 200 families for each clergyman—a number not greater than, if vigilant, he is able to instruct. It is evident, that the moral effect of such a body of men daily mixing with their people, must be very great, more especially as they are quite independent of them for subsistence.

" Let us now look at the episcopal church of the United States, and see what moral effect it can have on the population as a source of christian instruction; for this, after all, is the true foundation on which to introduce a comparison between it and the church of England; and if in this it greatly fail, the comparison falls to the ground. Now I shall give you every advantage in this matter, and instead of taking the United States generally, by which my argument in favour of England and ecclesiastical establishments would be much strengthened, I shall confine myself to the State of New York, where the episcopal clergymen are more numerous, in proportion to the population, than in any other state, and superintended by the most active Bishop.

"In this large State, the clergy of the episcopal church are in number 136; the population two millions, or upwards of 14,000 souls to each; the square miles 46,000. Hence the parishes, if we may so denominate them, contain 338 square miles, and are rather equal to an English county than an English parish. The influence of the two churches, as confined to England and New York, is as one to seventy; and, if the comparison be taken with all the States, it becomes much more favourable to England. Such influence on the manners and habits of the people is next to nothing, and yet you extol your church over that of England, and exclaim against establishments!

Add to this, the dependence of your clergy upon the people for support—a state of things which is attended with most pernicious consequences. The congregations frequently take offence at their pastors without a good reason, and in such cases the latter derive no protection from the Bishops, who are equally helpless with themselves. There are, doubtless, many splendid exceptions; but, in general, the clergy of all denominations in the United States, are miserably dependent upon their congregations. The result is, that they too frequently sink below the rank which they ought to hold in society, and whatever be their personal merit, they fail to command that respect from a vain, and thoughtless, and undiscerning people, which is necessary to secure attention to their instructions. It may be that, accustomed from their childhood to temporary engagements, the clergy partake of that restless disposition and desire of change so common in new countries, and think little of going with their families from state to state, in search of a new settlement. It cannot be supposed that clergymen so situated will at all times speak with that fearless disregard of consequences which the proper discharge of their duty may often require. The difference, then, of the two churches is this, that while in England the country is partitioned into parishes, over which a spiritual head is appointed, to be the moral and religious instructor of its population, and to add new converts to the faith by familiar and daily ministrations from house to house; the church in the United States presents only a few verdant spots, bearing marks of recent cultivation, distinguished chiefly by their contrast with the barrenness of the surrounding waste.

"Yet, notwithstanding all this, I admit that the progress of the Episcopal Protestant Church in the United States has been wonderful, and that she carries with her the divine blessing; and believing, as I do, that she will not only far outstrip all other denominations, but that the communion of which she is a part is destined to evangelise the whole world, I should have rejoiced in concurring entirely in the animated praises you pronounce upon her, had you not condemned ecclesiastical establishments, and placed her in her infancy above the mother church. In this you greatly err, and when you picture to your fancy England studded with parish churches, regularly served in all the beauty of holiness, and turn to this country, with a church at vast intervals, and a clergy not sufficient to supply the wants of one twentieth of the population, you must feel the advantages of an ecclesiastical establishment. In England, you behold the genius of true religion entering into every family; but here, unless in some favoured spots, you behold the spirit of false religion, infidelity, error and superstition, traversing the length and breadth of the land, and withering, with its pestilential breath, public as well as domestic and personal happiness and virtue."

" Sir," said the Bishop, interrupting the declaimer, " you are becoming too severe." He had hardly spoken the word, when the door opened, and a man from the Catskill Mountains was introduced, who told the Bishop that their missionary's time had almost expired, and that, being few in number, they could not engage him for six months longer, unless some aid could be granted them from the missionary fund. The good Bishop promised the necessary assistance, and on his departure said, with a smile, "How unlucky that my country friend should come in the midst of this discussion, to shew the nakedness of the land. He confessed that I had placed ecclesiastical establishments in a point of view which was somewhat new to him, and was pleased to conclude the conversation with observing, that whatever his opinion might be on ecclesiastical establishments, he loved with all his soul the Church of England."

Our departure from the shores of America was very hasty, and we had a very favourable passage. The vessel reached soundings in about seventeen days, and, in a little more than three weeks from the time of embarkation, arrived in London. Before leaving New York, I was invited by Dr. Milnor to dinner, and by Dr. Wainright to tea; but compliance was impossible. I experienced many favours from several Americans, and take this opportunity to acknowledge them. My impression, whilst in America, was, that the higher orders are in advance of the civil institutions of their country.

THE END.

BAYLIS AND LEIGHTON,
JOHNSON'S-COURT, FLEET-STREET.

Foreign Travelers in America 1810–1935

AN ARNO PRESS COLLECTION

Archer, William. **America To-Day:** Observations and Reflections. 1899.

Belloc, Hilaire. **The Contrast.** 1924.

[Boardman, James]. **America, and the Americans.** By a Citizen of the World. 1833.

Bose, Sudhindra. **Fifteen Years in America.** 1920.

Bretherton, C. H. **Midas, Or, The United States and the Future.** 1926.

Bridge, James Howard (Harold Brydges). **Uncle Sam at Home.** 1888.

Brown, Elijah (Alan Raleigh). **The Real America.** 1913.

Combe, George. **Notes on the United States Of North America During a Phrenological Visit in 1838-9-40.** 1841. 2 volumes in one.

D'Estournelles de Constant, Paul H. B. **America and Her Problems.** 1915.

Duhamel, Georges. **America the Menace:** Scenes from the Life of the Future. Translated by Charles Miner Thompson. 1931.

Feiler, Arthur. **America Seen Through German Eyes.** Translated by Margaret Leland Goldsmith. 1928.

Fidler, Isaae. **Observations on Professions, Literature, Manners, and Emigration, in the United States and Canada, Made During a Residence There in 1832.** 1833.

Fitzgerald, William G. (Ignatius Phayre). **Can America Last?** A Survey of the Emigrant Empire from the Wilderness to World-Power Together With Its Claim to "Sovereignty" in the Western Hemisphere from Pole to Pole. 1933.

Gibbs, Philip. **People of Destiny:** Americans As I Saw Them at Home and Abroad. 1920.

Graham, Stephen. **With Poor Immigrants to America.** 1914.

Griffin, Lepel Henry. **The Great Republic.** 1884.

Hall, Basil. **Travels in North America in the Years 1827 and 1828.** 1829. 3 volumes in one.

Hannay, James Owen (George A. Birmingham). **From Dublin to Chicago:** Some Notes on a Tour in America. 1914.

Hardy, Mary (McDowell) Duffus. **Through Cities and Prairie Lands:** Sketches of an American Tour. 1881.

Holmes, Isaac. **An Account of the United States of America,** Derived from Actual Observation, During a Residence of Four Years in That République, Including Original Communications. [1823].

Ilf, Ilya and Eugene Petrov. **Little Golden America:** Two Famous Soviet Humorists Survey These United States. Translated by Charles Malamuth. 1937.

Kerr, Lennox. **Back Door Guest.** 1930.

Kipling, Rudyard. **American Notes.** 1899.

Leng, John. **America in 1876:** Pencillings During a Tour in the Centennial Year, With a Chapter on the Aspects of American Life. 1877.

Longworth, Maria Theresa (Yelverton). **Teresina in America.** 1875. 2 volumes in one.

Low, A[lfred] Maurice. **America at Home.** [1908].

Marshall, W[alter] G[ore]. **Through America:** Or, Nine Months in the United States. 1881.

Mitchell, Ronald Elwy. **America:** A Practical Handbook. 1935.

Moehring, Eugene P. **Urban America and the Foreign Traveler, 1815-1855.** With Selected Documents on 19th-Century American Cities. 1974.

Muir, Ramsay. **America the Golden:** An Englishman's Notes and Comparisons. 1927.

Price, M[organ] Philips. **America After Sixty Years:** The Travel Diaries of Two Generations of Englishmen. 1936.

Sala, George Augustus. **America Revisited:** From the Bay of New York to the Gulf of Mexico and from Lake Michigan to the Pacific. 1883. 3rd edition. 2 volumes in one.

Saunders, William. **Through the Light Continent;** Or, the United States in 1877-8. 1879. 2nd edition.

Smith, Frederick [Edwin] (Lord Birkenhead). **My American Visit.** 1918.

Stuart, James. **Three Years in North America.** 1833. 2 volumes in one.

Teeling, William. **American Stew.** 1933.

Vivian, H. Hussey. **Notes of a Tour in America from August 7th to November 17th, 1877.** 1878.

Wagner, Charles. **My Impressions of America.** Translated by Mary Louise Hendee. 1906.

Wells, H. G. **The Future in America:** A Search After Realities. 1906.